Devil's Thumb

Dansketinde
Staunings Alps

Unemak
Fjord

Gunbjornsfjeld
Watkins Mts

Cumberland
Peninsula

Tête Blanche

Mt Atter   Mont Forel

Cape Farewell

Brooks Range

Mt McKinley

Alaska Range Mt Logan

Coast Range

Rocky Mountains

Mt Rainier

Gr. Teton

Mt Washington

Sierra Nevada

Yosemite

Pikes Peak

Sierra Madre

Popocatepetl

Huascaran

Andes

Pumasillo

Aconcagua

Ruapehu

Mt Cook

FitzRoy

Mt. Paget

World Atlas of
Mountaineering

World Atlas of
Mountaineering

Edited by Wilfrid Noyce and Ian McMorrin

The Macmillan Company

Library of Congress Catalog Card Number: 70-88209

First American Edition 1970

Published in Great Britain in 1969 by Thomas Nelson & Sons Ltd, London

The Macmillan Company

Phototypeset by Oliver Burridge Filmsetting Ltd, Crawley, Sussex
Printed in the Netherlands by L. Van Leer & Co. N.V.
Bound in the Netherlands by Proost En Brandt N.V.

Contents

4 The Mountains of Australasia

5 The Mountains of North America
George Bell

6 The Mountains of South America
Kim Meldrum and Eric Shipton

7 The Mountains of the Polar Regions

Colour Plates

Principal Maps

Credits for black-and-white illustrations

Notes on Contributors

George Bell is a theoretical physicist. He has climbed widely in both North and South America. He was a member of expeditions which made the first ascent of Yerupaja in 1950 and Salcantay in 1952, and was a member of the American Expedition which attempted K2 in 1953 and the International Himalayan Expedition to Everest-Lhotse in 1955. He led the American–Pakistan Karakoram Expedition which climbed Masherbrum in 1960.

Wally Herbert has travelled widely in South America, North America, and Greenland. He spent two and a half years with the Falkland Islands Dependencies Survey and was a member of the Scottish Spitsbergen Expedition and the New Zealand Antarctic Expedition 1960–1. He was leader of the 1968–9 British Trans-Arctic Expedition and is author of *A World of Men*.

Alexander Khrguian is an experienced climber and Professor of Geography in Moscow University. He has been a member of many mountaineering and scientific expeditions to the Caucasus and the mountains of central Asia. He has made ascents of East Shchelda and Ullu-Tau, and has written widely on atmosphere physics.

George Lowe, a New Zealander, is familiar with the New Zealand Alps, though he has visited the Himalaya four times and was a member of the 1953 Everest Expedition. He was also a member of Sir Vivian Fuchs' Trans-Antarctic team 1956–8 and the Anglo-Soviet Expedition to the Pamirs in 1962. He is the author of *Because It Is There* and is at present headmaster of the Grange School in Santiago.

Ian McMorrin has climbed widely in east, central, and southern Africa as well as in Britain and the Alps. He was a member of the British Antarctic Survey and was based at Stonington Island from 1961 to 1964. During this time he made extensive sledge journeys on the east coast of Grahamland, surveying much new ground and making a number of first ascents. He is a teacher and a member of the Alpine Club of Great Britain.

Fosco Maraini is an Italian ethnographer who has travelled extensively in the Himalaya, Tibet, and Japan. He was a member of the Italian expedition which climbed Gasherbrum IV in 1958, and in 1959 led an expedition to Saraghrar in the Hindu Kush. He is the author of many books, including *Karakoram*, *Meeting with Japan*, *Secret Tibet*, and *Where Four Worlds Meet*.

Kim Meldrum has climbed widely in the Alps and also in the Canadian Rockies. He was a member of the Cambridge Andean Expedition which climbed Pumasillo in 1957 and leader of the Oxford Andean Expedition to Allinccapac in 1960. He is principal of White Hall Outdoor Pursuits Centre in Derbyshire.

John Neill is a chemical engineer who has climbed extensively in Britain, Norway, and the Alps, and was a member of the British Caucasus Expedition in 1958. He is widely known as an author and editor of climbing guide books.

Wilfrid Noyce was in the older tradition of British mountaineers, being a scholar and poet as well as an outstanding climber. He visited the Himalaya seven times, was a member of the successful Everest Expedition in 1953, and leader of the Anglo-American Karakoram Expedition in 1960. He was killed in 1962 during the Anglo-Soviet Expedition to the Pamirs. His many books include *South Col*, *Climbing the Fish's Tail*, *To the Unknown Mountain*, *They Survived*, and two volumes of poetry.

Eric Shipton is perhaps the most widely experienced of living British mountaineers. After climbing extensively in Africa, he made the first ascent of Kamet in 1931 and subsequently visited the Himalaya/Karakoram eleven times, including five expeditions to Mount Everest. With H. W. Tilman he reconnoitred the approaches to Nanda Devi in 1934, and in 1951 led the reconnaissance expedition which discovered the southern approach to Everest.

He has also travelled widely among the mountains of Central Asia during periods spent as Consul-General at Kashgar and Kunming. More recently he has made six expeditions to Patagonia. He was president of the Alpine Club from 1964–7, and his many books include *Nanda Devi*, *Blank on the Map*, *Upon that Mountain*, and *Mountains of Tartary*.

Preface

This *World Atlas of Mountaineering* has been completed as Wilfrid Noyce envisaged it. The book has been designed to present a concise summary of mountaineering activity, but while it is an Atlas, it is not a Gazetteer. It is hoped that it will be read for interest, and even for enlightenment, not used merely as a work of reference. The main concern throughout has been with general tendencies, with the result that some peaks and some personalities are not mentioned, simply because they have no integral place in the picture presented. Similarly, some ranges, though big, are remote and inaccessible and receive scant mention, while others, like the British hills and the Alps, though smaller, are exceptionally rich in climbing history and therefore receive more attention than their size warrants. It has been a prime purpose that the photographic record should be as full as possible, and that the captions to the photographs should complement the text by telling their own story.

The contributors to this volume all have personal acquaintance with the continent or range described, yet each can know personally only a tiny fragment of his area. This is perhaps as well, since the better one knows a district the harder it is to condense its charms into a small compass. It is hoped, however, that each section conveys something of the atmosphere of the particular area while at the same time telling the story of its exploration against a background of history, political conditions, people, climate, structure, fauna and flora.

A book such as this naturally draws heavily on the writings and personal experience of others, and this debt is gratefully acknowledged, as is the debt owed to those who have contributed photographs. Especial appreciation is extended to Dr John Keates, of Glasgow University, who drew up the two-colour maps; Dr Brian Sissons, of Edinburgh University, who supplied most of the notes on geology and structure; Mr T. S. Blakeney, who gave much valuable advice; and Mr D. F. O. Dangar, who read the proofs and advised at many stages. Thanks are also extended to Professor Kenneth Mason and to the staff of the Central Asian Research Centre for their help with the Russian section. Particular appreciation is extended to David Cox for his Foreword. Finally, thanks are extended to the publishers and their designer and cartographers for their part in the planning of this book.

Ian McMorrin

Foreword

At the time of his death in the Pamirs in 1962 Wilfrid Noyce had been working for some time on a *World Atlas of Mountaineering*. The project was ambitious, very different from any of his previous literary undertakings; but he had already made considerable progress, both with the general planning of the book and with the writing of those sections for which he was to be responsible. Nevertheless, a great amount of work – the bulk of it, in fact – remained to be done, and as late as the end of 1965 it was still possible that the Atlas might have to be abandoned. That this did not happen, and that the Atlas as it now appears is essentially the book as it was at first conceived, is due to the work of Ian McMorrin. Despite his own major share in the book, he always saw its completion primarily as a tribute to Wilfrid Noyce, whom he originally met when the Atlas was being planned and soon came to know as a friend.

Wilfrid was a man whom it was impossible not to like and admire. He had an unusual combination of gifts, diverse enough for anyone who did not know him to be forgiven for thinking that there were two distinct sides to his character. Some people saw him as a dreamy, rather abstracted person, and in this there was an element of truth. He was very much at home in the world of thought, art, poetry and books, and even on an expedition he would spend much of his leisure time in reading and, above all, writing. But this was only a part of the picture. He was very far from being an unpractical academic. For a number of years, to take a minor instance, he was active in local government work; or again, he was very effective as a lecturer and public speaker. Also, of course, he was a mountaineer who ranked with the greatest of his day.

For most climbers, the skills and the stamina needed for mountaineering have to be painfully acquired. Wilfrid was one of the rare people to whom both came naturally. He had a superb sense of balance, which often made him seem unaware of steepness or difficulty. Equally, without there being any sort of conscious toughness about him, he appeared hardly to be affected by cold or storm or lack of food. Nor did he ever seem to feel the effects of tiredness.

These, of course, were physical advantages which he was fortunate to possess. They could hardly fail to make him an exceptional climber, whether on British rocks, or in the Alps, or in the bigger ranges further afield. But an exceptional climber is not necessarily also a great mountaineer. Wilfrid's contribution lay only partly in the many fine climbs which he made, sustained though these were over a period of twenty-five years. It lay also – and this was important in an age when competitiveness in mountaineering was increasing – in the fact that he thought so little in terms of mere performance of exploits and so much in terms of the wider enjoyments which he found in mountains.

Thus, while he understood, better than most, the challenge of a new Himalayan peak or a great Alpine traverse, he never saw the element of struggle in mountaineering in any distorted proportion. His relationship with mountains was almost a personal one, in which he looked for much else besides difficulty: 'The mountain itself and action upon it, companionship and an indefinable sense of greatness,' as he himself once wrote when examining his own motives.

Wilfrid sought these things in many of the ranges described and illustrated in a *World Atlas of Mountaineering*. Nothing could be more fitting if the book which he initiated assists other people to do the same.

David Cox

Introduction

In reply to that most difficult of questions 'Why climb mountains?' many have pointed to the fact that admiration for mountains and even an interest in what happens on them has little to do *a priori* with a desire to climb them. Indeed, the peaks, valleys and lakes, glaciers and passes, peoples and pastures were there long before men thought of scrambling up the steeper sides. For many centuries pious Hindus have felt themselves purified by looking on the snows of Himachal, without feeling at all impelled to tread them. Olympus and Parnassus were held sacred by the Greeks because they were the abode of mysterious powers, not because they had good routes. In Western Europe the mountains were for many centuries regarded with superstitious awe and finally, in the Age of Reason, as a 'Uniformity of Barrenness'. Even when, seen through the sentimental telescope of Rousseau or the Romantic spectacles, they came into favour, it was normally as cathedrals, to be admired from afar, not as gymnasia in which to practise feats of skill.

What, then, does make us climb them? There are, it would seem, several obvious reasons, and one or two which are not so easy to put into words. Moreover, a distinction must be drawn between the urge to reach a top and the desire to advance technical skill towards the overcoming of difficulty. Both are instinctive urges and may be combined, but chronologically the first becomes apparent before the second. It was the first urge which took the priests of the seventeenth century up the mountains, and it was a canon of the St Bernard Hospice to whom the first of the big peaks, the Velan, yielded. In the case of Mont Blanc, a scientist, de Saussure, gave part of the impulse, but the ascent of 1786 was made by a local doctor and guide, impelled both by patriotism and an ambition for the summit. In the years that followed science laid a cloak of respectability over the infant sport. Conscientiously, the respectable mountaineers boiled kettles on their peaks, noted temperatures and took samples of rocks.

I wonder how far the scientific motive was integral, how far a disguise? It was discarded as a reason for climbing, but has returned in the twentieth century as a sufficient reason for exploring distant high ranges. Discarded also was the aesthetic pretext; the long pages describing sunrise and sunset, valley scenery and summit grandeur slowly disappeared. Leslie Stephen could argue, combating Ruskin's attacks on the youthful Alpine Club, that the mountaineer had a fuller aesthetic experience than the non-mountaineer, since he alone savoured all the dishes from valley to peak top; but it was becoming obvious that enjoyment of scenery, like science, could be only part of the reason for climbing. Another important aspect lay in the urge to develop skills towards the overcoming of steep surfaces.

This became apparent in Europe when all the major peaks had been climbed by their easiest way. After Everest had been climbed people asked 'What's left now?' Well they might have wondered, after 1786, what remained to be done in the Alps. It was only then that climbing as an independent skill properly began, with all that accompanies any arduous skill: co-ordination of mind and nerve and eye, self-reliance, appreciation of risk, team work. The technique of climbing steep and even overhanging places safely has developed to a point beyond the wildest imaginings of the Alpine pioneers.

Perhaps mountaineering appeals nowadays to so many because itself it has so many facets. You can content yourself with climbing 'voies normales' behind a competent guide, or you can go for the Himalayan peaks, which require less of a high degree of specialization than a capacity to do ordinary things equally well at high altitude, when the oxygen is short. Or you can feel dissatisfied unless you are stretched on exceptionally severe rock. Many young climbers feel that they have not climbed unless they have gone near a limit, pushing that limit ever further and further ahead. Thus among the attractions of climbing (as against those of reaching summits) is that of developing technique, and so developing personality, overcoming fear, and co-ordinating one's own movements with those of others. For it is a special satisfaction of climbing in combination that the rope, skilfully used, links one climber with another in spirit as well as in body, and can, in doing so, often break down barriers of class or nationality.

It must be confessed that the specialized forms of climbing can be practised without regard for the mountains as such. In Britain, for instance, many people spend days on the crags without ever bothering to visit a summit. To confine oneself to such climbing would be to miss the deepest reason of all for mountaineering, one which links the canon of the St Bernard Hospice with the New Zealand bee-keeper and the Sherpa who first set foot on the top of Everest. By climbing mountains, by extending himself beyond the bounds of everyday experience, a man can set up a new relationship with something bigger than himself. At times, on a lonely summit at evening or as he crosses a dawn-filled glacier, he seems to acquire a rhythm which escapes the most ardent mountain-gazer. This both satisfies him with a deep intensity and gives him a certainty that on the other side of those mountains, the largest objects on his earth, there is something even bigger, of which he knows little but senses much.

It is for those who understand something of this urge to visit high places, and who are intrigued by the immense variety both of mountain scenery and of mountaineering experience, that this book is intended.

Wilfrid Noyce

1 The Mountains of Europe
The Alps

General Introduction

Five hundred miles long and up to 150 wide, the Alps extend from the Mediterranean coast through south-western France, Switzerland, north Italy, and Austria, to terminate near Vienna. They contain numerous peaks exceeding 12,000 feet, with Mont Blanc supreme at 15,771 feet. Formed during Tertiary times, they are built of great folds, including overfolds and nappes, believed to have been produced by powerful thrusting from the south. The broad arcuate pattern of the mountain system as a whole reflects the opposing pressures exerted by the ancient resistant blocks of France and southern Germany against and on to the edges of which the folds were thrust.

Along the northern and western flanks of the Alps limestones predominate, and peaks include the Eiger and Wetterhorn of the Bernese Oberland. The southern flank, as far west as Lake Maggiore, is also dominantly limestones and includes the Dolomites. The central zone between these two belts includes shales and slates, but is formed mainly of very resistant crystalline rocks, such as the granites of Mont Blanc and the Aiguilles Rouges.

The present relief shows only limited correlation with the geological structures, for the original folds have been severely eroded. The major folding culminated in mid-Tertiary times, after which much of the Alpine area was reduced to fairly subdued relief. In the late Tertiary renewed earth movements raised the mountains to their present altitudes, but these movements were mainly the uplift of large faultbounded blocks. During the last million years or so, the Alps, except for their highest peaks, have been several times submerged beneath a great ice sheet that reached out to the bordering lowlands to north and south at its periods of maximum extent. The ice has bitten deeply into the mountains and has gouged out the great U-valleys and cirques, leaving, between the latter, frost-shattered arêtes and 'Matterhorn peaks'. The present glaciers, although the largest on the European mainland, are tiny compared with the former ice sheets and are shrinking rapidly.

Historical

The place of the Alps in history is more important, perhaps, than that of any other range. Their barrier allowed the Roman Empire to germinate, and the breach of them by Hannibal came nearer to destroying that Empire in infancy than did any other feat. For centuries they were a shield, studded with Roman forts, of which the remains, in Val d'Aosta, for instance, still impress us.

When, finally, the dam broke and the empire dissolved, the Alps became a place of mystery; a place of refuge, too, for in the Middle Ages were founded the monasteries, such as the Grande Chartreuse formed in 1085 near Grenoble. Politically the picture becomes confused, both by the slow birth of Switzerland and by the part played elsewhere by the great houses. Switzerland, a Federation of twenty-two states differing in language, customs, and religion, shook off the Habsburg yoke during the fifteenth century, though the Bund was not constitutionally complete until 1874. It is now one of the most prosperous small countries in the world.

West of Switzerland, the House of Savoy became Italian, then finally French. To the east, the main range is predominantly Austrian, and many are the monuments to the House of Habsburg. Only for a few years, during the early nineteenth century, did Andreas Hofer raise the standard of revolt in the Tyrol. During the First World War some of the fiercest fighting took place in the Dolomites; as a price for her intervention Italy demanded, and received, this German-speaking region. That she has retained it since 1945 remains a point of friction with republican Austria.

Life in the Alps

Snow lies generally down to 9,000 feet while pine forests reach up to 7,000 feet. Below, the Alpine peasant carves out pockets of flat ground to hold his corn crops. Sheep and goats he pastures in summer on the high alps, cattle below. But modernization has hit the Alps. The tourist trade booms; the population drift is towards the cities; while in the valleys big engineering schemes flourish. In some parts whole villages are being deserted.

Alpine flora is a study of its own, the traditional association being with crocus, gentian, edelweiss, many types of saxifrage and primula. Of the fauna, preserved in many parts, one must mention chamois, steinbock, marmot, and eagle.

Early mountaineers

The Alps are the birthplace of mountaineering. In 1336 Petrarch made the first recorded ascent of a mountain for its own sake, climbing Mont Ventoux (6,273 feet) near Avignon. In 1492 Antoine de Ville used mechanical devices to climb Mont Aiguille (6,842 feet) in the Vercors. But, in general, to the farming and pastoral communities of those days, the mountains appeared frightening, the abode of dragons and demons and the source of terrible stories.

To the eighteenth century they were, on the whole, a

'Uniformity of Barrenness' (Dr Johnson). The sport was born of two parents: an awakening sense of their natural beauty and a scientific interest in them as evinced by von Haller and de Saussure. The first ascent of Mont Blanc, however, was made for patriotic reasons by a local doctor and a guide, who claimed the reward offered by de Saussure. The boldness and importance of their feat, however straightforward the route now seems, can be judged by the slowness with which its example was followed on other peaks. And however great the impulse of science, it was to the individual adventurer that these peaks usually yielded. Father Placidus claimed many; the Gross Glockner fell to a bishop, the Jungfrau to guides, the Ortler to chamois hunters (guides in embryo), the Finsteraarhorn to a scientist, though admittedly, he did not go quite to the top. The Swiss led the way, before the 'official' opening of the Victorians' campaign.

The 'Golden Age'

It is difficult to see why Alfred Wills's ascent of the Wetterhorn in 1854 should be regarded as the opening date of modern mountaineering. But it is true that from then on, for the next thirty years, the British virtually held the field. Aided by the growing body of local guides, they ranged up and down the Alps, sweeping everything before them. Apart from the Mönch, climbed by an Austrian rope, and the Meije, nearly all the remaining great peaks yielded to them. In 1857 the Alpine Club was formed, with John Ball, famous for his guide book, as first president. John Tyndall, E. S. Kennedy, Sir Leslie Stephen, H. Walker, A. W. Moore, the Rev. C. Hudson, Edward Whymper, C. T. Dent; these were giants, each claiming his share of achievements. It is perhaps unfortunate that Whymper's triumph and tragedy on the Matterhorn should be so popular a focus of attention. After the Matterhorn, only the Meije among major summits held out, to be claimed, in 1877, by a French party.

This was the 'Golden Age', and much has been written of the collection of lawyers, dons, scientists, parsons, and professional men who fled a too prosperous England to make it so. The Victorians were tough, aristocratic in outlook, reliant on their guides. Men like the great Jean-Antoine Carrel, an amateur in his passion for the Matterhorn, Michel Croz, Melchior Anderegg, Christian Almer, gained a vast experience. As time passed, science, and the contemplative aesthetic of Ruskin, both gently mocked by Stephen in *The Playground of Europe*, gave way to an unashamed quest for the new: for minor summits and untrodden flanks. Outstanding collector of peaks was W. A. B. Coolidge, author, with Martin Conway, of the Conway/Coolidge guide books, and among the first winter mountaineers. On new flanks, the Brenva Ridge of Moore's 1865 party was followed by such noble lines as the south-west ridge of the Schreckhorn, the Viereselsgrat of the Dent Blanche, the Zmutt of the Matterhorn, and finally the great Peuterey Ridge of Mont Blanc.

Before 1914

A. F. Mummery, the dynamic leader who first climbed the Grépon, with guides, and claimed the Requin guideless, looked forward to an age, and a technique, of which most Victorian pioneers had not dreamed. Guido Rey and others still climbed with guides; but Mummery's habit of guideless climbing was carried on by G. Winthrop Young. Young's finest climbs, however, whether up granite wall or airy ridge, were done with Joseph Knubel. This party joined with the great Franz Lochmatter, V. J. E. Ryan, and Joseph Lochmatter for the dramatic south face of the Täschhorn.

Between the Wars

St Niklaus, the little village below Zermatt, was renowned for its great guides. But after 1918 pockets were drained; besides, people had begun to enjoy climbing on their own. The Alpine Club had been followed by the Swiss, French, Italian, and Austrian Alpine Clubs, and these built and maintained huts from which summits could be reached easily within a day. Only on exceptional climbs was it necessary to bivouac as the Victorians had done. Guide books made it possible easily to choose one's area and climb. Some guides, like Armand Charlet, still reigned supreme. But in general this was the age of young men, in particular of young men equipped with pegs or pitons.

Perhaps because they did not sympathize with peg-work, the British were not conspicuous during this period. Three great lines on Mont Blanc were claimed by them, and the north ridge of the Dent Blanche. But the major struggles were for the north faces inaccessible by hitherto known techniques, and Italian or German names came to predominate. The north face of the Matterhorn fell to the Schmid brothers in 1931, while the Italians advanced the standard of pegging on the smooth overhangs of the limestone Dolomites. Transferring his technique to granite, R. Cassin led, first the north-east face of the Piz Badile, then the Walker Spur of the Grandes Jorasses. This feat was followed very shortly after by the first ascent, after several disasters, of the Eigerwand by an Austro-German party.

Today

Even between 1939 and 1945, the Swiss, maintaining a neutrality more than ever precarious, continued to climb, as did the French under the Occupation. Meanwhile, over the passes, strange acts of war were rumoured. In 1946 the crowds returned, continuing what Sir Arnold Lunn calls 'The Iron Age'. More 'last' problems have been solved, most conspicuously on the Aiguilles of Mont Blanc and in the Dolomites. In the general trend towards rock, the British have joined as heartily as any, and the standard of peg-work has risen very high indeed. It is the vertical sides of the Alps, now, that are the 'Playground of Europe'.

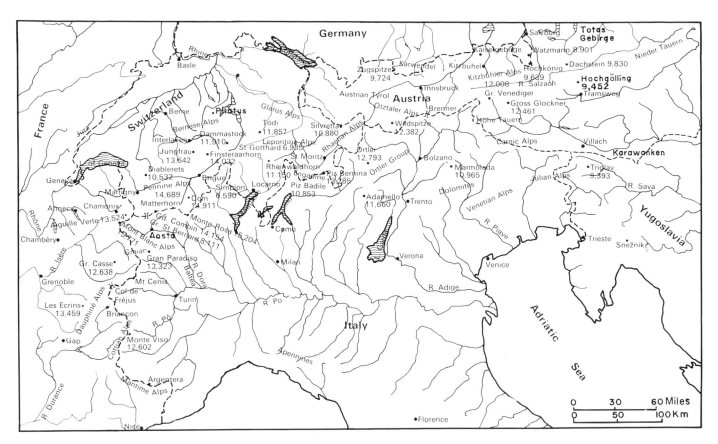

Ski and Winter mountaineering

The winter playground is on the snow slopes, and a word should be said in conclusion about skiing. Introduced from Norway in the nineteenth century, skiing took firm root and is nowhere more practised than here, French and Austrian being chief rival schools. Originally an aid to mountain travel, skiing developed a strong 'downhill only' appeal, with all the paraphernalia of beaten *piste*, cable-car, and competition. *Piste* skiing has been likened by Sir Arnold Lunn (himself a pioneer of downhill racing) to the cream, which some enjoy for its own sake without noticing the mountains that go to make the whole dish.

Ski mountaineering is an important craft. Good knowledge of the very varying snow conditions is essential, as well as mastery of ski technique. Since 1897, when a German party traversed the Oberland, the sport has caught on. Kurz and A. Bonacossa are said to have visited every district. In 1925/6 members of the French G.H.M. climbed all the Dauphiné peaks. Guides took to instructing in winter and some, like Armand Charlet and L. Terray, became great ski mountaineers.

There is no space to do justice to winter mountaineering on foot. It has had its advocates ever since the pioneer days of Coolidge and Miss Brevoort, above all of Mrs Le Blond in the 1880s. The great peaks having all been climbed in winter, the great routes started to fall also: climbs of the 6th standard in the eastern Alps to Germans and Austrians, and on Mont Blanc big climbs to Charlet and A. Roch, T. Gobbi, A. Ottoz, and W. Bonatti. The Eigerwand was climbed in winter by Germans in 1961 (T. Hiebeler and party), and the north face of the Matterhorn by a Swiss pair in 1962 (Hilti von Allmen, P. Etter).

The South-western Alps

First come the Maritime Alps, north from Nice and south from Turin, though some would begin with Mont Ventoux, the 6,273-foot summit reached by Petrarch which lies to the west, above the Rhône Valley. North of the Maritime Alps, with their spring delights of crocus and sunshine, the Cottian Alps boast Monte Viso (12,602 feet), a superb isolated peak with a neat route up its east face which was pioneered by Guido Rey. Northward again, the French Dauphiné is a distinctive region, a land of long stony valleys and upstanding peaks.

British mountaineers were early associated with the Dauphiné. Whymper climbed Mont Pelvoux (12,947 feet), and the highest point, the Barre des Écrins (13,459 feet). W. A. B. Coolidge was active on the Meije (13,068 feet), but its highest top, the Grand Pic, resisted for twelve years after the Matterhorn, yielding in 1877 to E. B. de Castelnau and the guides Gaspard. The traverse of the great comb-like ridge, first taken by the Brothers Zsigmondy and Purtscheller, is still a classic of the Alps, as are the south face and other climbs. Among other peaks, the Ailefroide (12,969 feet) should be mentioned, particularly its north face, climbed by G. Gervasutti and L. Devies.

La Bérarde is the chief centre, La Grave the second. Neither is more than a village, the sophistication of some Alpine resorts having largely spared the Dauphiné. It is in this district that history places the first steps in Alpine rock climbing with the ascent in 1492 of Mont Aiguille (6,842 feet) by Antoine de Ville with artificial aids.

Outlying the area of highest peaks are the ranges of the Grandes Rousses and Belledonne. The Dauphiné is profuse with its flowers, as are the Graians to the north with their wild life. The south-western Graians lie in France, peaks like the Grande Casse (12,638 feet) being approached from Val d'Isère, now a fashionable ski resort at the foot of the 9,088-foot-high motor pass over the Col de l'Iseran. Lower down, the valley has now been blocked to make a reservoir, and the village of Tignes has disappeared.

The Italian Graians are most easily approached by the Val d'Aosta, either from Turin or over the Little St Bernard from France. All along this valley stand testimonials to the strength of Roman architecture: forts and castles and walls, and at Aosta itself a fine theatre and arch. Descending from the south come four roughly parallel side-valleys, the most easterly, Valnontey, holding the little town of Cogne, 5,000 feet up. But the others also are worth exploring: unsophisticated, with rich hay for bedding, kindly peasants, and little-known peaks. A particular charm is the wild life; in this former game preserve of the King of Italy, chamois are almost tame, marmots peep from their rocks, and the *steinbock* gambol in greater numbers than they do anywhere else in the Alps.

Among the summits approachable from Cogne are the north-lying and graceful Grivola (13,022 feet), with its fine north ridge, the Herbetet (12,395 feet), and the highest peak, the Gran Paradiso (13,323 feet). This is usually climbed the easy and dullest way, from the luxurious Victor Emmanuel hut; but its north side, and the peaks to the east, have better sport to offer. There are few huts in the vicinity and bivouacs remain as much in order as they were in the days of Whymper.

On the south face of the Meije.

The Val d'Aoste, North Italy.

Perhaps the most beautiful of the Dauphiné peaks; the Barre des Écrins (13,459 feet). The north face can be seen rising steeply from the head of the Glacier Blanc. On the left is the Pic Coolidge (12,382 feet).

The Herbetet (12,395 feet) and the Gran Paradiso (13,323 feet). The latter is the highest summit in the Graian Alps.

Massif of Mont Blanc

Mont Blanc (15,771 feet) is the highest peak of Western Europe. In the Alps it is undisputed monarch. Its summit was the first of the great prizes to be won, and the *voie ordinaire* lures thousands each year. On the flanks surrounding it some of the most arduous Alpine climbs have been made.

The massif is one of the best defined. It runs roughly south-west to north-east bounded by seven valleys. The French-Italian border passes along the crest, to Mont Dolent (12,543 feet), which stands on the borders of three countries; for Switzerland is here represented, in the Trient and Saleinaz peaks. Mont Blanc itself stands up like a great snow dome surrounded by the granite spires of its minarets, the Aiguilles. Much more extensive on the northern Chamonix side, these are weathered to extraordinary shapes, their rough, firm granite forming, in crack and slab, the perfect gymnasium. On its southern, Italian side, Mont Blanc sweeps mightily down in the waves of the Brenva, Peuterey, and Brouillard Ridges towards the Val Veni.

From the Mont Blanc summits, the crest wriggles north-east over the remarkable Dent du Géant (13,166 feet), to the Grandes Jorasses (13,806 feet) with its 4,000-foot north face. From near the foot of this the Mer de Glace winds an icy way towards Chamonix, as further east the longer Glacier d'Argentière does towards Argentière. The mountains north-east of the Argentière, though finely proportioned, are built on more normal lines.

The French and Italian sides of the range have for long had a close kinship and much French is spoken at Courmayeur. The completion of the tunnel linking the two valleys should encourage yet closer ties. The southern slopes have remained Italian since the eleventh century; the northern, part of Haute-Savoie, have changed ownership several times, though the inhabitants have probably hardly noticed. The area belonged to the House of Savoy and through them passed to Italy when

The south face of Mont Blanc showing the three great ridges, Brouillard, Innominata, and Peuterey, and the Brouillard and Frêney Glaciers. In the centre can be seen the Brouillard Pillars, which provide a number of excellent routes. The Frêney Pillars are visible above the plateau at the head of the Frêney Glacier.

the capital moved from Nice to Turin. Since 1860 it has been French, but the frontier, apart from the Mussolini period, has remained very easy of passage.

In 1760 the Valley of Chamonix was a simple place, agricultural below, supporting sheep and goats on the slopes. Mont Blanc was the *Mont Maudit*, the 'cursed mountain', feared for its storms and booming avalanches. In that year the young Genevese scientist, H. B. de Saussure, offered a prize to the first men to reach the summit. After a number of attempts Dr M. G. Paccard, with a guide or porter named Jacques Balmat, made the ascent in 1786. This climb, perhaps the most important milestone in mountaineering history, was followed by an unhappy aftermath of controversy.

The early date of the ascent is particularly striking. For years the climb, done from the Grands Mulets, was considered highly dangerous, as indeed it was when undertaken by large

The immense Brenva Face of Mont Blanc, which lies between the Peuterey Ridge, the upper part of which forms the left skyline, and the Brenva Ridge, which is visible in the centre. In the foreground is the Frontier Ridge of Mont Maudit.

parties having very little idea of rope technique. At the same time poets had begun to turn men's eyes towards the beauties of snow and ice: Wordsworth, Coleridge, Shelley, and Byron among them. The ascents multiplied slowly, and with them the accidents. In 1808 Maria Paradis made the climb, in 1838 Henriette d'Angeville. In 1851 Albert Smith's ascent and lectures began the commercial exploitation of the mountain. Then came the Victorians.

The impetus of the British, here as elsewhere, was enormous. They were everywhere, and there were very few peaks and passes that they did not mark with their signature. Among major summits the Grandes Jorasses, Aiguille Verte, Aiguille d'Argentière, Mont Dolent, and Dent du Géant stand out. The names of Whymper, Walker, Reilly, Stephen are joined with those of their guides, many of them local, like Croz and Charlet. The ascents of this period were not made easier by the absence of huts. Mountaineers either bivouacked or walked through the night. But the Victorians seemed to welcome discomfort, in contrast to the too great comfort of their homes.

The Drus, bold outliers of the Aiguille Verte, dominate the Montenvers across the Mer de Glace. The ascent of the Petit

Dru by two guides in 1879 turned attention to the whole range of towering Aiguilles overlooking Chamonix. In 1881 Mummery climbed the Grépon (11,424 feet) with the guides Venetz and Burgener. But it was with his friends J. N. Collie, G. Hastings, and W. C. Slingsby that he climbed the Dent du Requin (11,228 feet), boldly anticipating a later generation. The greatest climb of the century, however, the Peuterey Ridge of Mont Blanc, was made in four days by the party of which Christian Klucker was guide. This immensely long ridge gave a third snow and ice route up a flank hitherto breached only by the Brenva route, which was done in 1865, and J. Eccles's remarkable line of 1877.

The climbs in the Mont Blanc massif are very varied. The Aiguilles give rock climbs as sharp and strenuous (cracks being a speciality) as any in the Alps. The big ridges of Verte or Jorasses give airy lines of arduous rock and snow. The monarch itself provides mountaineering of almost Himalayan proportion. One with an eye for all three was G. Winthrop Young, operating in the years before 1914 with Joseph Knubel and with friends. The Mer de Glace face of the Grépon, Twin Ridges of the Grandes Jorasses, and Brouillard Ridge of Mont Blanc are classics of three different kinds. In the same years, V. J. E. Ryan, with the Lochmatters, was making history among the Aiguilles, and climbed the Ryan-Lochmatter Route on the Aiguille du Plan in the remarkable time of thirteen hours from the Montenvers.

The spread of guideless climbing after 1918 did not stop Armand Charlet, doyen of Argentière, from riddling the Aiguille Verte in particular with wonderful routes of his own. On the great side of Mont Blanc the Innominata Ridge (1919) was followed by the Red Sentinel and Route Major (F. S. Smythe and T. Graham Brown) and the Pear Route (T. Graham Brown with Alexander Graven). But here, as elsewhere, the attention of the virtuosi turned to the north faces. The Frenchmen P. Allain and R. Leininger claimed the Dru. The biggest prize, the Walker Spur of the Grandes Jorasses, went to the Italians led by R. Cassin, expert in Dolomite tactics, in 1938.

Even during the Second World War first ascents were made, by French guides like G. Rébuffat and L. Terray; while the Pillars of Frêney on Mont Blanc were pioneered from Italy by G. Gervasutti in 1940. Since 1945 the accent has been more and more pronouncedly on rock, and Chamonix has become a Mecca. In 1952 the west face of the Dru yielded to the shock tactics of G. Magnone's party and its South-West Pillar, in 1955, to an astonishing solo *tour de force* by W. Bonatti, who had already forced the east face of the Grand Capucin. Attention turned to the great pillars which buttress Mont Blanc at the head of the Frêney and Brouillard Glaciers. In 1959 Bonatti and Oggioni climbed the Central Pillar of Brouillard, and in 1961 D. Whillans and C. J. S. Bonington solved an outstanding problem in the very high Central Pillar of Frêney. The right-hand Pillar of Brouillard yielded to Bonington,

A party on the Brenva Ridge. Behind lie the Dent du Géant and the Grandes Jorasses, with, in the distance, the Matterhorn and Monte Rosa.

The north face of the Grandes Jorasses showing the Walker and Croz Spurs. The former, climbed by R. Cassin's party in 1938, is one of the great classic routes of the Mont Blanc Range. On the left is the Col des Hirondelles and the Hirondelles Ridge leading to the Point Walker.

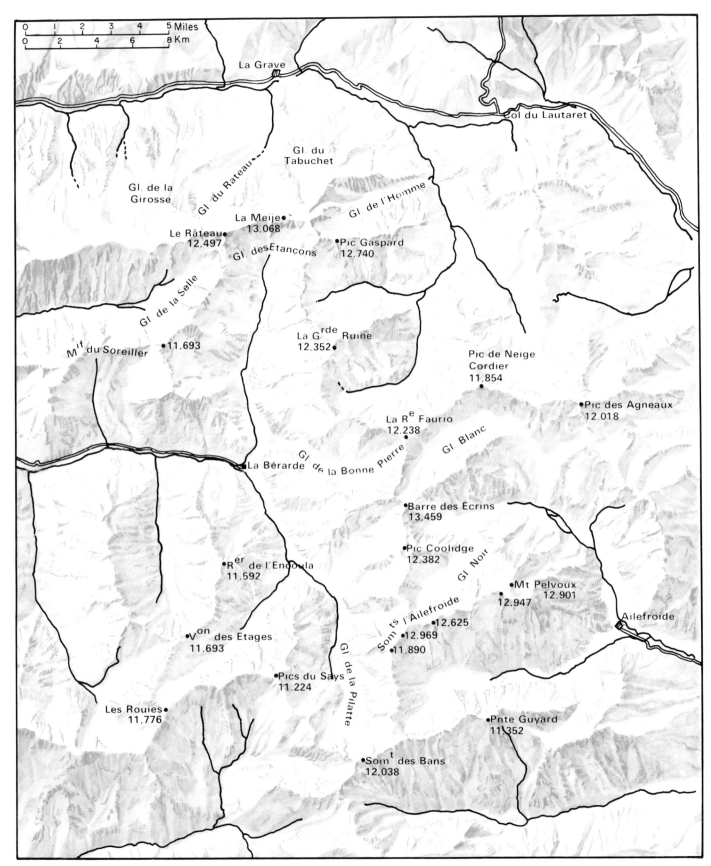

1. The Alps: The Barre des Écrins and the Meije in the Dauphiné.

2. The Alps: the Mont Blanc massif.

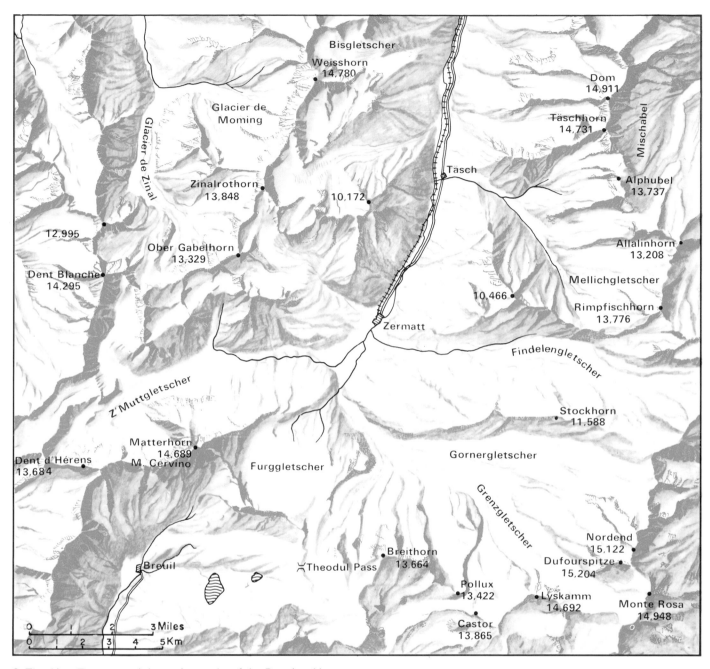

Bisgletscher

Weisshorn
14,780

Glacier de
Moming

Dom
14,911

Täschhorn
14,731

Mischabel

Täsch

Zinalrothorn
13,848

10,172

Alphubel
13,737

Glacier de Zinal

12,995

Ober Gabelhorn
13,329

Allalinhorn
13,208

Dent Blanche
14,295

Mellichgletscher

10,466

Rimpfischhorn
13,776

Zermatt

Findelengletscher

Z'Muttgletscher

Stockhorn
11,588

Matterhorn
14,689
M. Cervino

Furggletscher

Gornergletscher

Dent d'Hérens
13,684

Grenzgletscher

Nordend
15,122

Breithorn
13,664

Dufourspitze
15,204

Breuil

Theodul Pass

Pollux
13,422

Lyskamm
14,692

Monte Rosa
14,948

Castor
13,865

0   1   2   3 Miles
0   1   2   3   4   5 Km

3. The Alps: Zermatt and the major peaks of the Pennine Alps.

4. The Alps: The Bernese Oberland.

(*Above*) The Aiguilles République, Charmoz, and Blaitière.

(*Below right*) The Mer de Glace face of the Chamonix Aiguilles. From left to right they are Aiguille du Plan, Dent du Crocodile, Dent du Caïman, Aiguille du Fou, Aiguille de Blaitière, Aiguille du Grépon, Aiguille des Grands Charmoz, and Aiguille de la République.

Harlin, Baillie, and Robertson in 1965. A significant new factor has been the introduction of American techniques perfected on the Yosemite walls. The effectiveness of these methods was borne out in the direct ascent of the west face of the Dru by J. Harlin and R. Robbins in 1965.

Nowadays comfortable huts obviate the long walks of the pioneers and smooth the rock climber's approach. It is seldom necessary to bivouac, and Chamonix grows each year, adding winter sports to its other attractions. But on the great south flank of Mont Blanc there is still solitude, and the sleeping-bag can still be useful. Here, especially, the ghosts of the pioneers seem to linger.

(*Opposite*) The north and west faces of the Petit Dru, with, to the left, the Nant Blanc face of the Verte.

The Hörnli Ridge of the Matterhorn.

The Matterhorn (14,689 feet) from the north-east, showing the Furggen, Hörnli, and Zmutt Ridges and the north face. To the right is the Dent d'Hérens (13,714 feet) and, in the distance, the Mont Blanc massif.

The Pennine Alps

The line of the Aiguilles Rouges, north of Chamonix, is continued through peaks like the Dents du Midi (10,686 feet) towards the Rhône Valley by the Lake of Geneva. The main backbone turns east, along a line followed on the High Level Route from Chamonix to Zermatt by climbers and skiers, to broaden into the Pennine Alps. Here the Visptal, running south from near the Italian border to join the Rhône Valley, is flanked by more high summits than any other valley in the Alps. It has worthy neighbours, such as the Val d'Anniviers and the Val d'Hérens to the west, the Saastal, dominated by the Dom (at 14,911 feet the highest mountain entirely in Switzerland) to the east, and the Italian valleys running south from the main wall.

Rousseau, in *La Nouvelle Héloïse*, hymned the pastoral delights of the Valais. Vines, the highest in Europe, flourish in the Rhône Valley. The steepness of the hillsides above the tributary valleys makes agriculture a hard livelihood. To the mountaineer this area became, by the mid nineteenth century, one of even greater interest than the Haute-Savoie, since here a whole series of mighty peaks stood waiting to be claimed, and above all the incomparable Matterhorn (14,689 feet). The village of St Niklaus down the valley from Zermatt has been the home of the great guide families, of Lochmatters and Knubels, Pollingers and Gravens and Biners and many more.

The rock of the Zermatt peaks has not the granite-firm sharpness of Chamonix. The Matterhorn itself has been described as a heap of rubble glued together with ice. Thus the great routes here are usually of snow, or of mixed rock and snow. Including the mass of the Grand Combin (14,154 feet) to the west, many major peaks lie athwart the frontier, which swings round to allow Monte Rosa (15,204 feet) to present its huge glaciated east face, the largest in the Alps, to the Val d'Anzasca in Italy. The gentler Swiss slopes allowed Monte Rosa to be climbed in 1855. Then came a campaign which over the next ten years forced every major stronghold of the Pennine Alps, the majority falling to the ubiquitous British. In this most anglicized of Alpine districts Arolla, the charming

centre set 6,000 feet up at the head of the Val d'Hérens and surrounded by accessible summits, still has its English church. The Weisshorn (14,780 feet) fell to John Tyndall's party, the Dent Blanche (14,295 feet) to T. S. Kennedy's, the Zinal Rothorn (13,848 feet) to Sir Leslie Stephen; and finally the coveted Matterhorn to Whymper.

The Matterhorn luridly illustrated the technical deficiencies of the time. Whymper climbed the mountain by the Swiss Ridge (1865), easier in fact though apparently steeper than the Italian. The great guide J-A. Carrel of Breuil turned back that day, but climbed the Italian Ridge later. The tragedy of

(*Above*) The Zinal Rothorn (13,848 feet) and the Weisshorn (14,780 feet) from the south-east.

(*Below*) Steep ice climbing on the north face of the Matterhorn, with the Dom (14,911 feet), Täschhorn (14,744 feet), and other peaks of the Mischabel group in the background.

Whymper's descent, on which four climbers lost their lives through a slip and a broken rope, is the best known in mountaineering history. But the flood of exploration could not now be checked, for all the lofty disapproval of Queen Victoria and John Ruskin.

After the great summits, the great ridges. The Viereselsgrat of the Dent Blanche and the Schalligrat of the Weisshorn are two of many noble lines. Mummery, arriving with Burgener, made his ascent of the great twisting Zmutt Ridge of the Matterhorn, a mountain that was to captivate Guido Rey. In this district, as at Chamonix, the association of great guide with gifted amateur seemed to reach a high point with the ascents, shortly before the First World War, of Ryan and the Lochmatters, Winthrop Young and Knubel. The two parties combined on the south face of the Täschhorn in bad weather, a climb led by Franz Lochmatter and immortalized in *On High Hills*. Winthrop Young was also strongly attracted by the artistic possibilities of lines up mountain faces; with Knubel he neatly rounded up all three faces of the splendid Weisshorn.

Another face that had already attracted attention was the great Italian wall of Monte Rosa. The first route had been made by two Britons with Swiss guides as early as 1879. Another fell to Achille Ratti, later Pope Pius XI, and his guides. But here, as elsewhere, it was after 1918 that the short of pocket but increasingly expert amateur turned seriously to the great but often dangerous walls. Italians like E. Zapparoli and Frenchmen like J. Lagarde and L. Devies worked out great routes on Monte Rosa. On the north face of the Lyskamm (14,692 feet), and particularly of the Dent d'Hérens (13,714 feet), W. Welzenbach made bold direct lines. In 1931 the Schmid brothers from Munich climbed the north face of the Matterhorn; a route which repetition makes no easier. The other faces yielded after a struggle, as did the Furggen Ridge Direct, which 'went' with pitons in 1941 and, now that these have been removed, provides an exciting few hundred feet on difficult rock above the Furggen Shoulder. Since the Second World War there has been less rush for new routes here than at Chamonix; understandably, since the important rock faces are fewer and of poorer quality. (The east face of the Rothorn is an exception.) Perhaps for this reason, Zermatt, Saas Fee, Arolla, Macugnaga retain more of the atmosphere of the past than do many other centres. Outside hotels rows of brown-faced guides still wait for the daily '*Matterhornganger*'. Their lantern lights are now dimmed by the glare of the vast hydro-electric schemes which have been blossoming in but not beautifying these valleys, while in winter the Gornergrat railway and the ski lifts transform Zermatt into a ski resort of fashion and charm.

The Dent Blanche (14,295 feet) from above the Zmutt Glacier showing the Viereselsgrat and the north ridge.

The Bernese Alps

The Bernese Alps lie to the north of the Pennines and are separated from them by the Rhône Valley. These Alps contain no political frontier; some villages speak French, some German, some are Catholic, some Protestant. It is a big region, divided north–south by the line of the Lötschen Pass under which the Lötschberg Tunnel runs.

The West Bernese Alps are divided by short steep valleys descending to the Rhône into five masses. Important peaks are the Balmhorn (12,169 feet), Wildstrubel (10,640 feet), and

Diablerets (10,532 feet). The northern valleys are well known for winter sports, but those of the southern slopes are off the beaten track and inbreeding still produces occasional cretinism in the villages. The best-known north–south pass, the Gemmi, leads under the Balmhorn and Altels (11,907 feet), a classic traverse, whose east side dominates Kandersteg and looks across at the Blümlisalphorn (12,021 feet).

The Oberland, east of the Lötschen, is more intricate: an irregular complex of peaks and great glaciers. Unlike most Alpine chains, it presents a huge rock wall to the north, clearly

(*Above*) A party on the east ridge of the Doldenhorn (11,975 feet).

(*Below*) The Finsteraarhorn (14,022 feet), the highest peak in the Bernese Oberland.

seen in the well-known views from picturesque Berne and the
Lake of Thun. Thus, travelling south-west from Meiringen
over the Grosse Scheidegg, one has on the left first the sharp
peaklets of the Engelhörner, where now is a rock-climbing
school, then the Wellhorn and Wetterhorn (12,142 feet). Continuing the line is the Eiger (13,025 feet), with its 5,000-foot
limestone wall overshadowing the ski and mountaineering
village of Grindelwald. Beyond the Jungfrau (13,642 feet) the
wall takes a more westerly turn towards the Blümlisalp group.

Since 1912, when a great feat of Swiss engineering completed the Jungfraujoch railway, the interior of the Oberland
can be rapidly reached from the north. From the luxurious hotel
at the Jungfraujoch (11,400 feet) between the Jungfrau and
Mönch (13,449 feet) a paradise for all-the-year skiers can be
seen in the upper reaches of great glaciers, particularly the
Aletsch Glacier, the longest in the Alps. If one walks down
that in the direction of the Concordia (hut and hotel), even
the Jungfrau and Aletschhorn (13,763 feet) look no more than
excrescences above a great highway.

Below the Aletsch is the resort of Belalp, once more popular
than now, and at its head the Lötschenlücke, the gap leading
over to the Lötschental from which the isolated Bietschhorn
(12,907 feet) is climbed. East of the Aletsch and accessible from
Concordia the Finsteraarhorn (14,022 feet), monarch of the
Oberland, can be reached, or beyond that the Schreckhorn
(13,379 feet). The glaciers descending very low towards
Grindelwald from these peaks, and the size of the Aletsch,
are indications of the heavy snowfall of the Oberland.

The Jungfrau was climbed as early as 1811 by two Meyers
(Swiss), and the Finsteraarhorn in 1829 by two guides while
their Swiss employer, F. J. Hugi, stopped 200 feet short of
the summit. The highest summit of the Wetterhorn group,
the Mittelhorn, was reached in 1845, nine years before Wills's
much-publicized ascent of the lower Hasli Jungfrau, which
had also already been climbed. In 1857 came the Mönch,
led by C. Almer, in 1858 the Eiger, led by C. Barrington. The
Schreckhorn remained for Stephen's party.

As elsewhere, the great ridge climbs followed the great
summits. The south-west ridge of the Schreckhorn fell to
the great guideless combination of C. Wilson, J. H. Wicks,
and E. H. F. Bradby, who climbed it direct from Grindelwald.
In the days before huts many preferred a walk through the
night to an uncomfortable bivouac. The obvious but difficult
north-east ridge of the Jungfrau resisted till 1911. Meanwhile
the Swiss Alpine Club, founded in 1863, was as active here as
anywhere. Huts sprang up, the Gleckstein and Strahlegg are
monuments to Swiss building, the Concordia has developed
from a *gîte* in a damp cave to a palatial residence. With the
club there developed a tradition which rivalled that of St
Niklaus: Rubis and Steuris, Laueners and Jossis.

The Eiger north face: the upper section.

With one or two notable exceptions, the Oberland has remained better known for its snow and ice routes, and for its
skiing (Jungfraujoch for ski mountaineering, Mürren, Wengen,
Grindelwald for *piste* skiing) than for rock. It is also well
suited to winter ascents. The Nollen route up the Mönch and
the 1932 Guggi route up the Jungfrau are typically good ice
routes. Among the major peaks two rock faces are especially
conspicuous: the north faces of the Wetterhorn and Eiger. The
former yielded to N. S. Finzi with guides in 1929. The latter
remained a 'last problem'. In 1932 an unartificial line was
worked out on the slopes left of the limestone face proper by
H. Lauper's guided party, but this did not satisfy the piton
school. After some fatal accidents, an Austro-German party
climbed the face in 1938, taking four days. Since then ascents
have multiplied; so, too, have the number of fatal accidents.
In 1961 the first winter ascent was made by a German party
and in 1966 a direct route was completed by a combination of

(*Left*) The Eiger north face: Layton Korr and Dougal Haston
climbing the First Band during the first ascent of the Harlin
Route on the north wall.

(*Centre*) Traversing across the top of the second ice-field
during the first winter ascent of the Eigerwand by Hiebeler,
Kinshofer, Mannhardt and Almberger in 1961.

(*Above right*) On the Traverse of the Gods, Eigerwand.

1. Mont Blanc du Tacul and Mont Blanc from Aiguille du Plan.

British-American and German climbers (Lehne, Strobel,
Haston, Hupfauer, Votteler). J. Harlin, the leader of the
British-American party, was killed in a fall from above the
Second Ice Field. Controversy continues to surround a climb
which is exposed to objective danger and risk of bad weather.

The Central Alps

The Bernese Alps continue beyond the Grimsel Pass in less exciting peaks like the Dammastock (11,910 feet). Beyond this point the main chain divides into three. Northward lie the Glarus Alps and the massif culminating in the Tödi (11,857 feet), 'King of the Little Mountains' and easily accessible at week-ends to Swiss parties from Lucerne and Zürich. From Zürich, largest city of Switzerland and a clean, prosperous industrial town, home of the Swiss Foundation for Alpine Research, one takes the rail towards the Austrian frontier.

Due east from the Oberland, the central line is continued in the Lepontine Alps, a milder range crossed by four major roads and frequented by the Swiss though not greatly by the foreigner. Here, at the hub of the whole Alpine chain, we are on the frontier again. The steep southern wall drops towards the Italian valleys and the great lakes, which can be reached picturesquely either by the four roads or by the Simplon Pass to the south-west.

More important to climber and skier are the Engadine peaks. To their west the Val Bregaglia continues the line of the Upper Engadine westwards, towards Chiavenna north of Lake Como. The Bregaglia, with its well-placed Sciora hut and granite towers like Piz Badile (10,853 feet) and Piz Cengalo (11,057 feet), is becoming as popular with the advanced rock climber as Chamonix. The north-east face of the Piz Badile, 3,000 feet of rock first climbed with pitons by R. Cassin's party in 1937, has become a classic, although harder routes have been made on either side. Outlying this group to the south, in Italy, is the fine looking Monte della Disgrazia, first ascended by Sir Leslie Stephen with his favourite guide Melchior Anderegg.

The great peaks of the Engadine proper group themselves roughly round the highest, Piz Bernina (13,285 feet); to its west lies Piz Roseg (12,934 feet), to its east Piz Palü (12,811 feet); Piz Bernina yielded in 1850 to a Swiss party. Later, the name perhaps most closely associated with the region was that of its greatest guide, Christian Klucker, who climbed the north faces of Piz Roseg and Piz Scerscen with L. Norman Neruda, and others elsewhere, between 1889 and 1891. An outstanding winter pioneer of that time was Mrs Le Blond, who made the first ascent of Piz Palü in winter in 1898 and led guideless parties both in winter and spring.

Like the Oberland, the Engadine is a country of great snow routes; as such it has not, in recent years, had the attraction of novel rock routes exercised by the neighbouring Bregaglia and Dolomites.

Mention should be made of the great health centres in this area such as St Moritz and of Davos and Arosa to the north. Eighty-five years ago Nietzsche was writing enthusiastically

2. The Pennine Alps from the summit of the Dom.

The north-east face of the Piz Badile in the Bregaglia. First climbed by Cassin in 1937, it is one of the major north faces of the Alps.

of the healthful air of the Engadine. Nowadays enormous sanatoria for tuberculosis contrast with the atmosphere of luxury in this 'West End' of Switzerland, as R. L. G. Irving calls the eastern Swiss Alps. Here there is a more leisured environment than in the western Alps. In winter these resorts are the scene not only of the world's most fashionable skiing but of the great ski races on carefully prepared tracks.

(*Right*) A party on the Biancograt of the Piz Bernina.

(*Below*) The Piz Bernina (13,285 feet), the highest summit in the Engadine.

The peaks of the Sciora and Bondasca groups in the Bregaglia. Because of their remoteness, these peaks are not much visited, but they have much to offer the climber anxious to escape the crowded centres.

Austrian Tyrol and Bavarian Alps

Divisions of districts are artificial, for boundaries change with war. The Austrian Tyrol is generally taken to cover the peaks overlooking the Inn River, and when that turns north, the line of the Zillertal Alps and Hohe Tauern, by the Salzach. But the Ortler (12,793 feet), now in Italy, is really the highest peak of the Tyrol, and before 1918 it lay on the Austro-Italian border. It is in character more Tyrolese than it is akin to the sharp Dolomitic limestone of its nearest neighbours to the east. The Ortler was ascended as early as 1804 by Austrian chamois hunters.

The Tyrol has a character perceptible to the traveller immediately he crosses into the Vorarlberg. This mountainous corner of the Habsburg realm was a favourite of emperor and empress; the wonderful town of Innsbruck remains redolent of Maximilian I (sixteenth century), of the Empress Maria-Theresa and her consort. Only in the early years of the nineteenth century did the peasant Andreas Hofer raise the patriotic standard, saving the Tyrol from Bavaria and France. But he was betrayed by the emperor and sacrificed to Napoleon in 1809. The agricultural and pastoral Tyrolese turned back to concentrate on the hard job of wresting a livelihood from the mountains.

With the collapse of the Habsburgs and the loss of South Tyrol after 1918, eyes turned ever more inward. When the German columns came marching over from Munich in 1938, what could a small hill people do but escape to the hills? There is still an element of escapism in the attitudes of a delightful race which has produced some of the finest climbers and skiers of our time.

The Arlberg is the region associated with Hannes Schneider and the Austrian school of skiing. Even the children are experts; but knowledge of snow conditions is necessary for reasons other than those of sport, for in these parts some of the worst winter avalanches have destroyed whole villages, notably Blons in 1954. The peaks and passes of the Tyrol are particularly suited to ski mountaineering and touring: not too high, and provided with wide expanses of comparatively safe glacier.

Descending the Inn Valley from the Arlberg Pass, one is struck by the different nature of its two sides. Northward lie the *Kalkalpen*, bare limestone shapes whose highest point is the Parseierspitze near Landeck. The best known are the Karwendel, north from Innsbruck and the ski centre of Seefeld. Here gaunt grey buttresses contrast with rich pastures and birch woods. The Lalidererwand, first climbed by A. Dibona's party and now criss-crossed with harder routes, rises to the Laldidererspitze (8,474 feet). Of a similar nature are routes on the peaks around the Zugspitze, at 9,724 feet the highest peak in Germany to the west. The Zugspitze is accessible by railway, but on the steeper flanks the young Munich climbers train themselves with arduous rock climbs at week-ends, turning in winter to the ski slopes. In the Bavarian Alps the leather

The Karwendelgebirge to the north of Innsbruck. Because of their accessibility and sound rock, these peaks have become a training ground for the 'sixth degree' climbers from Innsbruck and Munich.

shorts and breeches of the Tyrolese pattern, and, of course, the felt hat, are still worn. Particularly between the wars, the Bavarian school of climbers was noted for daring artificial climbs and for winter ascents, such as on the east face of the Watzmann (8,901 feet) to the east, which sometimes involved dangerous rescue operations.

The range south of the Inn is built on more regular Alpine lines, the crystalline rock of the central fold predominating. Omitting the Silvretta, which belongs in Switzerland, the Ötztal, whose highest peak, the Wildspitze (12,382 feet), is a skier's joy, Stubaital, Zillertal, and Hohe Tauern are for the traditionalist the glory of the Tyrol. The first two of these groups are divided from the second two by the Brenner Pass, notorious highway for invaders of Italy. High, provisioned huts, like the Brandenburg in the Ötztal or the Berlin hut in the Zillertal, and not too high summits which necessitate no very early start, make the district ideal for beginners. The Austrians are companionable, lovers of song; the high pastures reach to the foot of charming peaks, the most shapely, perhaps, being those of the Zillertal. Of these, in a manner reminiscent of Skye, it is possible to traverse several in a day along the ridges. Among the Hohe Tauern to the east the Gross Venediger (12,008 feet) and Gross Glockner, at 12,461 feet the highest in Austria, were climbed early: the former by a large and distinguished Austrian party in 1841, the latter by the Bishop of Gurk's party in 1800, sixty-one persons reaching the summit. The Gross Glockner does, however, present a more precipitous flank, on which there lie difficult snow and ice climbs.

The Dolomites

The term Dolomites is usually used to cover all the limestone mountains of the Alto Adige and Trentino, east from the Bergamo Alps, though strictly it applies only to the formerly Austrian South Tyrol.

To a visitor the whole area looks more Italian than Austrian: there is more sun than in the Austrian Tyrol, whose weather is not of the best, and the valleys descend to the lakes and plains of Italy. Limestone favours a profusion of flowers to delight both botanist and ignoramus, some, like *Lloydia*, being a speciality. And dominant everywhere are the fantastic yellow and reddish-brown spires into which the original limestone plateau has weathered: towers and buttresses climbing dizzily above pastures, above blinding white waterless scree slopes, into a blue sky. Yet by Alpine standards the peaks are not high, and there are very few glaciers.

If one allows Örtler and Königsspitze to be part of the central chain, one must also allow the granitic Adamello (11,660 feet) and Presanella (11,667 feet). These are cut off by the upper Sarca Valley from the dolomitic limestone of the Brenta group: the Crozzon, Guglia, and Fulmini di Brenta and the Cima Tosa, the highest and easiest. The Dolomites proper are divided from these by the deep valley of the Adige, which descends from its confluence with the Isarco near Bolzano, capital of South Tyrol. A big massif, they are cut up by high passes like the Sella and Pordoi (high point of the road), and all within reasonable reach of the fashionable ski and climbing centre of Cortina d'Ampezzo. Indeed, the reddish-yellow south face of Punta Fiammes dominates the tea shops and dance halls of the town.

This region used to be part of Austria and the majority of its population is still German-speaking. Some of the fiercest fighting of the First World War took place here and the scars still show; on the Colle di Lana, for instance. The Treaty of Versailles gave the South Tyrol to Italy, and the peace of 1945, after both Italy and Austria had been on the losing side, did nothing to reverse the decision. It has remained a source of friction with Austria; the situations that build up are illustrated in H. Klier's *Etschland Ballade*.

After visiting Primiero in 1869, Stephen wrote: 'I hoped at the time that some of the peaks might turn out to be inaccessible.' His hope has been frustrated, and moreover the fine roads which zig-zag over the passes (particularly the Dolomite

The huge south face of the Marmolata (10,965 feet) from the Col Coldai on the Civetta.

road opened in 1909), as well as the hotel-huts, would have filled him with horror. In condensing the story of Dolomite exploration, it is hard to pick out the significant names and developments among so many peaks similar in character. It can be said, however, that, in the evolution of rock climbing, Dolomite climbers were well in the fore: apart from their steepness and exposure, the climbs here are long, rock is sometimes friable, and route finding difficult. In addition, the weather can change a climb quickly.

The region at first attracted continental rather than British mountaineers, though John Ball claimed Monte Pelmo (10,398 feet) in 1857 and E. R. Whitwell the Cimon della Pala in 1870. British climbers in general went where there was snow and ice. Pride of place must be given to P. Grohmann of Vienna, who claimed the Grosse Zinne, Cristallo, Marmolata (at 10,965 feet the highest peak), Langkofel, and three points of the Tofana. Surprising are the number of solo feats. G. Winkler made his first ascent of the hardest of the Vajolet Towers, alone at the age of eighteen, in 1887. P. Preuss climbed the Guglia di Brenta alone in 1911, a climb not repeated for seventeen years. H. Dülfer should be mentioned, and T. Piaz, the Italian who in 1906 reached the Guglia de Amicis by lassoing the summit, and who together with Guido

Rey first surmounted the great south face of the Marmolata.

But the development of Dolomite rock climbing can be illustrated most clearly on the Drei Zinnen, or Tre Cime di Lavaredo as they became after 1918. The routes of Grohmann and others took the straight-forward southern flank. Dibona nibbled at the great northern cut-off with his north-east ridge of the Cima Grande in 1909. E. Comici led his 1,600-foot north face piton climb in 1933, a route whose first 720 feet overhang. But this route now looks almost easy beside the *Direttissima* of L. Brandler's party in 1958. The same development has proceeded on the Cima Ovest, where the north face direct and Squirrel's Route attack some of the most formidable overhangs in the Alps.

Brief mention should be made of Dolomite skiing. For long day-tours—the circuit of the Sella Group is an instance—it is ideal. It has variety: *piste* near the centres, or seclusion and charm of view round the less frequented groups, luxury or simplicity.

The north face of the Civetta from Caprile. This face has a number of difficult routes, such as the classic Solleder Route and the Philipp-Flamm Route on the Quota I.G.M., which is one of the hardest 'free' routes in the Alps.

The Torre Trieste in the Civetta group from the south-west. The south face route, which starts at the top of the broken rock on the right, is one of the hardest free and artificial climbs in the Dolomites.

(*Right*) A party on the 'Spigolo Giallo', a popular Grade V route on the Cima Piccola, Tre Cime di Lavaredo.

The Tre Cime di Lavaredo group from the north. From left to right, Cima Piccolissima, Punta di Frida, Cima Piccola, Cima Grande, and Cima Ovest.

Artificial climbing in the Tre Cime di Lavaredo group: the start of the Couzy Route on the Cima Ovest.

Artificial climbing in the Tre Cime di Lavaredo group. The final roof of the Couzy Route.

The Langkofel group from St Ulrich.

The Eastern Alps

Eastward from the Brenner Pass the main line of the Hohe and Niedere Tauern continues north-north-east. The Carnic and Julian Alps swing southwards, into the Balkan countries.

The Julian Alps of Yugoslavia, though limestone like the Dolomites, are of weathered, faded, and forked appearance. Unlike the soaring dolomitic towers, these limestone shapes, even when precipitous like the Montasch, seem part of the country around. Some fifty years ago Dr Julius Kugy records that one could stand upon a summit and look round a horizon of unclimbed peaks. Even now the country is very wild and not the easiest of entry. Yugoslav climbers have done much, but new routes are still to be found. Triglav (9,393 feet), the highest peak, holds small glaciers and one of the largest rock faces in the Alps, the north face, first climbed in 1906 by K. Domenigg, H. Reinl, and F. Konig. The Route of the

Seven Lakes, starting from the Wocheinersee, is among the pleasantest. Perhaps the most handsome summit of all is the Jalouc (8,671 feet). The traveller is struck particularly by the poverty of the district and by the deep valleys, wooded below, which bite into this huge limestone plateau. East of the Julian Alps lie the Karawanken, on the borders of Austria, notable for the warm lakes and milder sunnier climate.

East of the Hohe Tauern, to the north, the Niedere Tauern extend a longer, less dramatic line of peaks culminating in the Hochgolling (9,452 feet). More exciting is the line of summits north of the Rivers Salzach and Enns. First the Kaisergebirge, that 'perky offshoot' of the Alps which came into prominence with the development of the piton school of Munich. To take an example of the harder and harder routes still being done

Valley near Bleiberg in the Gailtal, Carnic Alps.

Skrlatica in the Julian Alps, northern Yugoslavia.

The south face of the Dachstein (9,830 feet).

here: the south-east wall of the Fleischbank (H. Dülfer alone 1913) was superseded by a much harder south-east wall in 1925. Now the east wall direct is said to make even the south-east wall look like an easy day for a lady.

South from the Kaisergebirge is the high ski resort of Kitzbühel, known for the number and variety of its runs. The Berchtesgaden Alps eastwards culminate in the Watzmann, which has the highest rock face of the eastern Alps, scene of much drama and of a solo winter ascent by H. Buhl in 1953.

The River Salzach turns north, to the town of Salzburg at the foot of the Berchtesgaden Alps and Tennengebirge, and with its castle the picturesque centre of art and music festivals. The ease–west line of the Salzach is continued by the Enns, and still the more exciting ranges lie along the northern horizon. The Dachstein–Torstein group attracts thousands of climbers from all over Austria each year. Since the direct

(*Opposite*) The summit of the Klein Glockner (12,349 feet) in the Hohe Tauern, Austrian Tyrol.

route was first climbed by the Steiner brothers in 1909, the great limestone south face of the Dachstein (9,830 feet) has been criss-crossed with passages of every difficulty.

Eastwards again is the Totes Gebirge, the region of 'dead mountains'. Here, as on mountains as low as the Sparnfeld (7,366 feet), formidable rock faces are found comparable with, though still much larger than, those on which British climbers exercise themselves at week-ends. But it is for gentler delights that the extreme east end of the chain, like the Ligurian hills of Italy, are to be sought. At last the Alps subside peacefully into the vineyards of the Danube Valley near Vienna.

Wilfrid Noyce

The Pyrenees

Introduction

The Pyrenees, which rise to over 11,000 feet, divide France and Spain. The northern slopes where the plains are much nearer to the peaks are better watered, and the main glaciers occur on the north flanks of the Central Pyrenees. But even these are shrinking rapidly.

Climate and flora change greatly as one passes from west to east. The western climate is oceanic with high precipitation, and the north-west is the most thickly wooded area. The flora is that of Northern Europe, whereas that of the drier Eastern Pyrenees is Mediterranean. Besides saxifrages are several rare plants found only here in Europe. Among the fauna is the rare Pyrenean ibex, and bears are still reported on the Spanish side.

Special features of the scenery are the small lakes, the tortents or *gaves*, and the tremendous waterfalls, that of Gavarnie being the highest. There are low passes only at the extremities of the range, where the principal roads and railways between France and Spain run, but few roads cross the mountains.

Thus the range is an admirable natural frontier, and attempts to disregard it have always ended in failure. The most romantic legendary association is with Charlemagne's retreat, during which Roland with his sword supposedly hacked out the huge limestone cleft of the Brèche de Roland above Gavarnie. (Legend has a cheerful way of disregarding geology.) Important also in history has been the long-lasting culture of the Basques, not only in the Basque province of the Spanish side but in France too, where the proximity of towns like Pau, Lourdes, and Perpignan has been important to the culture of the near-by hill people. At the same time, the Pyrenean highland peasant, particularly on the Spanish side, remains little changed. Unmoved he has witnessed strange scenes in times of war, and he helped those who fled the Nazi occupation. Who can blame him if he makes his little bit out of smuggling across the passes?

View from the Pic Longue on the Vignemale (10,820 feet) towards Gavarnie. In the foreground is Montferrat (10,574 feet).

The Central Pyrenees: a view from the south-west of the Punta Maladetta (10,991 feet) and the highest summit in the Pyrenees, the Pic d'Aneto (11,168 feet). These summits, which lie wholly within Spain, provide good routes at a moderate standard.

Western Section, to Val d'Aure

It will be convenient to consider the districts from west to east.

The first important summit is the easy Pic d'Anie, west of Lescun. It is generally much more difficult in the Pyrenees than in the Alps to pick out important summits where many groups are known rather for their routes and ridges than for their tops; but the Pic du Midi d'Ossau, standing out north of the frontier and east from the Val d'Aspe, is known as the finest of all *pics* (9,465 feet). Accessible from Pau up the Ossau Valley, it was first ascended before 1797 by an unknown shepherd. Since those early days every variety of rock climb, up to P. de Bellfon's extremely severe South Pillar of 1959, has been made.

Eastward again stands the schistous Vignemale (10,820 feet), the highest frontier summit. A great plateau surrounded by flanking walls, it harbours on its eastern flank the largest glacier, and in the Couloir de Gaube (North Face), an ice route first climbed in 1889 and still extremely severe. It has also, in the limestone north face of the Pique-Longue, the highest Pyrenean wall; and it has been a most popular peak ever since the first ascent in 1838 (by Miss Lister and the guides Cazeaux and Charles) by the long and relatively difficult Ridge of the Prince of Moscow. Later it became the passion of Count Henry Russell, who made thirty-three ascents and excavated grottoes, even, finally, in 1893, at its top.

Among climbers the cliffs of the Cirque de Gavarnie are the most popular. Dominating the Gavarnie valleyhead is a ridge of limestone summits overlooking the great wall and slashed towards the west by the cleft of Roland's breach. The highest summit of the district, the limestone Mont Perdu (10,981 feet), stands aloof to the south. Not notable for rocks, this holds a magnificent ice climb in the north glacier, first climbed in 1888 when the ice was more extensive. It overlooks the fantastic 'Spanish canyons', the Niscle and Arrazas Valleys above which high grade climbs have been done by J. A. Gavin and others.

But it is the north flank which most attracts climbers, and here the C.A.F. has been active. From valley to the top of the Marboré (10,573 feet), the wall sweeps over 5,500 feet up in huge steps on which, rather than on the summits, attention is focused. Climbs of every degree of difficulty continue to be discovered. In the drier months from July to September they swarm with climbers; to the mountain lover they are more impressive when mantled in winter snow.

Cauterets and Bagnères de Bigorre (observatory on Pic du Midi de Bigorre) have developed as resorts, whence many gentler summits may be visited. Nearer to Gavarnie is the granite massif culminating in the Pic de Néouvielle (10,144 feet), and south of this is the Pic Long (10,479 feet), the highest French peak. Due east from Gavarnie come the cirques of Estaube and Troumouse (highest point the Pic de la Munia, 10,235 feet). Though less sensational in general, Troumouse is graced with two spectacular and difficult Sisters.

East from Aragnouet

Accessible from the Aure and Luchon Valleys are granite massifs like the Hourgade, Perdighero, Crabioules, and Quaïrat. But the high summits are soon once more on the Spanish side, the range at this point forming two parallel lines briefly overlapping at the centre. The bridge between is the grassy Bonaiguë Pass, at the head of the Val d'Aran, and the Maladetta group (Punta Maladetta, 10,991 feet, and Pic d'Aneto or Néthou, 11,168 feet) stands south of the bridge, in Spain, separated from the Pic des Posets (11,040 feet) by the deep Esera Valley, in which is the picturesque Bénasque (reached from Luchon over the Port de Bénasque).

The Aneto, highest Pyrenean summit, had been attempted in the eighteenth century long before its ascent in 1842. From the Rencluse hut the ascent of this peak and Punta Maladetta is not difficult, but in the sharp Fourcanade (9,400 feet) the group provides north face lines of sterner quality. In the Pyrenees in general, but particularly over the border, camping rather than huts is the answer to an expedition's accommodation.

(*Right*) The Cirque de Gavarnie, Pyrenees. Only recently has attention focused on the great walls above the cirque which offer climbs of great difficulty.

The Sierra dos Encantados in the Spanish Pyrenees. Spring thaw in the Gerbe Valley, with, in the background, A'Mitjes (9,344 feet).

The Aiguilles de Travessany in the Sierra dos Encantados, Spanish Pyrenees.

3a. Weisshorn from the Täsch hut.
3b. On the south face of the Aiguille du Midi.

Eastward is the Montarto massif, and east again, set among their secluded valleys and lakes, the cirques of Colomés and Sabouredo, and the limestone Encantados above Espot. The 9,000-foot lower summit of these twin peaks is perhaps the one Pyrenean summit offering no easy route. Colonel Brulle and Count d'Astorg climbed it in 1902; the north face yielded a difficult route in 1926.

These Spanish peaks are comparatively little visited and have the charm of new country. The same can be said of the frontier chain which starts again beyond Val d'Aran. While it still forms a mountain barrier, it has no glaciers, little perpetual snow, and its flanks are less steep. To the mountaineer it has little of great technical interest, but to the general traveller it is fascinating, and the little principality of Andorra, accessible without difficulty from France, lies tucked away in its recesses. Climate, vegetation, and people become more Mediterranean in character as one approaches the sea.

To sum up: the Pyrenees have few great ice climbs, but numerous Alpine-type rock climbs of every difficulty, on limestone and granite. Being lower than the Alps, the mountains are more easily accessible from hut or camp; since almost all have an easy way, the district is ideally suited to less experienced parties. In the remoter parts there is still much exploration to be enjoyed: wild country and its proudly unsophisticated inhabitants.

Wilfrid Noyce

Other European Areas

Italy south of the Alps

Though few other climbers get beyond the Alps, the mountains of the Italian peninsula are deservedly popular with the Italians. The C.A.I. authorizes guides and maintains huts, and there is also good skiing all down the peninsula.

The northern Apennines are mainly slatey and sedimentary; but the Apuan Alps, standing apart from the main Apennine chain, are real marble mountains; for example, the striking Pizzo d'Uccello capped with limestone. Further south, in the Abruzzi, Corno Grande in the Gran Sasso group is, at 9,616 feet, the highest summit outside the Alps. In these broken limestone peaks there is climbing of a high standard, and they are easily accessible from Rome. Near Naples is Vesuvius and the more precipitous Monte Sant'Angelo with its limestone climbs. Further south again, the wild dry mountains of Italy's toe are comparatively little known.

Germany (excluding the Alps)

The ski and fell country of the Harz, Riesengebirge, Böhmer Wald, and Black Forest should be mentioned. The sandstone pinnacles of 'Saxon Switzerland' are freaks; but in many valleys, accessible from towns like Regensburg and Nüremberg, are vertical limestone cliffs and pinnacles, popular at week-ends and a training ground of the piton school.

For the Bavarian Alps, see the Alpine section (page 35).

France (excluding the Alps)

There is a great deal of outcrop climbing in France, much of it highly specialized and on big outcrops. Near Paris, the sandstone of Fontainebleau offers a wide variety of routes, some of them trick problems. To the east the well-known limestone pinnacles of the Ardennes extend into Belgium and Luxemburg.

Discovered by M. Martin in 1939, the 200-foot limestone overhangs of Le Saussois above the River Yonne at the gateway of Burgundy are now the most popular training ground of French '7th degree' tigers.

Further south, the Massif Central culminates in the Auvergne at Mont Dore (6,188 feet). The rounded Cevennes, celebrated by André Chamson, are famous for their hot summers and fiercely cold, snowy winters.

The best-known sea cliffs, the limestone Calanques near Marseille, rise in places to 1,000 feet and have been popularized by G. Rébuffat and others. They yield extremely severe routes, free and artificial, amid soft Mediterranean scenery.

4. The Welsh peaks: Lliwedd, Snowdon, and Crib Goch.

Spain beyond the Pyrenees

Spain is a country of big mountain massifs and broad plains. Generally, the northern mountains are of limestone; the most striking are the Picos de Europa, a group reminiscent of the south-east limestone Alps in which, from the years before the First World War, very hard ascents have been made. The other limestone districts have been extensively explored by Spanish clubs.

The highest peaks of South Spain, the Sierra Nevada, lie close to the Mediterranean, in Andalusia. Composed mainly of shales, they attain their highest point in Cerro de Mulhacén (11,420 feet). Due to the unstable nature of the rock, they are of interest chiefly for the fine views, the skiing, and the richness of their vegetation.

Mediterranean Islands
Corsica

The mountains of Corsica are divided into two groups, the western being granitic on the Alpine pattern and including the highest peak, Monte Cinto (8,890 feet), while the eastern group is composed of crystalline schists which have not stood up to erosion. This group is not of great interest to climbers.

The early political history of the country was stormy. After nearly 200 years under Genoese rule, the Corsicans broke away in 1729 and set up their own short-lived monarchy. Despite British intervention and the efforts of Pasquale Paoli, Corsica was taken over by France in 1769. Apart from a two-year period from 1794, and again briefly in 1814, it has remained French, and is proud to have given birth to Napoleon.

The coast has been modernized, but, inland, Corsica remains simple, even primitive. It has largely escaped the advance of tourism which is rendering parts of the Alps unsightly. Here lingered the *vendetta* celebrated in Mérimée's *Colomba*, and even in recent times bandits have lurked, harmless to the mountaineer and a source of interest to the villagers.

For climbing, the most attractive season is May and June, when apart from the hunter of *mouflon* the climber will have the mountains to himself, when the snow still lying adds thousands of feet to their stature, and when the *macchia*, or mountain heath, is in bloom. The streams are well stocked with trout. It is usual to camp out, huts being less common than in the Alps.

In the centre of the island and east of the watershed stands Monte d'Oro (7,842 feet), accessible from Vizzavona. The traverse of this amenable peak, which has all the Corsican features of pine forest, lake, good granite, rough scree, is a

Icy conditions on the Punte la Porte, which lies at the head of the Restonica Valley, Corsica.

classic climb. Monte Rotondo (8,610 feet) near by is the second highest peak on the island.

The most important massif is that of Monte Cinto. It was climbed from the south by E. Rochat in 1882, but most probably by shepherds before, since it is not a difficult peak. It dominates the surrounding valleys and commands a splendid view. It is usually climbed from Calacuccia. Northwards lies the cirque of Bonifato, noted for low-lying but fine rock climbs. South-west stands the splendid Paglia Orba (8,275 feet), the 'Matterhorn of Corsica'. Climbed most easily from the west, it has a harder east face which was climbed by G. I. and M. Finch in 1909. Harder still are the Amstutz/Risch route on the south-east ridge and V. Moroni's south face which, like the east face direct, reaches Standard 5. Paglia Orba overlooks the Viro Valley, and behind it, to the west, is the impressive Capo Tafonato, noted for the great hole 400 feet below its summit and for the short, Dolomite-style climbs that abound on it. The most enjoyable climb, however, is undoubtedly the traverse of the peak across both summits.

Other groups, like the Bavella, are very worthy of attention. In the way of detailed routes much remains to be worked out on peaks that are small by Alpine standards yet give a great impression of height. They also have the attraction of remote country which is still accessible to the traveller with only a week to spare.

Sardinia, Sicily, and Crete

Sardinia, the 'forgotten island', is loved by those who know it. The highest point is Punta la Marmora (6,009 feet); but it is the fine granite slabs and pinnacles of the Monti di Limbara, and the coast rocks, which form a novel and attractive climbing ground. Access from Italy is easy.

Though not a climber's country, Sicily should be mentioned for the great volcano of Etna (10,741 feet). Etna is a good mountain for skiing and is usually climbed from Nicolosi.

Crete is about the size of Corsica and equally mountainous. Though composed of limestone, its peaks are of little interest to the rock climber, but for the general traveller they and their hospitable shepherds have a peculiar charm, particularly in spring, when the snow is down.

There are three principal groups: the White Mountains in the west, the most extensive and important group, containing the highest point, Pakhnes (8,045 feet); Mount Ida in the centre (8,143 feet); and, in the east, the range culminating in Mount Dikte. The island belongs to Greece and is easy of access.

Wilfrid Noyce

The Carpathians

In this great horseshoe of mountains those of most interest for the climber are the Tatra, lying on the Polish/Czechoslovak border. For the general traveller, the Transylvanian Alps of Romania have the charm of wild, heavily wooded country, the hills being more dome-like than craggy and covering a wide area. Negoi (8,920 feet) boasts an impressive south-east face.

In extent the Tatra are small: thirty miles long and some ten across. In the west or Low Tatra, limestones are prominent. The High Tatra, south-east from the resort of Zakopane, are granitic and give both the best climbing and the two highest summits: Gerlach (8,737 feet) and Lomnica (8,642 feet). They run on into the Belan (Bielskie) Tatra, and have at least two small glaciers. The lower reaches and valleys are covered with spruce, silver fir, and pine, and the Tatra lakes are famous. The occasional (protected) bear can be found, and marmots and eagles are seen. Unfortunately Tatra weather has well earned its bad reputation.

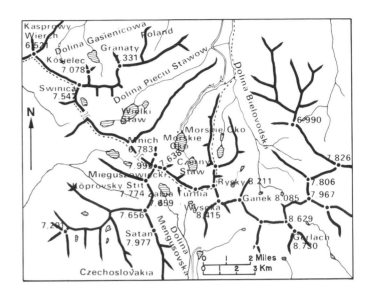

The High Tatra.

The High Tatra: Mieguszowiecki (7.999 feet) from Morskie Oko Lake. Several difficult routes lie on this, the north face, including the fine Alligator's Route, a Grade VI climb which has not often been repeated. On the right is Mnich (6,783 feet), which also offers fine climbing at a high standard.

Frontiers have fluctuated ever since the Magyar hordes settled in the southern valleys. Robbers were for long a Tatra speciality, but it is of interest that, until Hitler sent his divisions over the passes in 1939, there had been no organized fighting here for 1,000 years. The inhabitants are hard-working mountain shepherds, farmers, artisans, more inclined than Alpine peasants still to wear traditional costume, and great lovers of their traditional dances.

The Englishman R. Townshend climbed Lomnica, the most attractive of the peaks, in 1793. He was followed by John Ball, who made the first ascent of Lodowy (8,629 feet), and German, Hungarian, and Polish pioneers, including Dr Chalubinski, who first penetrated the forests on the Polish side in the 1880s. The ascent of rocky Mnich (6,783 feet) in 1879 by Pawlikowski and the guide Sieczka marked the beginning of serious rock climbing in the area.

The Tatra being Alps in miniature, and their most attractive feature being the airy, crenellated ridges above deep corries, climbing development followed the Alpine pattern.

The limestone faces of the West Tatra did not offer so strong an attraction; but by the 1930s climbers like Birkenmajer who climbed the west face of Lomnica, W. Stanislawski, and others were devoting themselves to the solution of all difficult face problems, routes being of the 3,000-foot order. Since the Second World War and with the advance of piton standards, much more has been done and the listed climbs number some 2,500. The Slovak club J.A.M.E.S. has been active on the south side, and one noticeable development has been in winter climbing, which has reached a high standard.

In winter, it goes without saying, skiing is as popular all over the Carpathians as in the Alps. There are fashionable centres for the sport, while many racing events are held here and there is also plenty of opportunity for ambitious ski-mountaineering.

Wilfrid Noyce

The High Tatra: the Mieguszowiecki group from near Bukowina.

Scandinavia

Introduction

The Scandinavian range is the longest in Europe, stretching over 1,100 miles. It also holds, along with the islands off its coast, the best opportunities for new routes. Faces 5,000 feet high at which nobody has looked seriously are still to be found.

The rock is inviting, since granites often alternate with the magnificent gabbro of which the Lofoten Islands, for instance, are composed. Difficult ice climbing is comparatively rare, though heavy precipitation causes extensive glacier fields, often tricky in the north where the low angle of the sun causes melting of the underlips of crevasses. Up here are the great snow caps, such as Jaegevarre. The heavy precipitation, due to the near-by Gulf Stream, makes the weather unreliable– though perhaps not more so than that of the British Isles–and causes a luxuriance of bracken and other growths which can present a hindrance in the valleys.

While skiing originated in Norway and remains popular, mountaineering made a slow start. The explorations of the greatly revered W. C. Slingsby opened the eyes of Norwegians to the possibilities of their own country, and Norwegian mountaineers have now made outstanding contributions in many ranges.

For parties prepared for camping and a variety of travel by boat, train, bus, car, or on foot, there is enormous scope, including some arctic travel. The range does not divide countries, and in the north the high mountains, like Kebnekaise, are over the Swedish border. Moreover, in these northern regions the nomadic Lapps move from place to place with their reindeer, caring nothing for frontiers; the traveller, in a more circumspect way, can do likewise. In all his travels he will be gratified by the hospitality of Scandinavian farmers and fishermen: by bowls of creamy milk, fresh fish, and berries for his camps, and, when the weather turns, by the welcome of some Lapp shanty or fisherman's hut.

South-west Norway

In all Norwegian travel, one is limited by the fjords, which bite at right-angles to the main core. Thus, 'Norway from end to end' would hardly be possible, while simply to work round one fjord, as J. M. Edwards did, may demand many days and much difficult rock climbing. The easiest access to the south-western peaks is by sea to Bergen, thence by coastal steamer and bus; or one can take the train from Oslo, passing the Havanger. Usually a combination of boat, train, and bus travel is the answer.

From Bergen up the Sogne Fjord one reaches Turtegrö,

Store Skagastølstind (7,888 feet), a magnificent peak in the Hurrungane group of the Jotunheimen, which was first climbed by Slingsby in 1876. The Hurrungane group offers good climbing on gabbro.

centre for the fine and popular Horungtinder. The finest peak, Store Skagastølstind (7,888 feet), was climbed first by Slingsby. A little north, in the Jotunheimen, stand the two highest Scandinavian summits: the shapely Galdhøpiggen (8,098 feet) and Glittertind (8,009 feet). North again are the Troldheim, on which steep ice as well as rock may be found. For the rock climber, interest centres in the easily accessible coastal districts of Sunnmöre, Romsdal, and Nordmöre, a land

(*Left*) The unbroken slabs of Stetind (4,530 feet) in the Tys Fjord region. The first ascent was made by A. B. Bryn, C. W. Rubenson, and F. Schjelderup in 1910 by way of the south-east ridge.

(*Below left*) Looking towards the mountains of Swedish Lapland from the Jiekkevarre icecap.

associated in Norwegian Saga with the 'trolls' and now well equipped with hotels, huts, and guides. In Sunnmöre, from the centre of Öye, gabbro peaks with still unclimbed ridges can be found. The peaks above Romsdal Fjord, approached from Andalsnes, are equally popular: Dronninga (5,144 feet), Juratind (5,124 feet), particularly Kvanndalstind (5,826 feet), climbed in 1885 by C. Hopkinson, W. C. Slingsby and L. Jansen, and the Romsdalshorn (5,102 feet), first climbed in 1827 but now with a variety of hard routes by A. R. Heen and others. Finally, there is the great jagged ridge of the Trolltinder (5,886 feet), containing the immense wall of the Trollryggen. This 4,500-foot wall, perhaps the steepest in Europe, was climbed in 1965 by J. Amatt, A. Howard, and W. Tweedale.

Looking south to the Jiekkevarre (6,012 feet) from the Trolltind, Lyngen.

In the Nordmöre area round Sunnalsöra, we find Slingsby's 'awful chimney of nearly 6,000 feet' on Harstadnebba. This is, in fact, a wall whose immensity had attracted a number of climbers from different countries. It was finally climbed by R. Hoibakk and O. Innerdal in 1961.

Arctic Norway and Sweden

Best known are the superb gabbro peaks of the Lofoten Islands. The Lofoteners live largely by cod fishing; and it was here, in March 1941, that the most successful Allied raid of the Second World War took place.

Though not high (the highest peak is Möysalen, 4,152 feet), the peaks gain in stature through rising straight from the

Peaks of the Jegervasstind group, Lyngen Peninsula, Norway.

fjords which bite into the islands. Svolvaer, on North Austvagöy, is a usual starting-point, for here the coast boat puts in. Above it rises the spectacular 1,000-foot 'Goat', for climbing whose horns Slingsby received the freedom of the town. But by taking a small boat one can reach the start of many climbs on other islands; indeed, one can begin climbs straight from the boat. Notable peaks are the Trolltinder (3,428 feet), Trakta (3,248 feet), and Rulten (3,485 feet) above the great gash of the Troll Fjord cutting into Austvagöy from the Raftsund. But particularly on Hinnöy, the largest island,

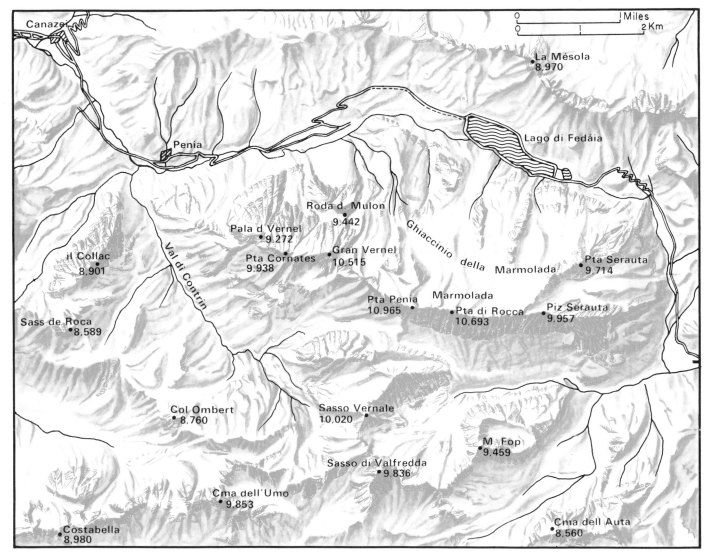

5. The Alps: Marmolada in the Dolomites.

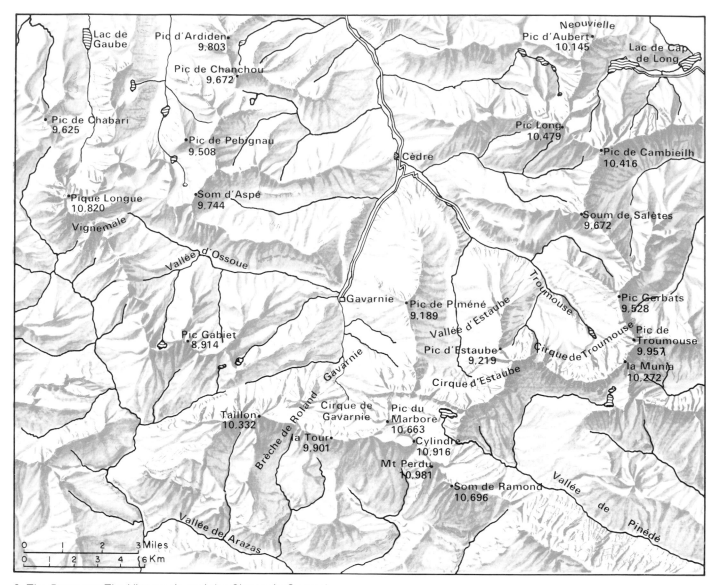

6. The Pyrenees: The Vignemale and the Cirque de Gavarnie.

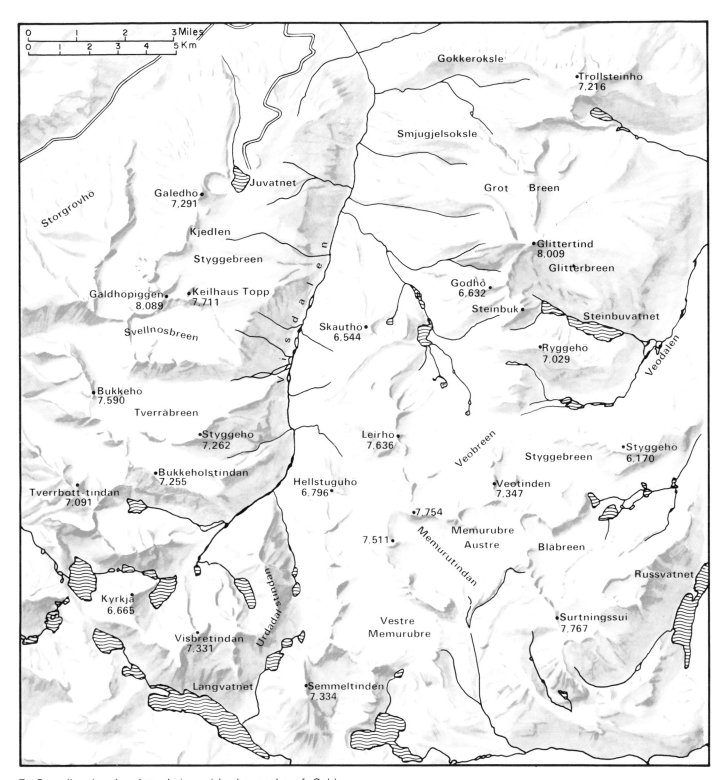

7. Scandinavia: the Jotunheim with the peaks of Gald-
hoppegen and Glitterstind.

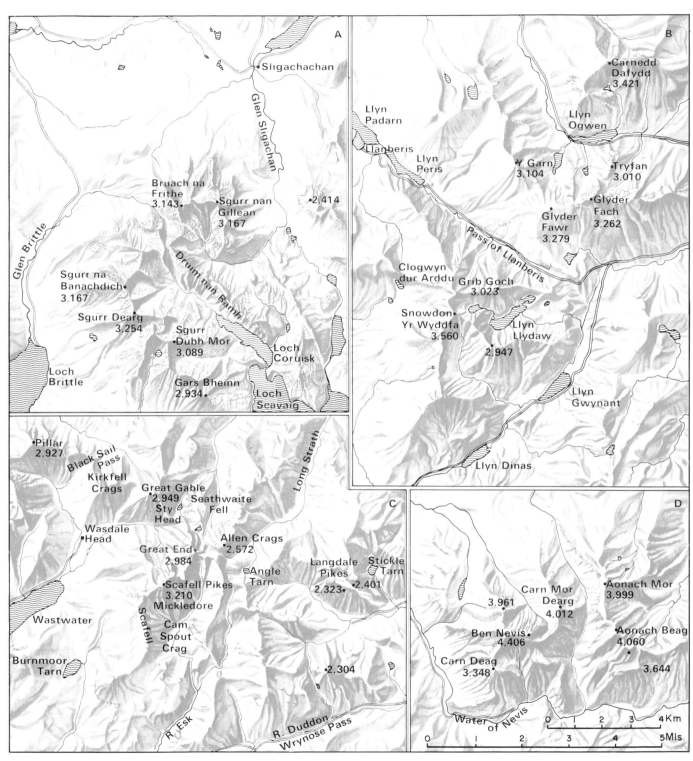

8. Some British peaks: (A) the Cuillin Hills, Skye; (B) Snowdonia; (C) The Lake District; (D) Ben Nevis.

there is a wealth of new routes, and even some new peaks waiting to be climbed.

Returning to the mainland, we find the high mountains are now in Sweden. The peaks culminating in Kebnekaise (6,965 feet) are well glaciated and arctic in appearance. Arctic also is travel in the Sarek district, the most extensive and wildest of Lappland. Tents must be carried and the only local food in the fine summer months is a profusion of wild berries.

More exciting to the climber, as the coast boat pursues its journey north, is the 5,000-foot Stetind, a granite obelisk which was attempted by Slingsby, who termed it 'the ugliest mountain in the world', and climbed by a Norwegian party in 1910. Very severe artificial routes have more recently been

The Trolltind wall in Romsdal.

worked out, in particular by A. Naess and E. Hertzberg.

East of Tromsö, the Lyngen peninsula provides long gabbro climbs on the Jegervasstind group, and south of that, the great snow cap of Jiekkevarre (6,012 feet), the 'Mont Blanc of the North', climbed in 1897 by G. Hastings and H. Woolley. Here, and among the other arctic peaks of Finnmark, there is a land of promise. In these countries of the midnight sun, with all their advantages and disadvantages to the climber, much remains to be done by those who have the time and strength to do it.

Wilfrid Noyce

The British Isles

Introduction

The hills of Britain here occupy, inevitably, a space quite disproportionate to their size. The major climbing areas of the world are almost restricted to mountains of geologically recent origin, and Britain possesses none of these. Instead, the present hills are the eroded and subdued remnants of great mountain belts of the geological past, such as the Caledonian system that extended from northern Ireland through Scotland to Scandinavia. The present altitudes are largely the result of modest block uplift and warping during Tertiary times. As uplift occurred, rivers carved out their valleys; but the main agent responsible for our present upland scenery was glacier ice. Glaciers were especially active in the higher ground of the wetter west and north, where they steepened the valley sides to produce many bare rock faces and enlarged the heads of their valleys to form steep-walled corries or cwms. In places adjacent corries were enlarged sufficiently to leave only sharp-crested ridges between them, but usually glaciation was less advanced and easy walking routes to the tops of most British hills are consequently available.

Apart from local activity on cliffs and escarpments, almost all major climbing in Britain is on igneous rock, such as the gabbro of Skye, the granites of Lochnagar, the Wicklow Mountains and Mourne Mountains, and the volcanic rocks of the Central Lake District, Snowdonia (apart from Twll Du), Cader Idris, and Ben Nevis. This is partly due to the normally superior quality of igneous rocks, but also results from the fact that these rocks, owing to their resistance to erosion, form many of the highest hills of Britain and are often associated with steep rock faces.

Historical

Sir Thomas Malory tells that King Arthur climbed a crag, perhaps Lliwedd near Snowdon. From that date on a series of travellers recorded in solemn tones their ascents of Snowdon, Scafell, and Ben Nevis (at 4,406 feet Britain's highest mountain). Outside Skye, however, all British mountains can be ascended without use of the hands. Cliffs of anything from 100 feet or less to the 2,000-foot buttresses of Ben Nevis are sought out for their own sakes. Thus, while the practice of scrambling must be as old as the hills, gradually figures like Parson Jackson of 'Pillar Stone' were observed openly to be hunting out the steeper faces.

The higher hills are of heather, grass, and rock. While it is true that the nineteenth-century pioneers used them as practice for the Alps, they also came to enjoy the slowly recognized sport of rock climbing. At first they sought safety in gullies, the natural line up a cliff. Towards the end of the century, 'balance climbing' brought them out on to the faces and walls. Climbers were usually limited to certain recognized professions, and would gather companionably at hotels like Pen y Pass

The north face of Ben Nevis from Carn Mor Dearg showing, from left to right, the North-East Buttress, Zero Gully, Observatory Ridge, Observatory Buttress, Gardyloo and Tower Gullies, and Tower Ridge. In winter Ben Nevis affords climbing of 'alpine' severity in arctic conditions.

(North Wales), Wasdale Head (Cumberland), and Sligachan (Skye) over Easter and Christmas.

Climbing had advanced a long way when, after 1918, pockets became shorter, the basis of the sport wider, and motor transport a factor making it easy for young towns-people to explore the Derbyshire edges, Snowdonia, the Lakes, or Glencoe easily at week-ends. In the early 1930s a wave of exploration seemed to exhaust the Lake District for the time being, while Clogwyn du'r Arddu under Snowdon became the Mecca of Wales.

Another formidable rise in the standard of rock climbing came some five years after the Second World War. Technique was learnt from the Continent and new methods made possible ascents up 'unclimbable' faces. As rock climbing for its own sake becomes ever more popular, sea cliffs, gorges, potholes, and sandstone and limestone outcrops are thronged at week-ends; while eyes have turned further afield, to northern Scotland, Ireland, and the lesser known cliffs of North Wales for the remaining possibilities of major new routes.

The Lake District

The Lake District is an area of grassy fells slashed by cliffs, covering some sixty square miles of Cumberland and West-morland. Unlike Snowdonia or Glencoe, it is a land without history, a land of shepherds and agriculturists. Sung by the Lake poets, it was natural perhaps that in these most English of mountains the sport of rock climbing should be born. Local men felt the attraction; the jutting Pillar Rock over Ennerdale was first climbed by a local cooper in 1826. Another immedi-ately challenging feature was Broad Stand, the rock hump barring the direct route from Scafell to Scafell Pike (3,210 feet), the highest point.

The Alpine pioneers were already here before, in 1886, W. P. Haskett Smith made his ascent of Naples Needle, a pinnacle on the flank of Great Gable (2,947 feet). The game began in earnest. Climbers turned to Pillar and the 400-foot north face of Scafell for routes of ever increasing difficulty. O. G. Jones, soon in the van of exploration, climbed Kern Knotts Crack, a short problem on the flank of Gable and one of the first to be climbed entirely 'for its own sake'. Among other crags the most popular were to be Dow Crag, a big cliff above Coniston Water to the south, and Gimmer in Langdale.

The beauty of the Lakes themselves, from Windermere, over ten miles long, to the tiny tarns, continued to attract tourists. The compact firmness of the igneous rock attracted

The birthplace of British mountaineering: Wasdale and Wast-water from the Sphinx Rock.

the climber, and obvious problems like Botterill's Slab on Scafell, Eagle's Nest Ridge on Gable, or Savage Gully on Pillar exercised them. In 1914 S. W. Herford rounded off a remarkable campaign on Scafell by leading the Central Buttress, a climb well ahead of the day's standards.

Wasdale Head had been the traditional centre for meets, but after the First World War Langdale, Borrowdale, Ennerdale, Buttermere, and Coniston came into their own. The Fell and Rock Climbing Club put up its huts, camping spread. Lakeland enthusiasts vaunted the discovery of the east face of Scafell, some 250 feet high and giving climbs of the high standard of Clogwyn du'r Arddu in Wales. Notable among them were M. Linnell, A. T. Hargreaves, C. F. Kirkus, and S. Cross. A. W. Bridge did his climb on Esk Buttress, which along with the low-lying crags was to be explored after the Second World War.

The effect of the war on climbing was, as elsewhere, to bring increasing numbers on to harder climbs now more safely done with the use of modern techniques. The seekers for novelty are still able to find something, for the area is large. Crags like Shepherd's Crag in Borrowdale are popular (the

The Langdale Pikes from Elterwater Village.

Lakes have not many cliffs near a road, as Wales has), and as far afield as Dovedale near Ullswater exceptionally hard routes have been found. At the same time the wave of post-war exploration does not seem to have hit the Lakes with quite the same force as it did Wales. However, the popularity of the district both with walkers and climbers is enormous.

The Pennines

To use the term in its broadest sense, this is the spine of England, running for some 150 miles up to the Scottish border. Since the opening of the Pennine Way it has been possible comfortably to walk the whole length. In Derbyshire, to the south, the fells are impressive for their breadth and size rather than for shape, Kinder Scout (2,088 feet) being a large plateau crevassed by peat runnels. The rock climbing here is usually on long gritstone edges, such as Stanage, which is over two miles long and some fifty to 100 feet high. There are also important limestone areas like Ilam Rock in Dovedale.

Gritstone prevails also on the Yorkshire and Lancashire edges and cliffs. Mountains like Ingleborough, a 2,373-foot limestone mass, are of pleasing shape, while the Yorkshire moors generally give splendid rough or smooth walking. It should be added that the Pennines have the most extensive caves in England.

There may once have been a 'gritstone school' which specialized in this type of short gymnastic rock climb; nowadays gritstone is climbed both as an end itself and as a training for longer climbs, being very accessible from big cities like Manchester and Sheffield. Piton climbing has become a speciality in quarries such as Lawrencefield and on the limestone cliffs of Kilnsey Crag in Wharfedale, and at Malham Cove.

Wales

Wales is a mountainous country, and fine walking can be had in the south, on the Brecon Beacons (2,906 feet), and the Black Mountains, in the centre on Plynlimmon (Pumlumon). Rock climbing centres itself in the northern group of mountains around Snowdon (3,560 feet), the highest point. Some is practised on Cader Idris (2,927 feet) and the Aran cliff of Cowarch, a little to the south.

The peaks of Snowdonia are among the most shapely of this country; but the valleys, more bare than those of the Lake District, did not attract early seekers of pleasure. This was, also, a foreign land with a strange tongue and a tradition of hostility towards the English. The mountain shepherd, the buzzard, and the fox were left in peace; even quarrying and mining, of slate particularly, only developed into a big industry in the last century. And the early travellers usually stuck to the established routes up Snowdon.

The earliest recorded rock ascent was made in 1798 by two clergymen up the east terrace of the cliff of Clogwyn du'r Arddu. As mountains emerged slowly into popularity, Pen y Gwryd, the hotel under Snowdon, became chief centre, the Kingsley brothers visiting regularly in the days of 'old Owen'. Mountaineers multiplied, and about the turn of the century Pen y Pass, 1,169 feet up and right under the peak of Crib Goch, was found more convenient. The Pen y Pass parties became a dignified tradition, joined at Christmas and Easter by the great names in climbing. Lliwedd, the 1,000-foot cliff of Snowdon's eastern arm, fascinated particularly; they also explored the Ogwen Valley, the Carnedds (second highest group), and Cwm Silyn to the west. They enjoyed the ice-filled gullies under Y Wyddfa (Snowdon).

The First World War provided a check. The next wave of exploration, in the late 1920s, involved the filling in of routes on cliffs discovered but little known, like Clogwyn du'r Arddu (A. S. Piggot, J. L. Longland, C. F. Kirkus) and the Devil's Kitchen cliffs (J. M. Edwards). The Welsh cliffs, larger than those of the Lakes, were also looser and required all-round technique. Edwards discovered the 'three cliffs' of the

(*Left*) The East Buttress, Pinnacle, and West Buttress of Clogwyn du'r Arddu, North Wales. This impressive crag contains some of the hardest rock climbs in Britain.

Troach, an extremely severe route on the East Buttress of Clogwyn du'r Arddu.

Llanberis Pass, which had then a reputation for vegetation (rowan, holly, and yew) and rottenness. They are now among the most popular.

The Second World War came, bringing after it the wider use of rubber soles, karabiners, and the occasional piton, which Edwards had scorned. Upon the explorations of P. R. J. Harding and A. J. J. Moulam followed a series of ascents which sent the standard rocketing again. J. Brown and D. Whillans, members of the *Rock and Ice* group, were young men from the cities, trained on gritstone. Brown led Cenotaph Corner in Llanberis Valley, and a series of climbs on the smooth walls between the cracks by which Clogwyn du'r Arddu had previously been approached. Since then a growing number have been able to lead these routes. 'Cloggy' has seen a number of new routes, and the enthusiasts are turning to the lesser-known crags, those at Tremadoc, in the Gwynant Valley, and the sea cliffs of Anglesey and the Lleyn Peninsula.

Scotland

The mountain area of the Scottish Highlands, traditional home of the red deer and the eagle, is the largest in Britain. The Highlanders are a mountain race apart, renowned for their cattle, their crofts, their kilts, and their own Gaelic tongue. For the climber, chief areas of interest are the North-West Highlands, the mass of the Cairngorms culminating in Ben Macdhui (4,296 feet), Ben Nevis, the peaks of Glencoe and the islands of Skye and Arran. While Ben Nevis was early and often climbed, Sgurr Alasdair (3,309 feet), highest peak of the Black Cuillin of Skye, yielded only in 1873. Climbing of an Alpine nature attracted the Alpine pioneers to the precipitous gabbro of the Cuillin ridges.

Rock climbing as a sport was slower to develop here than in the south, partly because of the greater distances involved and the long months during which snow covers the mountains, partly because, outside Ben Nevis, Glencoe, and the Skye gabbro, rock tends to be faulted horizontally rather than vertically. J. N. Collie and others, however, turned seriously to the rocks, and in 1889 the Scottish Mountaineering Club was founded. A few years later the great northern cliffs of Ben Nevis, the highest in Britain, were explored, and also the granite of Arran. It was even found that one could practice on Salisbury Crags, an outcrop on the doorstep of Edinburgh.

In 1900 the Abraham brothers climbed the exposed Crowberry Ridge in Glencoe. Soon H. Raeburn was proclaiming Scottish mountaineering to be even better training than Alpine, since it provided so great a variety. Collie continued to dominate Skye. The general tradition was still more Alpine than in the south; great walks were done in winter and efforts made to tick off 'Munros'–from a list of 3,000-foot summits compiled by Sir Hugh Munro.

Immediately after the First World War the English seemed to hold the field, N. E. Odell, for instance, claiming the fine 1,400-foot Chasm on Buachaille Etive. The 1928 guide book

to the Cairngorms contained very few rock climbs, even on Lochnager. Soon, however, climbers like J. H. B. Bell and G. G. Macphee were breaking new ground on rock, and on long snow, rock, and ice climbs like those of Ben Nevis. This sort of climb became the speciality of W. H. Murray and his friends. At the same time Scotland was found to have long and very severe rock routes to compare with those south of the border.

Distance was being annihilated by motor transport, and, particularly after the Second World War (when hitch-hiking became respectable), the young of Clydeside began to stream each week-end into the hills, sleeping in barns or caves if they could not afford tents. Along with the extremely severe new routes on better-known cliffs, Scotland can still provide the charm of fresh ground; in the Torridon area, for instance, and on the islands. Meanwhile winter ascents of the harder routes on Ben Nevis, in Glencoe, and on Skye keep the standard of ice climbing high and provide training for the Alps, Andes, and Himalaya. Notable, perhaps, among recent achievements has been the first winter traverse of the Cuillin Ridge. On a different plane, the extension of ski facilities in Glencoe and the Cairngorms has had the effect of opening the mountains to an increasing number of people. Skiing has come to Britain in a big way.

Glen Sligachan and the northern Cuillin, including Sgurr nan Gillean, from Blaven, Skye. The Cuillin give excellent climbing on gabbro and are perhaps the closest approach to Alpine climbing in Britain.

Ireland

For the walker, the scattered mountain groups of Ireland, unmarred by the litter and crowd that sometimes embarrass him in England, have for long been a land of pleasure. For the climber, this is also a land of promise. Only since the Second World War has intensive climbing started. The present Irish Mountaineering Club was founded in 1948.

Accessible from Dublin and giving fine routes of high standard are the granite cliffs of Glendalough in the Wicklows, whose highest point is Lugnaquilla (3,039 feet). In Northern Ireland the Mournes (Slieve Donard, 2,796 feet) have some compact small crags. But the seeker after solitude goes south and west, where fresh gullies of the old-fashioned type can be climbed alongside the most novel 'peg routes'.

In the southern counties, on the highest mountains of Ireland, the Macgillicuddy's Reeks, which include Carrantuohill (3,414 feet), red sandstone is not so favourable to climbing as other rocks. Clare, Galway, and Mayo have some of the wildest country and best opportunities. Among several mountain groups of different rock texture, the Twelve Bens and the north face of Ben Corr, in Galway, boasting climbs of 1,300 feet, should be mentioned. In Mayo stands the isolated Creagh Patrick (2,510 feet), ascended each year by pilgrims on the last Sunday of July, and in Clare the caving area of Slieve Elva.

Finally, the sea cliffs of western Ireland may one day be as popular as those of Cornwall. Major sea cliffs exist on the Dingle Peninsula in Kerry and on the north coast of Mayo. Donegal, in the north-west, has magnificent sea cliffs, as well as fine inland climbing grounds like Poisoned Glen, which has climbs of up to 1,000 feet.

Outcrops and sea cliffs

Though hardly deserving long notice, mention must be made of the week-end fervour for outcrop climbing. Londoners crowd the sandstone outcrops of Kent, only forty feet high. At Bristol the Avon Gorge provides limestone climbs of over 200 feet; Almscliff is a gritstone outcrop near Leeds; Helsby an important sandstone outcrop in Cheshire. There are climbs in Cheddar Gorge of up to 400 feet, and the Dartmoor tors provide short problem climbs. It is all training and good sport.

In about 1900, A. W. Andrews began to investigate the granite cliffs of the Cornish coast. The Commandos, practising cliff assaults during the Second World War, helped to promote this specialized form of climbing, on firm rock of up to 250 feet. Pembrokeshire provides similar opportunities and the limestone cliffs near Swanage on the south coast are now popular. The more extensive but almost untouched cliffs of Ireland have already been mentioned.

This is climbing for the sake of climbing, and though distinct from mountaineering is very enjoyable in its own right.

Wilfrid Noyce

Winter conditions on the Cuillin. This photograph was taken during the first winter traverse of the Cuillin Ridge made in 1965 by T. Patey, B. Robinson, D. Crabbe, and H. MacInnes.

The Caucasus

General description

The Caucasus, comparable in extent with the Alps, vies with those mountains–and can probably be said to excel them–as the finest mountain range in Europe, little known as it is to western climbers. Geographically, the range forms the boundary between Europe to the north and Asia to the south: an ethnological paradox, since the north side is peopled by Moslem tribes akin to those of Central Asia, while much of the south side was occupied by the former Christian kingdom of Georgia, which traces its origins back to the ancient Greeks and whose inhabitants, like the Basques, are basically of non-Indo-European stock.

Politically, the whole of the Caucasus lies within the Soviet Union, although much of the northern side is divided among native tribal regions which enjoy some degree of autonomy.

The south side is largely contained with the Georgian S.S.R.

The Caucasus range is usually considered as being divided into three sections: the western, central, and eastern Caucasus, separated respectively by the Klukhor Pass, linking Karachai-Circassia and Abkhazia, and the Krestovy Pass, which carries the Georgian Military Highway from Dzaujikau to Tbilisi, the capital of Georgia.

The western Caucasus starts as a low ridge near the swamps at the mouth of the River Don and rises to high mountains of

Caucasian valley scenery: the Shkhelda Valley from near the Spartak mountaineering 'camp'. The easy peak on the left is Pik Kavkaz. The head of the valley on the right is dominated by the north face of the Shkhelda ridge, up which run several fine and difficult routes.

Alpine character only in its eastern sector. Its climate is dominated by the Black Sea, being warm and humid, with the result that the valleys and lower ridges are heavily afforested.

The central Caucasus contains the highest mountains, the dominant altitude being about 3,000 feet higher than in the Alps, although the snow-line in the Caucasus being somewhat higher than it is in the Alps this does not make so much difference as it might otherwise do. The Black Sea still has a considerable influence on the climate, and the weather never seems very settled, with good snow and ice conditions only rarely obtainable. But the climate is drier than in the western Caucasus, with grassy terrain predominating in the upper valleys and the grazing of sheep as the principal economic activity. In the early nineteenth century the belief was held that the Caucasus contained no glaciers; in fact the range holds extensive glacier systems, although they are smaller than Alpine glaciers. Most of the main peaks are surrounded by formidable arêtes and faces of rock and ice similar in character to that of the Italian side of Mont Blanc. The ridges connecting the peaks are long and serrated, with few points offering access to their crests. Of all the main peaks, perhaps the extinct volcanoes Elbrus and Kazbek are the only ones with easy routes to their summits.

In the eastern Caucasus the climate becomes drier and the mountains no longer lie in glaciated chains but form isolated massifs. At the eastern end, near the Caspian Sea, snow-cap and grassland disappear and semi-desert conditions prevail.

Historical

The earliest history of the Caucasus is that of the Greek colonies established from the Black Sea. From this historical basis originates the classical knowledge of the Caucasus as the home of such legends as that of the Golden Fleece sought by Jason and the Argonauts (which arose from the methods used for the recovery of alluvial gold from the waters of the River Rion in Georgia), and that of the incarceration by the gods of Prometheus on Kazbek. Later, from the south, the Roman Empire extended to the crest of the range, until it was succeeded by the Eastern Empire and the Eastern Church. Thus arose the kingdom of Georgia, which survived with many vicissitudes in this corridor from Europe to Asia, despite Arab, Persian, and later Turkish advances, until the triumph of Tsarist and Soviet imperialism in the nineteenth and twentieth centuries. The Middle Ages were the hey-day of Georgia. This was the age of Queen Tamara and the poet Shota Rustaveli, author of *The Tiger in the Skin*, whose name is commemorated in one of the peaks of Shkhara. Because of their struggle for survival, both against each other and against mighty invaders throughout the centuries, the life of the peoples of Georgia and the neighbouring Caucasian highlands has always been a matter of blood and honour, as dark as in the highlands of Scotland. But fighting, drinking, and love-making are no longer the only fit occupations for a man,

and no longer is his costume decorated with cartridge belts. Hints of the former way of life of the Caucasian peoples are to be found only in their temperament, their distinctive headgear (of which many different forms, of wool or hair, are found in various parts of the range), and, in Svanetia, the upper valley of the Ingur, close to the central Caucasus, the tower-like houses from which every man defended himself against his neighbour.

The north side of the range, directly in the path of movements of people from Asia to Europe, has a history of repeated sweeps by barbarian hordes until the Russian armies advanced across the steppes to the foothills of the mountains. By the early nineteenth century the Black Sea coast and the western parts of the northern hills had been settled and the Caucasian watering places became fashionable to St Petersburg society. Life in the Caucasus at this period is depicted in the works of the Russian novelists Lermontov, Tolstoy, Gogol, and Herzen. But further east the story was different, and prolonged and bitter conflict took place before Russia overwhelmed the native peoples. The most noteworthy conflict was the Murid Wars (1834–61), when Shamyl the Avar led the people in repeated bloody struggles which took place mostly in Daghestan. Even later, in the 1870s, friction between Russia and Turkey coincided with native risings on both sides of the range. After the Russian Revolution the Caucasian peoples, with Allied support, again achieved independence until they were finally suppressed by the Russians in 1923. During the Second World War bitter struggles took place in the Caucasus, those around Elbrus being remembered in the song 'Baksan', popular among Russian climbers. Hitler's armies had advanced halfway to the Caspian Sea before they were driven back, and, as a reprisal for collaboration with the enemy (it is said that the Balkarians presented Hitler with a white horse), Stalin had several tribes deported to Central Asia. This exile lasted until the late 1950s.

Mountaineering in the Caucasus

The history of climbing in the Caucasus is bound up with political history. In a mountaineering sense the range was *terra incognita* until the Russian military conquest was completed. The first explorers, map-makers, and geologists came with the Russian armies, and it was to them that the first easy summits succumbed. In 1829 Russian soldiers and scientists visited Elbrus, the highest peak in Europe, and one of the natives accompanying them is alleged to have climbed the east peak of the mountain, though this is generally believed in the west to be unlikely.

The completion of the Russian conquest coincided with the end of the Golden Age of mountaineering in the Alps, and members of the Alpine Club turned their attention to the possibilities of the Caucasus. The first party, Freshfield, A. W. Moore, and Tucker, in 1868, explored the whole range from end to end, climbing Kazbek (16,546 feet) and the east

(*Above*) A Soviet climbing centre in winter: the Dombai mountaineering 'camp'. The jagged rock tower is the Tooth of Sofrudya. Sofrudya is a glaciated hump behind, out of sight, and is an easy climb.

(*Below*) The twin peaks of Ushba from Pik Kavkaz. Chatyn-tau is on the left, then Pik Shchurovsky, with Little Ushba behind it to the left. To the right is the beginning of the ridge of Shkhelda. The low double-topped ridge in front is Pik Woolley.

peak of Elbrus (18,442 feet), and brought back a glowing report of what the range had to offer. Moore returned in 1874 and extended these explorations, as well as climbing the higher western peak of Elbrus (18,481 feet). But the continued unrest in the Caucasus deterred any further visits, and only in 1884, when the Hungarian climber, de Déchy, visited the Adai-Khokh group, did the real attack on the main summits begin. In 1886 the English returned in earnest, and in the next ten years most of the great peaks fell to members of the Alpine Club and their Swiss guides. The year 1888 was an important one in the history of climbing in the Caucasus. It saw the capitulation of the supreme peaks: Dykh-tau to Mummery, Shkhara, Jangi-tau, and the north peak of Ushba to Cockin. It also saw the first climbing accident in the range, when W. Donkin and H. Fox disappeared on Koshtan-tau. Local searches having failed to find them, the Russians accused the natives of murdering them and visited Draconian punishments on the local population. The following year a search expedition sent out from England found incontestable evidence that a climbing accident had taken place and interceded with the authorities on behalf of the natives. The gratitude of the Balkarians to British climbers for this was long-lived and persisted even through their exile in Central Asia.

Continental climbers also took up the challenge, and many first ascents were made by Merzbacher, Sella, Fischer and Schuster, and Egger. Schulze's ascent of the difficult south peak of Ushba (15,453 feet) was among the greatest of pre-war accomplishments. It was followed by a complete traverse of the twin peaks of Ushba by another German party, involving six bivouacs, which was a precursor of the long traverses which are a Caucasian speciality. Russian climbing clubs were established during this period, but the achievements of Russian climbers were very modest.

The First World War and subsequent disturbances precluded activity until 1923, when climbing started again with ascents of easy peaks by large Russian and Georgian parties, a characteristic which has persisted and increased to the present day. Western mountaineers returned in 1928, and in the next nine years many continental parties, particularly German and Austrian, climbed in the range, ascending most of the virgin peaks and ridges and putting up face climbs on a par with those being made in the Alps at this period. Among the finest achievements were Müller's ascent of the north rib of Shkhara, Schwarzgruber's ascent of the north face of Jangi-tau, and Schmaderer's climbs on the west face of Ushba and the north face of Shkhelda (14,173 feet). Long ridge traverses carried out by the Austrians included the complete Bezingi ridge and the Dykh-tau/Koshtan-tau ridge.

Russian climbers accompanied some of these parties, and by 1931 had started themselves to tackle the harder peaks. In 1938 some of the first long ridge traverses by Russian parties were made. Numerous accidents caused the Russians to institute a rigorous control and grading system for both

The north face of Shkhara from Dykh-tau. The prominent buttress rising to the highest point is the north rib, up which lies Tomaschek's fine route. The 'frontier ridge' between Russia and Georgia lies to the left.

climbs and climbers. This promoted safety, but also a highly competitive atmosphere, which now prevails completely.

After the Second World War climbing was resumed at an intensified rate. Trade unions and youth organizations set up camps to train mountaineers and large numbers of young people were attracted to the hills. Most of the hard face climbs made by Western climbers have been repeated, and very hard new routes made by the Russians themselves. Those on the north faces of Pik Shchurovsky (13,974 feet), Shkhelda, and Dykh-tau, as well as even longer ridge traverses than before, are typical. Within the last few years the Mountaineering Federation of the U.S.S.R. has been set up to control the

Shkelda, showing the Central Buttress, which was climbed in 1959 by an 'Avangard' party led by B. Subartovitch.

The north face of Pik Shchurovsky. Two fine routes were made on this face in 1962: that of an 'Avangard' party led by L. Kensitsky, and that of a Ukrainian Spartak party led by Anatoli Kustovsky.

sport, and foreign climbers have returned to the scene; each year now several parties from either side of the Iron Curtain visit the Caucasus.

Western Caucasus

The western end of this section of the range, the 'Black Sea Flail', is topped by Fisht (9,358 feet). In the next part, up to the Marukh Pass, the peaks vary between 10,500 feet and 12,500 feet in height, being mainly memorable for their confusing names: Pshish (12,467 feet), Psyish (12,425 feet), and Pseashkho (10,580 feet).

The next part, between the Marukh and Klukhor passes, is the area of greatest climbing interest, with fine peaks of alpine

character up to 13,000 feet. Climbing is centred around the headwaters of tributaries of the River Kuban, particularly the Aksaut and Teberda (Amanauz) branches, where there are several permanent mountaineering 'camps'. From the Marukh Pass eastwards the main peaks are Kara-kaya (12,782 feet), Aksaut (12,828 feet), Ertsog (12,687 feet), Sofruju (12,428 feet), Amanauz (12,326 feet), Juguturlyuchat (12,864 feet), Ptyish (11,549 feet), Dombai-ulgen (13,255 feet), Bu-ulgen (12,838 feet), and Dottakh-kaya (12,677 feet). The traverses of most of these peaks are difficult, and ascent of their faces even more so. Aksaut and Amanauz have fierce north face routes.

The summit of Elbrus, with the Soviet equivalent of the images of the Virgin or crucifixes found on Alpine peaks.

Dombai-ulgen, the highest peak in the western Caucasus, is a splendid rock and ice mountain first climbed by Schuster and Fischer in 1914. Both north and south flanks have now been lined with difficult routes by Russian parties.

Central Caucasus

The Central Caucasus has a rather undistinguished beginning east of the Klukhor Pass, with the Kichkinekol group (Zamok, at 12,894 feet, being the highest peak hereabouts), Gvandra (13,068 feet), and peaks further east rising to 13,590 feet, with the Shtavler spur (13,166 feet) going off south. This part ends at the Azau, Jiper Azau, and Dongus-orun Passes leading into the Baksan valley, the main Caucasian climbing centre. Here climbing 'camps' abound, both in the main Baksan valley and in its tributaries, the Adyr Su and the Adyl Su. North of the Azau Pass is the great mass of Elbrus, with its glaciers radiating from the central extinct volcano, and its summit glacial carapace giving easy but laborious access to its twin peaks (18,481 feet and 18,442 feet). Elbrus is tamed more than any other part of the Caucasus; on it are climbing huts and *téléphériques*.

Returning to the watershed, the first peak is Dongus-orun (14,659 feet), with three summits giving a good traverse. A fierce route lies up the north-west face with its prominent final ice bulge. To the east, beyond the Betso Pass, is Shkhelda (14,173 feet), a formidable ridge with many jagged peaks. Both the ridge traverse and the many routes on the rock and ice of the north face are major expeditions. East is the Ushba Pass, reached from the Shkhelda Glacier by the Ushba Icefall

and giving access to one of the world's greatest mountains, Ushba. Its two peaks (15,453 feet and 15,400 feet) give a classical traverse, the approach to the south peak from the south being the most difficult part. The first ascent was from the east to the col between the peaks. A corresponding but much more difficult ice route approaches from the west, and the ridges and faces of the south peak give other long and difficult routes.

From the Ushba Pass, the main watershed continues past Chatyn-tau (14,318 feet) and Pik Shchurovsky (13,974 feet), with fierce north face, and, on Chatyn, south face routes, and easier access by their ridges; then Bzhedukh (14,012 feet), the Kashka-tash Pass, Ullu-kara (14,115 feet), Bashkara (13,914 feet), Cheget-tau-chana (13,484 feet), Ullu-tau-chana (13,803 feet), the Mestia Pass, Sarikol-bashi (13,648 feet), the Lekzir Pass, Bashil-tau (13,967 feet), the Lychat Pass, Bodorken (13,674 feet), the Tuiber Pass, Kulak-tau (13,327 feet), the Kitlod Pass and Tikhtengen (15,125 feet) to Salynen-bashi (14,265 feet) overlooking the Tsanner Pass and the Bezingi Glacier – to mention only the more important peaks and passes. Spurs go off to the north to Kurmichi (13,314 feet) and to Adyr-su-bashi (14,353 feet), Jailik (14,872 feet), and Tiu-tiu-bashi (14,747 feet), with many rock peaks containing routes of all degrees of difficulty.

Around the Bezingi valley cluster most of the great peaks of the Caucasus. The Bezingi Glacier is flanked at its head by the peaks of the Janga or Bezingi Wall. On the watershed are Lyalver (14,272 feet), Gestola (15,945 feet), with Tetnuld (15,922 feet), on a spur to the south, Katyn-tau (16,355 feet), Jangi-tau (16,571 feet and 16,529 feet) and Shkhara (16,529 feet). The peaks give a marathon ridge traverse, most

(*Above*) The great peaks of Shkhelda dominating the upper Shkhelda Valley. A view from the Spartak camp.

(*Below*) The twin peaks of Ushba from the Ushba Plateau. On the left is Little Ushba.

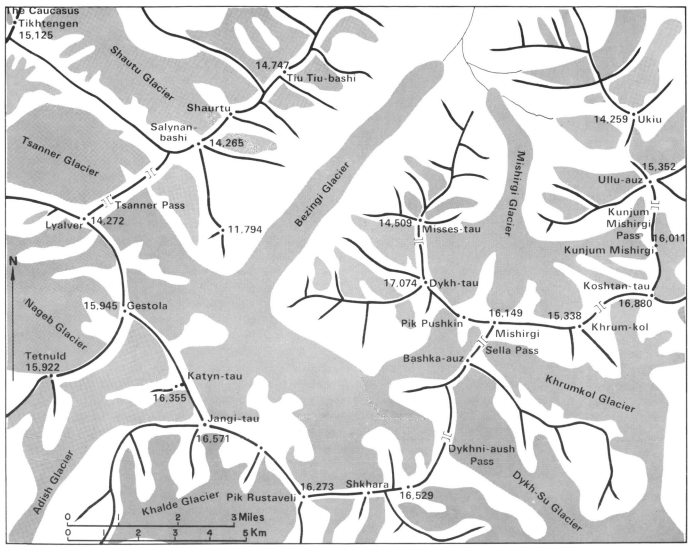

The Caucasus: Bezingi Basin and surrounding peaks.

Within the map:

The Caucasus
Tikhtengen
15,125

Shautu Glacier

14,747
Tiu Tiu-bashi

Shaurtu

Salynan-bashi
14,265

Tsanner Glacier

Bezingi Glacier

14,259 Ukiu

15,352
Ullu-auz

Kunjum Mishirgi Pass

Mishirgi Glacier

Kunjum Mishirgi
16,011

Koshtan-tau
16,880

Tsanner Pass

Lyalver 14,272

11,794

N

14,509 Misses-tau

17,074 Dykh-tau

Pik Pushkin

16,149
Mishirgi

15,338

Khrum-kol

Nageb Glacier

15,945 Gestola

Tetnuld
15,922

Katyn-tau
16,355

Bashka-auz
Sella Pass

Khrumkol Glacier

Jangi-tau
16,571

Dykhni-aush Pass

Adish Glacier

Khalde Glacier Pik Rustaveli

16,273

Shkhara

16,529

Dykh-Su Glacier

0   1   2   3 Miles
0   1   2   3   4   5 Km

(*Above*) The Caucasus: Bezingi Basin and surrounding peaks.   (*Below*) Pik Shchurovsky from the Shkhelda Glacier.

A bivouac on the north rib of Shkhara, showing the useful and easily erected Soviet bivouac tent held up by ice-axes tied together. In the background is Koshtan-tau.

(*Left*) Elbrus from Pik Shchurovsky.

Dykh-tau from the north rib of Shkhara. Twin buttresses rise to the twin summits of Dykh-tau. The left-hand buttress was in part used by A. F. Mummery on the first ascent, and was recently climbed throughout by a Polish party. The right-hand buttress was climbed by M. J. Harris and G. C. Band in 1958.

easily gained at either end or from the south. The north faces form the Bezingi Wall itself, a tremendous 6,000-foot face of snow, ice, and rock eight miles long, containing many fine and difficult routes. Perhaps the best are the Müller Rib on Shkhara and the Schwarzgruber Rib on the west peak of Jangi-tau.

To the north of the Dykhni-aush Pass beyond Shkhara lies the Dykh-tau/Koshtan-tau ridge, forming a horseshoe round the Mishirgi Glacier, which gives another fine ridge traverse. Dykh-tau (17,074 feet and 17,054 feet) is at the western end, a peak second in magnificence only to Ushba in the Caucasus. Fine routes lie up all its ridges. Mummery's original route lies mostly west of its south rib, while there are recent hard routes on the north-east face. To the east are Mishirgi (16,149 feet) and Khrum-kol (15,338 feet), both with hard north face routes, and Koshtan-tau (16,880 feet), with ridges radiating north-west, north-east, and south-east, on which are many fine peaks such as Kunjum-Mishirgi (16,011 feet), Ullu-auz (15,352 feet), Ukiu (14,259 feet), Tiu-tiun-tau (14,888 feet), and Tiu-tiu-bashi (14,747 feet).

Beyond Shkhara the main watershed continues via the graceful Ailama (14,840 feet), with a ridge branching off south to the Svanetian Range (Laila, 13,078 feet). East again are the Gevetsek Pass and the Laboda group (Laboda, 14,173 feet), with a further group dominated by Sugan-tau (14,734 feet) to the north. The last group much visited by Western climbers is the Adai-khokh group beyond the Gurjivtsek Pass (Adai-khokh, 15,243 feet), much of its exploration being carried out by H. Raeburn's parties. It is separated by the

highway of the Mamison Pass from Khalatsa-khokh (12,934 feet), and, further east, Tsilga-khokh (12,677 feet), from which a branch goes off to Tepli (14,525 feet), Jimarai-khokh (15,673 feet) and the much frequented and easy volcanic dome of Kazbek (16,546 feet), the easternmost 16,000-foot peak in the range.

Eastern Caucasus

This section of the range is of less interest and is not well known by climbers. The first group, east of the Georgian Military Highway, is dominated by Shan (14,532 feet). East of this is the Pirikitel range, with Tebulos-mta (14,744 feet), Komito-tavi (14,016 feet), Donos-mta (13,566 feet), and Diklos-mta (14,025 feet). Many of the main peaks in these two areas were first climbed by Merzbacher, the author of a monumental German work on the range. East again is the Bogos range, with Addala (13,619 feet) and Bishinei (13,475 feet). The peaks are then lower until the last high alpine region is reached with Bazar-juzi (14,698 feet), a mountain typical of the isolated snow massifs of this region and ascended by Baker and Yeld in 1890 (although there is a record of an ascent by the topographer Alexandrov in 1873). Near it are Shalbuz-dag (13,626 feet), the legendary home of the roc of the *Thousand and One Nights*, and Shagh-dag (13,944 feet). Beyond Baba-dag (11,884 feet) the mountains tail off, in the 'Caspian Flail', to the sea.

John Neill

2 The Mountains of Asia
Turkey and Iran

Turkey

Turkey is largely mountainous, but, as yet, little known by Western mountaineers. The Taurus range to the south borders the Mediterranean, while the northern range, with summits between 10,000 and 12,000 feet, such as Kaçkar (12,917 feet), receives moisture from the Black Sea. Between is a high, dry plateau from which rises the volcanic peak of Erciyas (12,851 feet). In the south-east corner the Hakkâri of Kurdistan culminate in the Sat Dağ and Cilo Dağ, while to the north, near the Iran border, rises the huge mass of Ararat (16,945 feet).

Thus the climate varies from sub-arctic to sub-tropical. In general the coastline regions are damp and relaxing, the inland plateau dry and bracing. The Taurus are at their best in June and July, Ararat in August, while in spring and autumn the limestone coastal peaks of Antalya are an attractive rock-climbing ground.

Exploration has been fragmentary; until recently access to the interior was made difficult by an oppressive officialdom. If we disallow Noah's ascent, J. J. F. W. Parrot was the first man to climb Ararat in 1829. The ascent, involving a three-day walk, is not difficult, although crampons are advised for the glaciated summit cone. Another German, H. Bobek, surveyed the Hakkâri and Taurus in the 1930s. R. A. Hodgkin and others were active in the Ala Dağ shortly after. In 1966 his party made the first ascent of Bobek Tepesi (11,549 feet) in the Sat Dağ.

Among the Turks themselves, hunters have been roaming the peaks for centuries. Only recently has mountaineering developed as a sport, and that in a small way. The hut on the fine massif of Ulu Dağ, only seventy miles from Istanbul, is still little patronized by climbers, despite the near-by limestone cliffs of Kuşakli Kaya and Zirve. A Turkish governmental organization has built huts, and the army is now active, running a rock-climbing school near Egridir Lake. Turkish climbers like B. Ergor are also becoming active.

First ascents are hard to trace, but much new ground was broken by the powerful Austrian parties of 1956 and 1958 and the British party led by T. Weir in 1958. The conspicuous Erciyas has a difficult snow-and-ice north-west face, now several times climbed from Hacilar village. It is also a popular ski mountain. The most rewarding area is probably that of the wild Cilo Dağ and Sat Dağ in the Hakkâri province of Kurdi-

The north face of Geliasin (13,681 feet), the highest peak in the Cilo Dağ, from the summit of Eckpfeiler (12,139 feet).

Peaks of the Cilo Dağ, including Eckpfeiler (12,139 feet) and Suppa Durak (13,320 feet), from Demir Kapu.

Hendevade (12,500 feet), the highest peak in the Sat Dağ.

stan, which, until quite recently, was a closed military zone and therefore little visited. Geliaşin (13,681 feet), the highest point of the Reşko Dağ, offers some interesting routes, including an impressive north face. A route on the east face was climbed in 1965 by R. Fedden's party, who also climbed the north face of Hendevade (12,500 feet) the highest peak in the Sat Dağ. The Taurus mountains, too, have been visited more

frequently in recent years. In the Ala Dağ peaks such as Demirkazik (12,225 feet) and Kaldi Dağ (12,251 feet) have much to offer the climber eager for new routes.

Those who have travelled among these mountains have testified to the hospitality of the pastoral inhabitants and been stimulated by the sight of bear, ibex, wolves, marmots–even panthers–as well as by the long vistas of unfrequented mountains. To the mountaineer who wishes to venture away from the beaten track the mountains of Turkey are an ideal prospect.

Peaks of the Ala Dağ. From left to right they are Hudut Dağ (c. 12,500 feet), Kaldi Dağ (c. 13,000 feet), and Ludut Dağ (12,200 feet).

Erciyas Dağ (12,851 feet), in Central Turkey.

Iran

The full mountaineering possibilities of Iran have only recently been appreciated. Much of the country is mountainous, and ski races as well as mountain expeditions are organized from Teheran itself. But, for the climber, the most important massifs are those of the Elburz Range south of the Caspian Sea. These (not to be confused with Elbruz, the derivation of which is the same) present a remarkable contrast. They separate the Persian plateau from the sub-tropical jungles of the Caspian, below the level of the Black Sea. On one side are uplands, dry and almost bare of vegetation, wind-swept and snow-covered in winter, arid in summer, peopled by roving shepherds and small agricultural communities. On this side the mountains are bare and brown, but to the north they plunge into a riot of forest, from evergreen through deciduous to sub-tropical, inhabited higher up by bear and deer, lower down by forms of jungle life including reptiles and even the rare Hyrcanian tiger. On both sides transport at the end of the motor road is by mule.

Demavend (18,603 feet), the highest mountain between the Atlantic and the Pamirs, is an extinct volcano lying some forty miles north-east from Teheran. The first recorded European ascent is that of Sir W. Taylor Thompson in 1836, and since then it has become almost a place of pilgrimage, like Fuji-san in Japan. From the south and west it is easy, but the north-east flank presents serious problems. The snowy north-east ridge was climbed by L. Steinauer and X. Gorter of a German expedition in 1936. The east ridge, climbed by B. Pierre's French party in 1954, gives a long and very fair climb on volcanic rock adorned, at 16,000 feet, with strange 'obelisks of yellow sulphur and lava'. The face between, involving a 3,000-foot ice couloir, fell finally to a French party in 1956.

The most interesting group of the Elburz is that of Takht-i-Suleiman, the 'Throne of Solomon', west of Demavend. The identity and location of these peaks was uncertain (though they had been seen by J. B. L. Noel) as late as 1932, when Freya Stark circumvented them. In the same year Sir Douglas Busk explored this intricate complex, of which Alam Kuh (15,880 feet) is the highest point, and in the next year he climbed the mountain from the east. This proved to be a second ascent, two German botanists, the brothers Bornmuller, having made the first in 1902. Though easy from the south, east, and west, Alam Kuh drops a formidable wall to the north. The ascent of this, 'the Persian Jorasses', was led by L. Steinauer up the north-north-east buttress in 1936, and repeated by members of B. Pierre's party, who followed it with a complete traverse. A north-north-west face climb, mostly on ice, was also added.

Takht-i-Suleiman itself (15,154 feet), north of Alam Kuh, was probably first climbed up the south ridge by L. Steinauer. The whole area was excellently mapped by H. Bobek in 1934 and 1936. The French in 1956, defeated on the north face of Alam Kuh direct, climbed the Haft Khan Ridge to the west, a route repeated shortly after by a Cambridge party.

Among other Persian mountains, Savalan Dagh or Kuh-i-Savalan (14,010 feet) in Azerbaijan to the north-west should be mentioned. This was climbed by Bobek in the course of his survey journeys. Zardeh Kuh (14,920 feet), the highest point in the long range of the Zagros Mountains to the south, was first visited in 1933 by an Italian party, and small glaciers were located. Kuh-i-Taftan (13,262 feet) is a frequently snow-capped volcano in Baluchistan.

The growing enthusiasm for mountaineering among Iranians has extended exploration, but there remains much new ground, if few major problems of high technical order. To travellers from abroad the ambiance of wide horizons, wild life, proud and courteous villagers still living in a tribal framework, is an even greater attraction than the possibility of new ascents.

Wilfrid Noyce

Demavend (18,603 feet), the highest peak in the Elburz Mountains.

(*Above*) Elburz Mountains: the Takht-i-Suleiman group from Rud Barak village. Takht-i-Suleiman (15,154 feet) is in the centre.

(*Below*) Elburz Mountains: the north face of Alam Kuh (15,880 feet), seen from Takht-i-Suleiman.

The Greater Himalaya

Introduction
Structure

The great mountain chains of the Himalaya–Karakoram, Hindu Kush, and Tyan' Shan'–splay out from the knotted mass of the Pamirs in the extreme south of the U.S.S.R. The Himalaya extend south and east along the borders of India-Pakistan and through Nepal for some 1,600 miles as a broad arc that embraces the high plateau of Tibet to the north and towers above the fertile Indo-Gangetic plains to the south. Millions of years of mountain-building movements and erosion extending through Tertiary time have produced the landscape we see today. The dominant feature has been compression of a great wedge of sedimentary rocks between the rigid block of interior Asia and that of peninsular India. In places, as along the southern border of the system in the Siwalik foothills, the structure is simple, anticlines forming ridges and synclines longitudinal valleys. But much of the area has a complex structure, the powerful earth-movements having produced overfolds and nappes, which later have been pushed forwards and upwards to the south and south-west along great thrust planes. Owing to the intensity of the folding and to deep erosion, highly resistant crystalline rocks, such as granites and gneisses, outcrop over wide areas of the main Himalaya.

The various ranges trend parallel with the system as a whole, following the main lines of folding and faulting. Repeated movements along faults have been associated with the uplift of large blocks to form the present mountain ranges. Numerous earthquakes show that this process is still going on.

As the mountains have risen, erosion has attacked them. Rivers have cut out great gorges and carried away the materials to build up the wide alluvial plains of the Indus and Ganges and their tributaries. Many of the rivers were in existence before the mountains were formed and the larger ones, such as the Brahmaputra, Sutlej, and Indus, whose sources lie to the north of the highest ranges, were able to maintain their courses across the rising mountains. The mountains are also being actively attacked by weathering, especially frost action, for the snow lies between about 15,000 and 20,000 feet, depending on precipitation and aspect. From the snowfields descend valley glaciers, including some thirty or forty miles long, although most are much shorter than this. Many of the glaciers carry great quantities of angular rock waste and their terminal parts often stagnate beneath a thick layer of this material–evidence of the rapidity of erosion on the mountain slopes above.

History

To confine the Himalaya, Karakoram, and Hindu Kush in so short a space is like squeezing an elephant into a rucksack. They occupy a huge area, some 1,600 miles long and sometimes 100 or 200 miles wide, shading off to the north into the peaks and uplands of Tibet. Climatically the extremes are wide, from the sub-tropical hothouses of Sikkimese and Bhutanese Valleys, with their orchids and giant butterflies and leeches, to the austerely arid Karakoram and Hindu Kush, which lie at a latitude north of Cyprus and to which the summer monsoon rains, governing factor of most Himalayan travel, do not penetrate. At the north-west extremity the range is also linked with the Pamirs of Russia.

The main Himalaya stand up like a barrier between India and the Tibetan plateau. Rising abruptly from the plains, they carry a life quite unlike that of the millions swarming at their feet. Yet great rivers like the Indus, Sutlej, and Brahmaputra cut through them; others, like the Jhelum and Ganges, have their source among them. To the Himalaya and their rivers pilgrims of many shades of faith come flocking every year. It is worth casting an eye over the varieties of belief and character found along the range.

The Hindu Kush extend along northern regions of fiercely independent Afghanistan into Chitral, and the inhabitants are predominantly Muslims, as are those of the Karakoram regions of north-west Pakistan: Muslims, but of various sects. Descending to Kashmir and Jammu, which comprise the rich Vale of Kashmir and the valleys round it, we find a largely Muslim population ruled over by Hindus; hence the friction between Pakistan, which has many claims to this area, and India, which got in first. Over the Zoji La we are in Ladakh, or 'Little Tibet', which is Buddhist under Indian (Hindu) rule. The nearer one comes to Tibet, the more Buddhist do the Himalayan hill people become. The dry plains and snowy peaks of Ladakh, like those of Spiti and Lahul to the south (but still north of the Himalayan divide), are closely akin to those of Tibet, while Kulu, south of the divide, is predominantly Indian in character.

The peak of Leo Pargial overlooks both the Spiti and Sutlej Rivers in a country Tibetan in character. But the next important knot of peaks, those of Garhwal and Kumaon, are in Hindu country, and to the town of Badrinath near the source of the Ganges pilgrims flock yearly to do homage. These peaks are southerly enough to be greatly affected by the summer monsoons of May or June, and vegetation thickens. Gorges are narrow and steep and the yak of the northern flanks gives way to mule or man as carrier. Nanda Devi (25,645 feet) used to be the highest summit of the British Raj. Soon we are among the tangled forests and 23,000-foot summits of West Nepal, home of the Dhotials and a country little known until very recently. Indeed, the whole of Nepal, where the biggest mountain giants stand, was, before 1949, a closed country in the grip of its Rana rulers. Only the recruitment of Gurkhas to the Indian Army gave a glimpse of some of its inhabitants. The southward valleys, Kathmandu and the Terai, are predominantly Hindu. Towards Tibet, notably in Sola Khumbu, the home of the Sherpas south of Everest, we are in a land of almost autonomous Buddhist communities. Buddhist also are the small, semi-independent states of Sikkim and Bhutan to the east, though the original inhabitants of Sikkim, the Lepchas, still preserve their own beliefs and customs.

It is natural that the Himalaya, the home of diverse nationalities and cultures, should have been at times the scene of bloodshed. The North-West Frontier, rather outside our scope, is famous in British history. Less known is the 1891 campaign of Hunza-Nagir in the Karakoram. The bloodshed that tinges Kashmir has been the result chiefly of the 1947 Partition and the dispute between India and Pakistan. On its other Kashmir front, in Ladakh, India has more recently found herself harassed by the Chinese, as also on her far eastern frontier, in Assam. The campaigns of Nepal, the Chinese incursions, and the aggressive Gurkha ascendancy will concern us later. In other Himalayan regions the British operated more in a police than a military capacity.

The mountaineer was preceded by the general traveller, but for centuries high passes demanding mountaineering technique have been crossed, by trader or herdsman or soldier, long before mountaineering as a sport was born. In the early nineteenth century names crop up, like that of the Gerard brothers, adventurous Scotsmen who climbed to 19,000 feet on Leo Pargial. Sir Joseph Hooker explored valleys round Kangchenjunga. In the Karakoram, surveyors had already been exploring, many years before Sir Francis Younghusband's well-known journey from Peking in 1887, during which he crossed the Muztagh Pass. The mountaineers, when they arrived fresh from the Alps, underestimated the scale of the Himalaya, understandably. Mummery tackled Nanga Parbat as though it were an Alpine peak and lost his life on it in 1895. D. W. Freshfield, on his journey round Kangchenjunga in 1899, reckoned that it would take at least three days to the top. Everest had been triangulated and named after the former Head of the Survey of India, Sir George Everest. More realistic in approach were explorers like C. G. Bruce of the Gurkhas, the Duke of the Abruzzi, who found the route up K2 but was prudent enough not to pursue it, T. G. Longstaff, who climbed the first twenty-three thousander, Trisul, in 1907, and the Workmans, who charted the Karakoram glaciers. C. F. Meade explored Garhwal and Dr A. M. Kellas Sikkim, ascending Pauhunri (23,180 feet) in 1911.

Progress in Himalayan mountaineering has been made in the first place over obstacles of altitude and logistics, only later over technical difficulty. At first it was thought that men could not breathe above 23,000 feet, then above 26,000 feet, then above 29,000 feet. The idea of tackling Everest came early, but only in 1921 was permission received to approach the mountain from the northern, Tibetan side. The first British party found the way; the second and third overcame tremendous psychological and physical obstacles to reach a height of over 28,000 feet.

Their example was followed by the Germans on Kangchenjunga, in two heroic attempts. The British held the keys to the mountains, and Everest remained their preserve. Nanga Parbat became the Germans' mountain, despite repeated disaster. The Americans, in 1938 and 1939, climbed very high on K2. But there seemed to be an invisible line drawn around the highest summits. Of peaks over 25,000 feet, only Kamet and Nanda Devi had yielded when war came.

After the Second World War, equipment had become lighter and protection against cold better. There seemed a certainty in the air that the tops could be reached. Tirich Mir (25,263 feet) and Annapurna I (26,504 feet) yielded in 1950, the latter owing to a reversal of Nepalese policy which now enabled parties to climb in Nepal. Attention turned to Everest and K2. The ascent of Everest from the south in 1953, due partly to greatly improved oxygen apparatus, opened an international Golden Age. Nanga Parbat was climbed the same year, K2 and Cho Oyu in 1954, Kangchenjunga and Makalu in 1955, Manaslu, Lhotse, and Everest again in 1956. There have followed three of the four 26,000-foot Gasherbrums and Broad Peak in the Karakoram, Annapurna II, and Dhaulagiri I in Nepal, as well as at least a dozen peaks of over 25,000 feet. In 1964 the Chinese climbed Gosainthan, which of the Himalayan peaks over 26,000 feet was the last to be climbed. A saddening feature of this zestful time has been the closing of the Tibetan frontier since China's unwarranted invasion of the country in 1947. Tibetan refugees streaming over the passes have added to the difficulties of both India and Nepal.

Apart from the highest peaks, it has been found possible, with greater confidence, to climb routes of Alpine difficulty on mountains of 22,000 or 23,000 feet. The Muztagh Tower, Machapuchare, and Ama Dablam are only three examples. Another development has been the advance in technique of Sherpas until now they, too, are reaching the summits. Everest, Cho Oyu, Annapurna II, and Nuptse all saw a Sherpa on top. More slowly, the Hunzas and Baltis of the Karakoram are also gaining experience.

The future is clouded with political doubts. Pakistan, India, and Nepal have natural fears of China, and incidents do occur. Travel is not quite so cheap or easy as in the old days of the British Raj. To set against these doubts are the awakened interest and pride of Indians, Pakistanis, and Nepalese; the Mountaineering Institute of Darjeeling, founded in 1954, is a sign of the times. Successful combined expeditions have been run which may well be the pattern of things to come and destroy the last taint of nationalism in greater mountaineering. There are still many blanks on the map to be filled, new and difficult peaks to be climbed, and a wealth of harder routes to be done on peaks already climbed by their easiest way. May the mountains, which have played so large a part in the cultures of these mountain peoples, help at last to break down barriers rather than to form them.

The Hindu Kush

The Hindu Kush, if taken in its whole extent, forms a range over 500 miles long, loosely connected at its eastern extremity with the north-west Karakoram. The mountains west of Charikar are lower and less well defined and are usually considered as part of the Koh-i-Baba system. The range starts along the Wakhan, the tongue of territory which Afghanistan projects towards China, and is at first wide and flat-backed, having no great peaks.

Turning south-west it soon gains in height, but the most important peaks stand not on the watershed, but south of it. Tirich Mir (25,263 feet), the highest summit, is part of a southerly spur projecting into Pakistan which dominates the long, narrow Chitral Valley. C. G. Bruce explored around it while on a military mission with G. S. Robertson and Younghusband (1893), and wrote of the Kafirs of Kafiristan, a district more thoroughly treated by Robertson. Tirich Mir was finally climbed in 1950 by a Norwegian party, the top being reached by P. Kvernberg, A. Naess, H. Berg, and H. R. A. Streather, the transport officer.

Since that time exploration of this high group, mainly in Afghanistan, has established the other summits. Istor-o-Nal (24,271 feet) was climbed by an American party in 1955 (J. E. Murphy, T. A. Mutch); Saraghrar (24,110 feet) by F. Maraini's party in 1959. In 1960 Noshaq, at 24,581 feet the second Hindu Kush summit, was climbed by Japanese and Polish parties–the latter approaching from Russia–within ten days of each other. All these are high snow peaks, similar in general character to the West Karakoram.

The accessibility of the Hindu Kush, coupled with its generally fine weather, has, in recent years, made it possible for small parties with limited means to climb among the high peaks. This increased activity has resulted in ascents of Nadir-Shah (22,356 feet), Urgend (23,091 feet), and Shachaur (23,347 feet), as well as of many others.

This section of the range is crossed by many passes. From the Dorah west to the Khawak (the easiest), the divide overlooks both Kafiristan and Badakshan, and separates the Oxus from the Chitral–Kunar–Kabul basin. Not many travellers have in recent times explored the wild mountains south of the Khawak. In 1956 a journey in lighter vein was undertaken by E. Newby and H. Carless, who attempted Mir Samir (19,059 feet). A German party climbed it in 1959 and found the rock exceptionally brittle. The Pamjshir Valley south-west from Mir Samir, already known to Wilfrid Thesiger among others, was visited by Mrs J. Dunsheath in 1960, and its head explored to the Anjuman Pass, despite minor trouble with f. and sometimes quarrelsome Afghan porters. The general structure of the mountains south of the Khawak is similar to that of the better known main Himalaya, though the uplift

(*Above*) The southern aspect of Noshaq (24,581 feet) from the Upper Tirich Glacier.

(*Below*) High peaks of the Hindu Kush. A panorama from the Upper Tirich Glacier showing, to the left, the south-west aspect of Istor-o-Nal (24,271 feet), and on the right the rounded summit of North Tirich (22,087 feet) as well as Tirich Mir (25,263 feet), the highest summit in the range.

(*Above*) The north ridge and summit of North Tirich (22,087 feet) from a camp on the Upper Tirich Glacier.

(*Below*) Porters resting during the ascent of Gunbaz-i-Safed (*c.* 22,310 feet). In the background are the northern slopes of Noshaq.

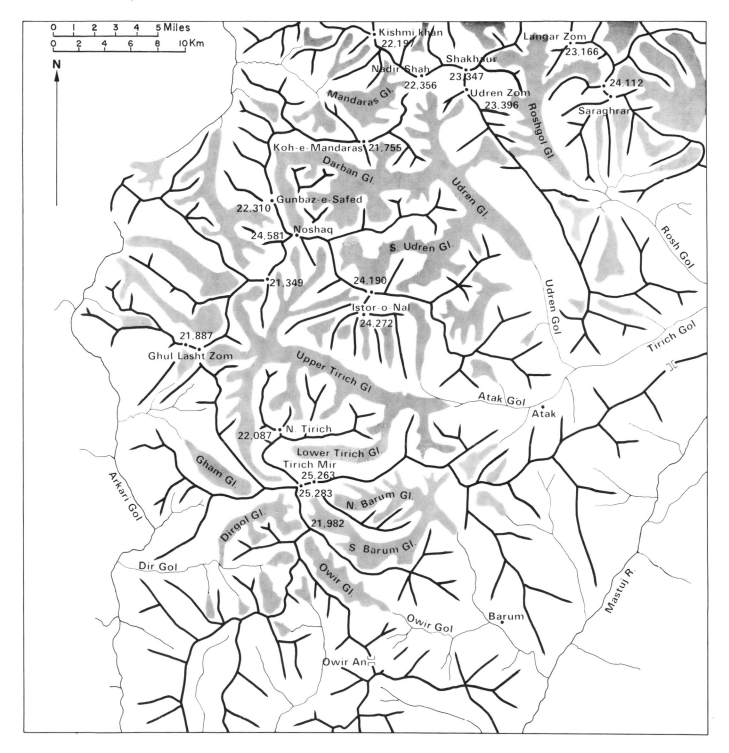

The Hindu Kush: Tirich Mir and Noshaq.

was later. This range, too, forms the face of a great tableland to the north.

Formidable as the barrier of the Hindu Kush seems, it has hardly ever been the boundary between important nations. The frontiers settled during the reign of Abdur Rahman Khan (1880–1901) with Russia and Britain took lines to north and south. Thus, except for parts of the Chitral stretch and the little-known Rosh Gol, and apart from occasional penetrations by the British and Russians, the area has been, and remains, Afghan territory.

The Karakoram

The Karakoram form an immense complex of groups, bounded on the west by the Ishkoman and Karumbar Rivers, on the east by the Upper Shyok; by the Shaksgam to the north and the Indus to the south. The western waters drain the Pamir edge; to the east stretch the uplands of Tibet. The main range lies in Pakistan, and since Partition the regions south and west of the cease-fire line are inaccessible from Indian Kashmir.

These regions are out of reach of the southerly monsoon. While the valley gorges are dry, the peaks are exposed to irregular but heavy snowfall which produces some of the largest glaciers in the world. Thus travel is difficult, large tracts of rocky desert or glaciated valley must be traversed with porters, and local food is scarce. Early travellers were few, bold spirits like the eighteenth-century Jesuit A. Desideri preferring to strike out east beyond Ladakh. The people of the range vary from the Hunzas of the west, through the Baltis, to the tough Ladakhi people of the east, polyandrous and closely akin to the Tibetans.

The range is usually divided latitudinally into Greater and Lesser Karakoram. The northern groups from the Batura along the north side of the Hispar, Panmah, Baltoro, and Siachen Glaciers form the Great, the southward groups of Rakaposhi, Haramosh, Masherbrum and Saltoro the Lesser. Purely for convenience I shall divide the area into West, Central, and East: West being everything west of the Muztagh Pass, Central the Baltoro groups, and East the groups east of the Turkestan Pass.

Hispar Muztagh: looking down the Gharesa Glacier towards Rakaposhi (25,550 feet), Karakoram.

Western Karakoram

East of the Indus bend, and north from Nanga Parbat, the Haramosh Range is the first to confront the traveller. Haramosh (24,270 feet) itself is a massive peak visible from Gilgit. Strangely, it was not attempted till 1957, when two of a four-man party were killed, and H. R. A. Streather and J. A. G. Emery won through after three nights in the open. It was climbed by H. Roiss's Austrian party in 1958.

Gilgit, traditional birthplace of polo, has for long been important as a strategic and trade post on the routes to China and Afghanistan. In 1889 the Gilgit Agency was established to control the Hunza and Nagir military activities, and it was to investigate Hunza raids that Younghusband made his 1889 journey. In 1891 a daring British detachment defeated the combined Hunza–Nagir forces at Nilt. Peace reigned, and next year Conway led the first serious Karakoram expedition, which mapped the Hispar and Biafo Glaciers. His survey was later continued by the Workmans, who also climbed peaks. But the attention of climbers had turned eastwards, and few ascents were made here until 1957. Much important survey work was done by K. Mason, the Vissers, H. F. Montagnier, C. J. Morris, and E. E. Shipton. Since Partition, and because of strained relations with China, Gilgit has gained in military importance what it has lost as a trade post.

The most obvious prize was Rakaposhi (25,550 feet), a huge, conspicuous pyramid having a number of possible lines. Several reconnaissances were needed before an Anglo-Pakistan Services expedition reached the top by the south-

Hispar Muztagh: the summit of Trivor (25,330 feet) from Camp 3.

Hispar Muztagh: Momhil Sar (24,090 feet) from Trivor, with the peaks of the Batura Muztagh in the background.

Hispar Muztagh: Disteghil Sar (25,868 feet) from the northwest ridge of Trivor.

west ridge in 1958. The summit pair were M. E. B. Banks and T. W. Patey. Meanwhile, the little-known peaks above the Batura Glacier to the north, surveyed by the Vissers, had received a strong German party under M. Rebitsch (1954). Ice conditions are peculiarly dangerous here and they retreated from the highest summit (25,540 feet) but climbed Pt 23,945 feet. In 1959 members of K. Warburton's international party disappeared somewhere above the dangerous Batura icefall.

Dr and Mrs P. C. Visser-Hooft were very active in 1928 around the Shimsal to the north-east, a river that shares with the Shyok the distinction of occasionally breaking its glacier dam and wreaking havoc in valleys far below. They mapped the north side of Disteghil Sar and their Hispar work was continued by Shipton, who in 1937 solved the problem of Conway's 'Snow Lake' at the head, and in 1939 mapped Hispar and Biafo, a continuous ice passage seventy-six miles long.

The Hispar drains into the Hunza River, on either side of which lie the narrow states of Hunza and Nagir. Both are ruled by semi-independent Mirs, the Hunzas claiming to be descended direct from three soldiers of Alexander the Great. They are distinctive in appearance, methods of agriculture, and language. Barley, buckwheat, and apricots provide staple diet, cultivation here as elsewhere being dependent on irrigation. Hunzas are natural hillmen and have accompanied major expeditions as porters.

A. Gregory chose the highest West Karakoram peak, Disteghil Sar (25,868 feet), for 1957. R. Lambert's Swiss party attempted it again in 1959, and the top was reached in 1960 by the Austrians G. Stärker and D. Marchart, substantially using Gregory's south side route. Meanwhile Kanjut Sar (25,460 feet) to the east had been claimed by G. Monzino's party of Italian guides in 1959, and in 1960 Trivor (25,330 feet) yielded to W. Noyce's Anglo-American party (W. Noyce and J. Sadler). In 1962 a joint British-Pakistan Forces expedition attempted Khinyang Chhish (25,762 feet), but withdrew after the death of two of the party in an avalanche. Khinyang Chhish and its neighbour, Pumarikish (24,581 feet), remain unclimbed. Momhil Sar (24,090 feet), which lies north-west of the Hispar glacier, was climbed by an Austrian expedition in 1964. In general, these peaks are snowy and dome-like, in

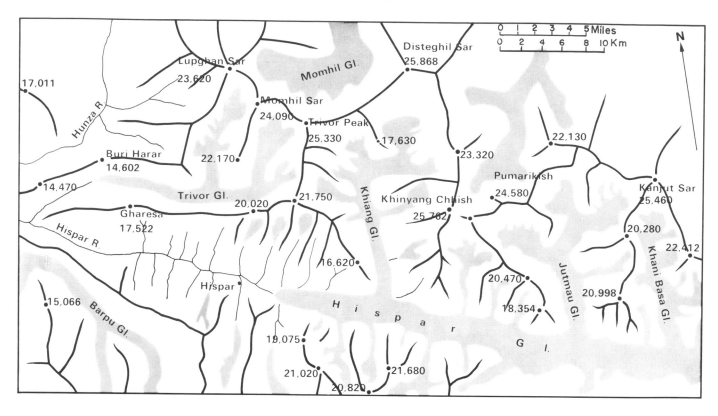

Karakoram: the Hispar Muztagh.

Hispar Muztagh: Khinyang Chhish (25,762 feet) from Trivor.

Buddhist reliefs on a rock near Skardu, Baltistan. This district, lying to the south of the Karakoram, was Buddhist up to the fourteenth century, but is now Moslem.

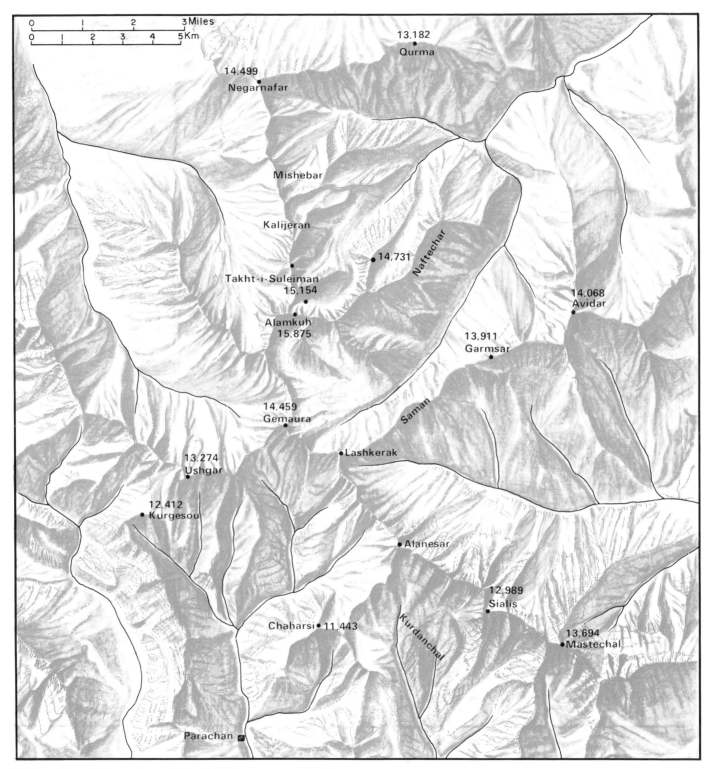

9. Iran: Alam Kuh and the Takht-i-Suleiman group in the
Elburz Mountains.

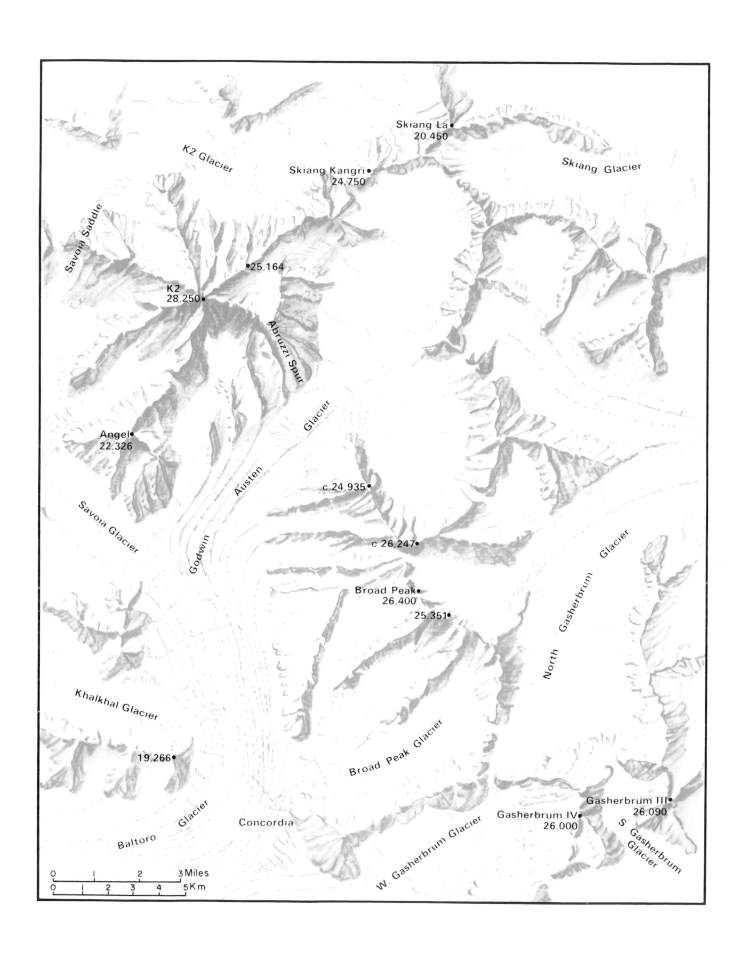

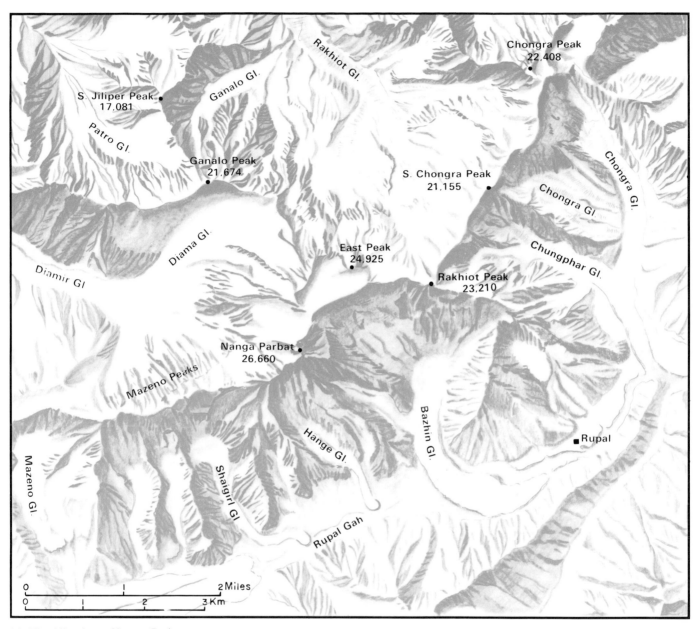

Chongra Peak
22,408

S. Jiliper Peak
17,081

Ganalo Gl.

Rakhiot Gl.

Patro Gl.

Ganalo Peak
21,674

S. Chongra Peak
21,155

Chongra Gl.

Chongra Gl.

Chungphar Gl.

Diama Gl.

Diamir Gl

East Peak
24,925

Rakhiot Peak
23,210

Nanga Parbat
26,660

Mazeno Peaks

Bazhin Gl.

Rupal

Mazeno Gl.

Shaigiri Gl.

Hänge Gl.

Rupal Gah

0   1   2 Miles
0   1   2   3 Km

11. The Himalaya: Nanga Parbat.

10. The Himalaya: K2, Broad Peak, and the Gasherbrum
Group in the Baltoro Karakoram.

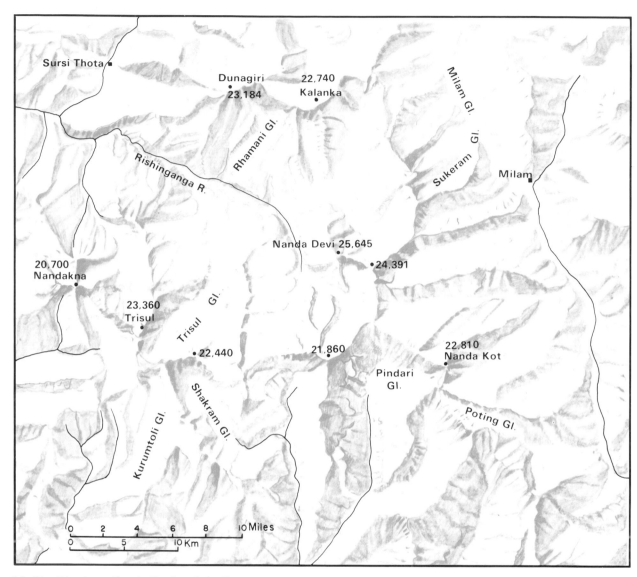

12. The Himalaya: Nanda Devi and the Sanctuary.

(*Above*) A caravan of porters on the Baltoro Glacier. Behind them are the granite spires which form the glacier's northern wall.

(*Right*) A Balti porter at Askole.

contrast to the more jagged Baltoro towers. Ascents have also been made among the southern ranges between Hispar and Chogolungma, notably Yengutz Har (23,056 feet) by a German party in 1955. Malubiting (24,451 feet), the highest summit in the group, is still unclimbed.

The Biafo Glacier descends south-east towards the Braldu River. But due east from the Snow Lake are the less lofty summits of the Panmah Muztagh, to the north of which descends Crevasse Glacier, the discovery of Younghusband.

Central Karakoram

H. H. Godwin-Austen and others had already done much surveying before Younghusband's classic crossing of the Muztagh Pass in 1887. He slept out at 18,000 feet and dared not light fires for fear of Hunza raiders. Two years later Younghusband was exploring the Shaksgam Valley to the north and the K2 approaches. After Conway's expedition had visited the Baltoro, the story of this glacier became mainly one of parties passing along to attempt one of the giants flanking its thirty-six-mile length.

The length of the glacier means a long approach march from Skardu to any peak, passing first the Masherbrum group (25,660 feet) on the right and the monolithic Muztagh Tower

Baltoro Muztagh: Masherbrum (25,660 feet) from the north. This difficult peak was climbed in 1960 by an American-Pakistan expedition.

Baltoro Muztagh: Gasherbrum IV (26,000 feet) from the Baltoro Glacier.

(23,860 feet) on the left. The 'Concordia', at the junction of the Baltoro and Godwin-Austen Glaciers, is the centre of one of the greatest mountain cirques. K2 (28,250 feet) and Broad Peak (26,400 feet) rise to the north, the Gasherbrums, four of them over 26,000 feet, to the east, the Chogolisa group (25,110 feet) to the south.

Conway sorted out some of the topography. In 1902 Eckenstein made a bold attempt on the north-east ridge of K2. The Duke of the Abruzzi's well-equipped party reconnoitred

Baltoro Muztagh: the western aspect of Gasherbrum I ('Hidden Peak') (26,470 feet), the highest peak in the Gasherbrum group.

the south-east (Abruzzi) spur in 1909, and also reached 24,700 feet on Chogolisa, for long a height record. International (1934) and French (1936) parties were defeated on Gasherbrum I ('Hidden Peak', 26,470 feet), but the former claimed Sia Kangri (24,350 feet). in 1938 a British party climbed very high on Masherbrum. R. A. Hodgkin and J. B. Harrison, the summit pair, were badly frostbitten.

In the same year an American party under C. S. Houston reconnoitred K2 and decided on the Abruzzi Spur. They climbed to above 26,000 feet. Next year an ill-led American expedition reached a greater height but resulted in the death of D. Wolfe and of three heroic Sherpas who tried to save him.

Since 1950 the Central Karakoram have had their full share of attention. Waves of climbers have followed the earlier waves of explorers. In the post-Partition fighting, Skardu changed hands several times, and when the next American expedition arrived in 1953, it was by air from Rawalpindi – an example followed by subsequent parties to Skardu and Gilgit. Moreover, Sherpa porters who had, till then, done the high-altitude carrying, were no longer allowed in Pakistan and Hunzas filled the bill. Baltis being considered unreliable. (More recently, some Baltis have proved very useful high-altitude porters.) This party, under Houston, was overtaken by prolonged bad weather at 25,000 feet. A. Gilkey was taken sick and died during an appalling ordeal of descent through storm.

K2 was climbed next year by a mammoth Italian expedition, using oxygen, under A. Desio. L. Lacedelli and A. Compagnoni reached the summit. Another sign of changing times was the ascent, in 1956, of the reputedly impossible Muztagh Tower (23,860 feet) by two parties, British and French, using different routes, both of high technical difficulty. The attention of continental parties focused on the Gasherbrums and Broad Peak. Gasherbrum II (26,360 feet) went to the Austrians in 1956 (F. Moravec, S. Larch, H. Willenpart), and Broad Peak to the small Austrian party of M. Schmuck, F. Wintersteller, K. Diemberger, H. Buhl – a bold venture marred by Buhl's subsequent death on Chogolisa. In 1958, after a desperate siege in bad weather, P. K. Schoening and A. Kauffman claimed Gasherbrum I, the Japanese (M. Fujihira and K. Hirai) Chogolisa, the Italians (W. Bonatti and C. Mauri) the fiercely sharp-edged Gasherbrum IV (26,000 feet) with its Alpine-standard summit ridge. In 1960, Masherbrum (25,660 feet) was claimed by an American-Pakistan expedition led by G. Bell. In all ascents the new attitude to technical difficulty at high altitude has been an important factor.

In this crowded survey much has been omitted, but a word must be added about the Shaksgam Valley to the north. After Younghusband's journeys, Mason (1925), the Duke of Spoleto (1929), and Shipton (1937 and 1939) did much to fix the course of this circuitous river, its relation to the Aghil Range to the north, and the glaciers descending to it. However, there still remain blanks on the map.

Baltoro Muztagh: Broad Peak (26,400 feet) and K2 (28,250 feet) from the north-east ridge of Gasherbrum IV.

Baltoro Muztagh: looking south-west from the summit of Broad Peak towards Masherbrum (25,660 feet), the Baltoro Glacier, and, in the distance, Nanga Parbat (26,660 feet).

Looking across the Shaksgam Valley towards peaks of the Aghil Mountains lying on the Tibetan border.

Eastern Karakoram

Containing less lofty peaks and being particularly hard to approach since Partition, the eastern massifs have received less attention than their neighbours. The best early pioneer work here was done by Longstaff's party in 1909. This located the Teram Kangri group and explored the forty-five-mile-long Siachen Glacier, which begins its course under Sia Kangri (24,350 feet), an outlier of the Gasherbrum group. It was followed by the Workmans (1911–12), who also attempted Saltoro Kangri (25,400 feet), the highest point of the southern chain. Twenty-four years later an expedition led by J. Waller reached about 24,700 feet on Saltoro Kangri. Heavy snowfall, a characteristic of these ranges, stopped the party. The mountain was finally climbed in 1962 by a Japanese-Pakistan expedition. Mount Ghent (24,280 feet), also in the Saltoro Range, was climbed by E. Waschak's Austrian expedition in 1961.

Finally, in the complex of glaciers east of the Siachen, the Rimo gives birth to the tempestuous Shyok River, notorious for dam breaking and explored by F. de Filippi (1914) and G. Dainelli (1930). In the Rimo Muztagh, as in the Teram Kangri group, stand many unnamed, unattempted peaks. The important Saser group to the south will be mentioned later, since it lies, under the present cease-fire arrangement, in Indian Ladakh.

Nanga Parbat

The Nanga Parbat massif (26,660 feet) stands alone, near to the Karakoram yet not part of them. Geologically the mountain is an isolated mass of gneiss, in whose composition metamorphosed sediments have had a share. It rises over 22,000 feet from the Indus Valley to the north, and presents a south face of nearly 15,000 feet. Being isolated, it attracts storm and snowfall and is notorious for avalanches.

It was natural that the 'Naked Mountain', towering above the Kashmir skyline, should attract climbers. Mummery, with Hastings, Collie, and Bruce, surveyed the south side in 1895; but he disappeared mysteriously with two Gurkhas above the Diamirai Glacier to the west. In 1932 a strong German party, approaching, as was usual, from Srinagar over the Tragbal and Burzil Passes, found the correct approach by the Rakhiot Glacier, Rakhiot Peak, and the east ridge, and a determined assault led by W. Merkl was made in 1934. The danger of the route lay in its great length and exposure to both avalanche and sudden weather changes. When the goal seemed within reach storm broke, and in the struggle to get back Merkl, with two other climbers and six Sherpas, died.

In 1937 a German party of seven climbers and nine porters was overwhelmed by an avalanche at Camp IV. P. Bauer, who flew out at once and found the bodies, led another expedition in 1938, supported by aircraft, but weather defeated him. After the loss of two British climbers in 1950, an Austro-German expedition led by Dr K. Herrligkoffer was finally

successful in 1953; but only through a solo *tour de force* by H. Buhl, who climbed the last 4,000 feet alone, reached the summit at evening, and stood out for the night under it, returning next day. This may claim to be the most remarkable single feat in Himalayan mountaineering.

In 1962 a German expedition, led again by Dr Herrligkoffer, climbed the mountain by the Diamir flank, the route which Mummery had selected and which was attempted by Aufschnaiter's party in 1939.

The history of Nanga Parbat has been a tragic one, for fourteen climbers and seventeen Sherpas have lost their lives on the mountain.

Though politically in Pakistan, and thus approachable by the Babusar Pass, it should be added that Nanga Parbat is structurally part of the Punjab Great Himlaya, which include the Sind peaks of Kashmir and Nun Kun. It used to be approached by the direct 'Gilgit Road' over the Burzil Pass. These Kashmir peaks we shall now consider.

Kashmir and Ladakh

The term Kashmir should rightfully cover the Karakoram, but it is usually applied to the parts of Kashmir which, along with Ladakh, are now under Indian rule.

This is the most 'European' stretch of the Himalaya. North, south, and east of the flat-bottomed Vale of Kashmir there rise peaks of Alpine stature, while in the valleys below them pine and birch, wild rose and columbine, apple and pear remind the western traveller of home. Even sparrows and tits display themselves alongside the vultures, choughs, and enormous lammergeier. The ranges continue into Ladakh, the antechamber of Tibet.

The Kashmiris are predominantly Muslim. By the lakes which are a feature of the vale near Srinagar, the capital, the Moguls built their pleasances: Shah Jahan that of Nishat, Jahangir the famous Shalimar. In those days the arts flourished. But Shah Jahan was deposed by the intolerant Aurangzeb, who once assisted a Ladakhi prince on condition of conversion to Islam. After Aurangzeb came the dissolution which made India an easy prey for the British. In Kashmir a period of Afghan oppression was followed by Sikh government (1815). An ally of the Sikhs, Gulab Singh, the Dogra Rajput prince of Jammu, took it upon himself to overrun Ladakh (1835–40). When the Sikhs fell foul of the British, Kashmir, and with it Ladakh, were handed over to him and he became Maharajah of Kashmir and Jammu–a Hindu prince governing communities that were largely Mohammedan or Buddhist. Both states are now under Indian rule, though parts of Ladakh are disputed by the Chinese.

Owing to its temperate climate, Kashmir has always been a favourite resort and refuge from the heat. The climbing in the area has been largely done by the British and Indians, since the peaks are not, apart from Nun Kun, conspicuous enough prizes to attract costly expeditions from the West.

However, both for traveller and climber, botanist and artist, this is a small paradise. Along main routes like the Sind Valley (north and then east from the vale) there are good rest-houses and ponies do the carrying. The Zoji La, at 11,578 feet the lowest pass over the Himalayan divide, lies between the contrasting landscapes of Kashmir, with its rich vale, Mogul mosques, and wooded Sind Valley, and the flat ochres and reds of Ladakh, soon a Buddhist country of towering monasteries, of *mani* walls and yaks and dromedaries, of hard winters and terraced barley fields and apricot groves. M. Pallis, visiting in 1936, sympathetically described the monasteries around Kargil, Spituk, and Leh – all in a different world from Srinagar. From Leh, reached by the Ladakh Treaty Road, the traveller can turn north-west to the Shyok and Skardu or north-east towards unexplored Ladakh.

E. F. Neve, who started a long climbing career here in 1886, is, with his brother A. Neve, a name closely associated with Kashmir climbing. In 1899 he climbed the highest summit of Haramukh (16,872 feet). (Bruce, who had already climbed here in 1892 with Conway and Eckenstein, made the second ascent.) His climbs included many in the Kashmir reaches of the Pir Panjal Range – south of the vale and part of the Punjab Lesser Himalaya – and culminated in his ascent of the east ridge of Kolahoi (17,799 feet), the highest point in Kashmir proper, climbed with Mason in 1912.

Skiing caught on in Kashmir, and after the First World War the Ski Club of India established its centre at Gulmarg on the south side of the vale, with a hut at Khilanmarg above. In 1929 M. D. N. Wyatt skied over the Pir Panjal and crossed the Zoji La. Climbing continued with more ascents of Kolahoi, which is easily accessible from Srinagar. In 1935 John Hunt and R. Brotherhood climbed its south face. J. Waller made a variation route in 1937, and climbed Thajiwas Peak in the Sind Valley above Sonamarg. Then the war came.

In 1944 Wing-Commander A. J. M. Smyth started the Aircrew Mountain Centre at Sonamarg, and later Gulmarg, for the training of aircrew in mountain country. Many climbs were done by aircrew and pupils. The meadows, summits, and glaciers of this part of Kashmir remind the pioneer of the Alps in the early days. Notable first ascents were done by instructors on Alpine-scale peaks of between 15,000 and 18,000 feet.

The most important peak of Kashmir proper is Nun Kun, dominating its own massif sixty miles east of Srinagar. It was explored early by A. Neve, and the easier Kun (23,250 feet) climbed in 1913 by Piacenza's expedition. Nun (23,410 feet) offers more serious obstacles and resisted Waller in 1934 and again in 1937, as well as another British party in 1946. All these early parties underestimated the difficulties facing them. In 1953 B. Pierre led a strong mainly French party supported by Sherpas. The climb was made from the south, finishing up the west ridge. Despite an avalanche, which injured Pierre and others, the attempt was pursued and the

Kolahoi (17,799 feet). This peak, which lies thirty miles east of Srinagar in the Vale of Kashmir, was first climbed by E. F. Neve and K. Mason in 1912.

Nun (23,410 feet), the highest peak of the Nun Kun massif, from Camp I on the west ridge.

summit reached by P. Vittoz, a Swiss, and Mme C. Kogan.

South-east from Nun Kun, and approached from Jammu, are important peaks of 21,000 feet and glaciers draining into the Bhazun explored by F. Kolb and L. Krenek in 1946.

If we consider the mountains east of the Karakoram and Saser Passes to be part of our area, it will be seen that northeast Ladakh has great tracts of high and largely unexplored mountain country, a part, really, of the Eastern Karakoram. The Shyok River descends from the Rimo Glacier and does a great loop, enclosing the Saser Kangri and Kunzang groups. Younghusband crossed the Karakoram pass in 1889 and Longstaff penetrated the area in 1909. The Vissers surveyed part of it in 1929 and important gaps were filled in by Mason and R. C. F. Schomberg. The highest peak, Saser Kangri (25,170 feet), was photographed as early as 1899 by E. F. Neve from a peak of 20,580 feet east of Panamik, and A. Neve and D. G. Oliver explored the area round Mamostong Kangri (24,690 feet) in 1907. J. O. M. Roberts reconnoitred the Saser group in 1946 and climbed Lookout Peak (*c.* 20,500 feet). An outstanding solo achievement was the ascent of Stok Kangri (20,723 feet) by Vittoz in 1951. In the whole of North-East Ladakh, difficult of access, there remains much to be explored.

Kulu, Lahul, and Spiti

The ranges south of Kashmir and west of Garhwal and Kumaon comprise a continuation of the Pir Panjal and Ladakh Ranges, the latter continuing in the Zaskar. Less striking than those to the north and the east, the mountains are for the most part curiously little known and have only recently been appreciated.

The states of Kulu, Spiti, and Lahul can be taken together, since Kulu, to the south, gives access to the other two. All are in India and Kulu is the most accessible of Himalayan districts. In the Beas Valley, famous for its cherries, apples, and pears, little has changed apart from the motor road constructed in the 1930s. Manali is the starting-point. From it the snowy dome of Deo Tibba (19,687 feet), part of the Pir Panjal and the objective of many parties, is approached. There was long a confusion between this peak and its neighbour Indrasan (20,410 feet). Deo Tibba was finally climbed in 1952 by J. de V. Graaff's party, forty years after the first reconnaissance. Indrasan was climbed by a Japanese university party in 1962. J. O. M. Roberts had already climbed 'White Sail Peak' (21,148 feet) in the Tos Nal in 1941.

From the Rohtang Pass (13,050 feet), one descends to the Chandra River. Lahul lies to the north, Spiti to the east. Both these states, lying north of the Himalayan divide, are Tibetan in climate rather than Indian: dry and bare, largely out of monsoon reach. Lahul is roughly triangular, bounded to the south and east by the Chandra River, to the west by the Bhaga River. In recent years particularly, it has been recognized that this and Kulu are ideal countries for the small party with a short time at its disposal. Bruce and others had pioneered,

(*Above*) A pony caravan in the Spiti Valley.

5. Machapuchare (22,956 feet) in the Annapurna Range.

6a. (*Overleaf*) Nanda Devi (25,645 feet) in the Garhwal Himalaya.

6b. (*Overleaf*) The Nepalese village of Tinkar.

but the location even of important peaks like Mulkila (21,380 feet) was for long in doubt. In 1939 L. Krenek's party thoroughly explored the Milang, tributary of the Bhaga River. In 1955 an R.A.F. party under Smyth went straight up the Kulti Valley into Central Lahul and climbed peaks of up to 21,000 feet. In the same year, H. McArthur's party climbed Tara Pahar (20,430 feet). At Darcha, beyond the administrative centre of Kyelang, one reaches the political 'Inner Line', beyond which indiscreet persons have been arrested by the Punjab police.

(*Above*) Crossing the Bara Shigri Glacier.　　　　　　(*Below*) Papsura (21,165 feet), in the Punjab Himalaya.

A Buddha in Kee Monastery, Spiti.

Kulu Pumori (21,500 feet) from a camp on the Bara Shigri Glacier. The north-west ridge is on the left. The first ascent was made by the south-west ridge, which is on the extreme right.

The least visited and perhaps most interesting region is Spiti, accessible over the 14,931-foot Kunzum Pass from Lahul, or by the Hindustan-Tibet road and the junction of the Sutlej and Spiti Rivers. The country is very dry, agriculture hard and practised by means of irrigation. Flocks and herds are maintained with difficulty. The inhabitants are Buddhist, and there are big lama communities at monasteries like Kee. The mountains have been very little climbed except for triangulation purposes. P. F. Holmes, after climbing in the south in 1955 with T. H. Braham, in 1956 forced a way up the Ratang Gorge and climbed peaks at its head, notably Ratang Tower (20,800 feet).

In the Zaskar Range, east of Spiti, stands Shilla, climbed according to tradition in 1860 by a solitary *khalasi* in the service of the Survey of India, and boasting a height of over

23,000 feet. Recent investigations have shrunk the giant; observations taken by Graaff's party from Mani Kang (21,630 feet) on the Bashahr frontier have reduced the height to 21,325 feet at most.

The highest peak of this part of the Zaskar Range, the great round-headed Leo Pargial (22,280 feet), stands near the junction of the Spiti and Sutlej Rivers and overlooks Spiti, Tibet, and Garhwal. The Gerard brothers climbed to over 19,000 feet early in the nineteenth century, and the summit was reached in 1933 by M. Pallis's party. Seven miles to the north stands Shipki (21,680 feet), still unclimbed and, like Leo Pargial, now out of bounds.

Garhwal and Kumaon

The Garhwal-Kumaon Himalaya are well defined by the Sutlej River to west and north, and the Kali River to the east, on the boundary of Nepal. Among these mountains rise the Ganges and its tributaries, the Jumna, Bhagirathi, and Pindar. The great Himalayan crest zone passes along the north side of the Baspa Valley, to the Satopanth (23,213 feet) and Chaukhamba (23,420 feet) groups, and on to Nanda Devi (25,645 feet). This is flanked to the south by the Dhaula Dar, which includes Bandarpunch (20,720 feet) and the Gangotri peaks, to the north by a continuation of the Zaskar, more Tibetan in character but including the Kamet group.

The whole of this area, lying as it did nicely within British India, has been excellently surveyed, particularly since G. Osmaston's monumental survey of 1935–8. One of the last blanks to be filled was that of Nanda Devi, which stands isolated within a ring of mountains seventy miles in circum-

View north-east from 19,500 feet and the slopes of Gangotri 1 (21,890 feet) in Tehri-Garhwal. The Rudugaira Valley lies below the glacier to the right of the photograph. Beneath the cloud lies the Gangotri Glacier and Gaumukh, one of the sources of the Ganges. The distant ranges include the Chirbas Parbat and Matri groups.

ference that is broken only by the Rishi Gorge to the west.

The climate varies between the monsoon-fed luxuriance of the southern valleys and the arid northern aspect towards Tibet. The lower reaches of Kumaon are noted for tigers, the northern villages of Garhwal for yaks. Both districts are administered by commissioners from the U.P. (Uttar Pradesh). Only Nanda Devi and Kamet exceed 25,000 feet, but for the pioneer there is a wealth of 20,000 to 23,000-foot peaks to be climbed, magnificent valleys of pine and deodar, ingeniously terraced barley fields, charming alps, and a sympathetic people in the sturdy, round-faced Garhwalis who walk along spinning wool for their home-woven garments. Kedarnath and Badrinath are towns of pilgrimage for pious Hindus, the latter lying near the source of the Alaknanda or infant Ganges. Both these towns and the villages around are evacuated in winter when the snows descend and the Garhwalis with them to lower levels. In summer, however, flocks are to be found on alps 15,000 feet up or more.

W. W. Graham and his guides anticipated modern exploration by trying to force the Rishi Gorge in 1883. In 1907 Longstaff, Bruce, and A. L. Mumm, with guides and Gurkhas, began the remarkable campaign which included Longstaff's ascent, with guides and one Gurkha, of Trisul (23,360 feet) from the north, the last 6,000 feet being climbed in one day. The party then made the first serious reconnaissance of Kamet (25,447 feet) and crossed the Bhiundhar Pass into the 'Valley of Flowers'.

C. F. Meade attacked Kamet doggedly in 1910 and 1912, and in 1913 camped on 'Meade's Col' (23,420 feet) between Kamet and Abi Gamin (24,130 feet). He would probably have climbed Kamet but for bad weather. A. M. Kellas visited the mountain in 1911 and 1914 and reached Meade's Col in 1920, at the age of over fifty.

Meanwhile a geological survey was begun, glacier snouts were measured and botanists became active in the well-flowered valleys. Sportsmen hunted among the lower hills. Stations like Ranikhet and Naini Tal became popular refuges from the summer heat. Deputy Commissioners of Garhwal, Almora, and Naini Tal travelled widely, and none more widely than H. Ruttledge, Deputy Commissioner at Almora. In 1926, with T. H. Somervell and R. C. Wilson, he tried to enter the Nanda Devi sanctuary from Milam to the northeast; next year, with Longstaff, he tried from the Nandakini Valley. All in vain.

Somervell had brought Chettan, a Sherpa porter from Darjeeling; in 1927 more Sherpas, including Lewa, were engaged. This was an innovation. For ordinary carrying, Dhotiyals, who come from western Nepal in the summer months, and Bhotias from the northern villages are used. These last proved their worth on F. S. Smythe's 1931 Kamet expedition, when the top was reached in less than a fortnight from base by climbers who included Lewa the sirdar and one Bhotia, Kesar Singh.

In 1934 Shipton and H. W. Tilman, with Ang Tharkay and two more Sherpas, solved the approach to Nanda Devi by forcing the Rishi Gorge and surveying the sanctuary. During the monsoon they explored the Gangotri–Arwa area, then returned to the sanctuary, to escape over the Sundardhunga col (18,110 feet) inspected two years before by Ruttledge. This was a brilliant first pattern of the light, self-contained party. In 1936, using the route found by Shipton and Tilman, a strong Anglo-American party climbed the mountain (Tilman and Odell).

More ascents have been made of Trisul, including an ascent in 1933 by P. R. Oliver with Kesar Singh. Both peaks of Nanda Devi were climbed again in 1951 by R. Duplat's French party, two of whom were lost while attempting the traverse to Nanda Devi East (24,391 feet), first climbed by A. Karpinski's Polish party in 1939.

Mountaineering has gone on happily up and down Garhwal and Kumaon, and only a brief summary can be given. Pallis's party explored Gangotri in 1933, C. F. Kirkus and F. E. Hicks climbing Peak 22,060 feet. Five Japanese and one Sherpa reached the top of Nanda Kot (22,510 feet), southeast from Nanda Devi over Traill's pass, in 1936. Smythe and Oliver campaigned in 1937 and Smythe climbed Mana Peak (23,860 feet). R. Schwarzgruber's party was in the Gangotri area in 1938, and in 1939 A. Roch and the Swiss had the first of two remarkably successful campaigns, climbing Dunagiri (23,184 feet) on the north ring-wall of Nanda Devi, and Rataban (20,230 feet). The second party in 1947, the last under British rule, climbed Kedarnath (22,770 feet) and Satopanth (23,213 feet), then moved east to climb Nanda Ghunti (20,700 feet), westerly outlier of Trisul.

During the Second World War short journeys by troops on leave filled in minor gaps. W. Noyce climbed peaks south and west of the Nanda Devi rim. Several attempts were made on Bandarpunch (20,720 feet), isolated above the source of the Jumna River. Bandarpunch was finally climbed by J. T. M. Gibson of the Doon School and a party of young climbers in 1950.

Since the war notable ascents have been Abi Gamin in 1950, by the Anglo-Swiss party, A. Tissières, K. Berrill, G. Chevalley, and R. Dittert, and Mukut Parbat (23,760 feet) in 1951, by the New Zealanders H. E. Riddiford and F. M. Cotter. J. B. Tyson's party climbed Gangotri peaks in 1952, and the coveted Chaukhamba (23,420 feet) went, in the same year, to a French party (V. Russenberger, L. Georges).

Indian mountaineers have played an increasingly active part since 1950. N. D. Jayal and Gurdial Singh both reached the summit of Trisul in 1951, and were members of the party which climbed Mrigthuni (22,490 feet) in 1958. In 1961 Indian mountaineers (O. P. Sharma and two Sherpas) climbed Nilkanta (21,640 feet), often attempted and one of the most shapely of all Himalayan peaks, and Nilgiri Parbat (21,240 feet). In 1964 they crowned their achievements by making the third ascent of Nanda Devi.

One little-known area remains, the Panch Chuli to the east, between the Ramganga and the Dhauliganga. Very few have visited here since Ruttledge in 1929, and these include W. H. Murray and H. Harrer. The highest peak, Panch Chuli (22,650 feet), is fine, but access is not easy.

Nepal Himalaya

These ranges have only seriously been explored since 1949, though peaks actually standing on a border, like Everest and

Kangchenjunga, have been approached from other countries.

Nepal, a rectangular country about the size of England and Wales, comprises the *terai* or southern lowlands, and high mountains to the north. It is drained by three main rivers, the Karnali, Gandaki, and Kosi. Its past history was stormy. The old régime of the Newars yielded to the vigorous Gurkhas, whose origin is obscure but who came in earlier days from the north. In 1768 they conquered the country and in 1790 invaded China, which in turn invaded Nepal and dictated terms in 1792. Then came the rise of the powerful Rana family, culminating in the seizure of power by the great Jung Bahadur in 1845. Though a supporter of the British in 1857, he kept to a policy of privacy which continued until the end of the Rana régime in 1948.

By a treaty with the British, who had a Resident in Kathmandu from 1816, Gurkha troops were (and still are) recruited, the name 'Gurkha' now applying to the Puns, Magars, and Gurungs of Central Nepal. But the British still were not admitted except on special occasions, and even for the 1925–7 Survey, British officers were not allowed in to supervise the Indian surveyors. In 1949 the first climbing party, led by Tilman and partly scientific, explored the Langtrang, Ganesh, and Jugal Himal. Since then, under the increasingly personal rule of the king, many expeditions have been allowed. All the major peaks over 26,000 feet have been climbed. Some of the twenty-four-thousanders have yielded, as well as a number of 'slightly stunted giants' of 20,000 feet and over.

The majority of the five million Nepalese are Hindu, but Kathmandu also has its Buddhist temples not far from the holy shrine of Pashpatinah. The country in which Gautama Buddha was born becomes rapidly Buddhist as one travels towards the Tibetan frontier.

Nepal is heavily affected by the monsoon, and like Garhwal has a pre-monsoon climbing season (April, May, and early June) and a post-monsoon season from September. It is rich in plant life, and in spring the valley sides are a blaze of rhododendron. In 1848 Sir Joseph Hooker explored the valleys west of Kangchenjunga; a hundred years later O. Polunin was listing the primulas, potentillas, saxifrages, Lloydia, and delphinium of the Langtang. Plant life goes up to over 19,000 feet. The eagle is found here; snow cock, *ram chikor*, minivets, redstarts, add colour below. Among the fauna are bears, snow leopard, mouse hares, *jharal* (like ibex), musk deer, martens—and, of course, the 'Abominable Snowman', or *yeti*, whose photographed tracks have led several expeditions up the garden path.

Karnali Section

Western Nepal is the least known. The Seti River cuts back into, but not through, the Api-Saipal group. Api (23,399 feet) was reconnoitred from the Kali to the north in 1953 by W. H. Murray and J. B. Tyson, and in 1954 was attempted by an expedition led by P. Ghiglione. Whether the summit was reached is not known as two of the party died high up. A lone Sherpa struggled down with the news. The first definite ascent was made in 1960 by a Japanese party. The Japanese also claimed Saipal (23,079 feet) in 1963. The main Humla Karnali River cuts through from Tibet, having Gurla Mandhata (25,355 feet) on the crest forty miles north of Saipal. Gurla Mandhata, now out of bounds to western climbers, was attempted in 1905 by Longstaff, who was carried down 3,000 feet by an avalanche and survived. Moving east one approaches the Kanjiroba Himal beyond Jumla. Much

Peaks of the Yokapahar Himal (left), Nampa (22,162 feet) and the eastern summit of Api (23,399 feet) from the Tinkar Lipu pass, West Nepal.

survey work has been done here by Tyson's parties since 1961. In 1962 a British women's party made several ascents in this group.

The Kanjiroba Himal is linked at its eastern extremity with the Dhaulagiri Himal to the south. Attention has focused on Dhaulagiri I (26,810 feet), reconnoitred by the French in 1950 and then attempted by Swiss, Argentinian, German, and Austrian parties. It was climbed by M. Eiselin's Swiss party in 1960, six members reaching the summit, up the north-

east ridge. The use of aircraft to land climbers and stores up to 18,000 feet (on Dambush Pass and North-East Col) was an innovation. There still remain four more Dhaulagiris, three of them over 25,000 feet. In 1962 J. O. M. Roberts, who climbed Putha Hiunchuli (23,750 feet) in 1954, attempted Dhaulagiri IV (25,064 feet) with an all Sherpa party. An R.A.F. party attempted the mountain again in 1965 with no success. This still comprises the largest area of really high unclimbed peaks in the Himalaya.

(*Above*) The highest summit of the Kanjiroba Himal (22,580 feet), seen from the summit of Bhulu Lhasa (20,016 feet).

(*Below*) The Dhaulagiri Range from the south-east. From left to right the peaks are: Gurja Himal (23,539 feet), Dhaulagiri IV (25,064 feet), Dhaulagiri II (25,427 feet), and Dhaulagiri I (26,810 feet).

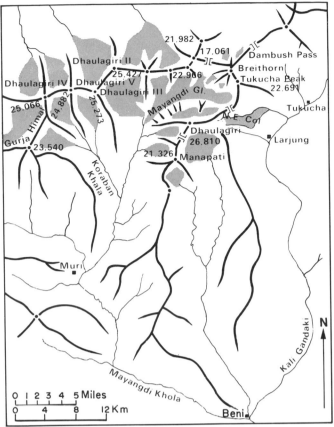

Gandaki Section

These groups are drained by the Gandaki River and its tributaries. The Kali Gandaki separates Dhaulagiri from the Annapurna Himal, a line of giants beginning with Annapurna I and ending with Annapurna II some twenty miles away. The Kali descends from Tibetan country beyond Mustang, and up it pilgrims come annually to the shrine in the cliffs above Muktinath, one of the four holy places of Hindu Nepal. The Tilicho and Thorungse Passes give access to Manangbot on the Marsyandi. South of the Annapurna Himal lie the plain and town of Pokhara, the goal of which early travellers like Bruce dreamed but to which they could never come. Roberts was the first British visitor here in 1950, and since then Pokhara has been linked with Kathmandu and India by an air service, particularly useful to the Gurkhas and their administrators.

In 1950 M. Herzog's party discovered the northern route up Annapurna I (26,504 feet), and the summit was reached by Herzog and L. Lachenal. They suffered frostbite and next day, with Terray and Rébuffat, were forced to spend a night in a crevasse on the way down. This was the first 26,000-foot peak to be climbed. The same year Annapurnas II (26,041 feet)

The Himalaya: the Dhaulagiri Himal.

The Annapurna Range from the south. On the left is Annapurna South (23,804 feet) with Annapurna I (26,504 feet) to the right of centre.

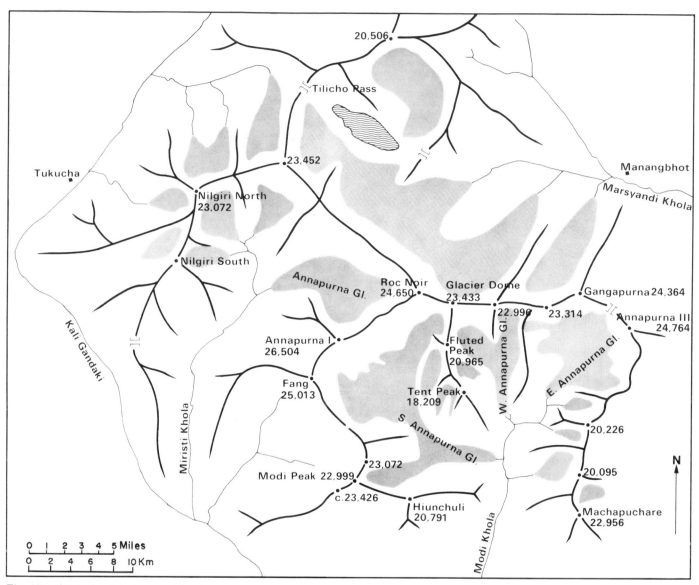

The Himalaya: the Annapurna Himal.

and IV (24,688 feet) were reconnoitred from the north by Tilman; the latter was climbed in 1955 by a German party (H. Steinmetz, H. Biller, J. Wellenkamp), the former in 1960 by Roberts's party using oxygen (R. H. Grant, C. J. S. Bonington, Ang Nyima).

To the south Annapurna I drops a 14,000-foot face into a huge sanctuary visited up the Modi Gorge by shepherds during the monsoon. Annapurna III (24,858 feet), which was climbed in 1961 by an Indian expedition, stands at the north-east corner, and from it a long ridge projects south, having at its end the extraordinary two-headed Machapuchare (22,956 feet), the 'Fish's Tail', a sacred mountain. Roberts led a party here in 1957; W. Noyce and A. D. M. Cox reached a point 150 feet below the summit. Several other peaks of note overlook the basin of the Modi Khola, Ganesh (23,804 feet),

Glacier Dome (23,802 feet), and Gangapurna (c. 24,375 feet). The first two were climbed by Japanese parties in 1964 and the latter by a German party in 1965.

North of the Annapurna group, the Peri Himal and the Larkya Himal continue the eastward line. The important peaks of Manaslu (26,760 feet) and Himal Chuli (25,801 feet) are part of a subsidiary north–south crest. Manaslu, seen by Tilman in 1949, became the objective of Japanese parties. Two reconnaissance parties and three full expeditions (the second was stopped by villagers on religious grounds) were needed before the summit was reached in 1956 from the Larkya Glacier to the north (leader, Yuko Maki). Oxygen was used, and both summit pairs, T. Imanishi and Gyaltsen Norbu, K. Kato and N. Higeta, made the final climb at remarkable speed.

Himal Chuli also yielded to a Japanese expedition four years

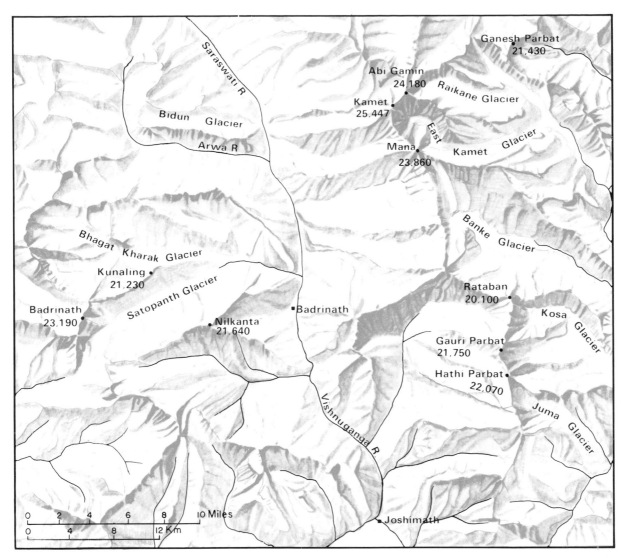

Ganesh Parbat
21,430

Abi Gamin
24,180

Kamet
25,447

Raikane Glacier

Saraswati R

Bidun Glacier

Arwa R

Mana
23,860

East

Kamet Glacier

Banke Glacier

Bhagat Kharak Glacier

Kunaling
21,230

Satopanth Glacier

Rataban
20,100

Kosa Glacier

Badrinath
23,190

Nilkanta
21,640

Badrinath

Gauri Parbat
21,750

Hathi Parbat
22,070

Vishnuganga R

Juma Glacier

0   2   4   6   8   10 Miles
0   4   8   12 Km

Joshimath

13. The Himalaya: Kamet and Abi Gamin and the neighbouring peaks, including Mana Peak, Hathi Parbar, and Nilkanta.

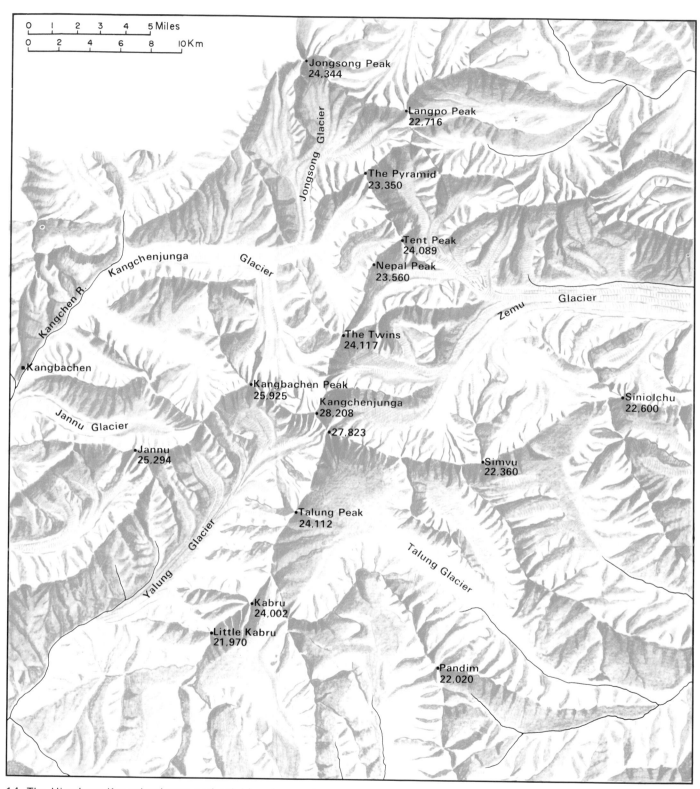

Scale:
0 1 2 3 4 5 Miles
0 2 4 6 8 10 Km

•Jongsong Peak
24,344

Jongsong Glacier

•Langpo Peak
22,716

•The Pyramid
23,350

Kangchenjunga   Glacier

•Tent Peak
24,089

•Nepal Peak
23,560

Kangchen R.

Zemu   Glacier

•The Twins
24,117

•Kangbachen

•Kangbachen Peak
25,925

Kangchenjunga
•28,208

•27,823

•Siniolchu
22,600

Jannu Glacier

•Jannu
25,294

•Simvu
22,360

•Talung Peak
24,112

Yalung Glacier

Talung Glacier

•Kabru
24,002

•Little Kabru
21,970

•Pandim
22,020

14. The Himalaya: Kangchenjunga and neighbouring peaks,
including Siniolchn, and Jannu.

West Rongbuk Glacier

Rongbuk Glacier

East Rongbuk Glacier

•Khartaphu
23,720

Khartu Glacier

Changtse
24,780

Lingtren•
21,972

•Kartse
21,350

Pumori•
23,442

•Khumbutse
21,785

•North Col
22,916

Khumbu Glacier

West Cwm Glacier

•Mount Everest
29,028

Kangshung   Glacier

South Col
26,200

Nuptse•
25,726

•Lhotse
27,923

•Pethangtse
22,080

Nuptse Glacier

West Lhotse Glacier

Lhotse Glacier

East Lhotse Glacier

Makalu II
25,130•

•Phalong Karpo

Makalu Col
24,310

•Taweche
21,463

Imja   East   Glacier

Makalu•
27,824

■ Dingboche

Barun   Glacier

•Baruntse
23,688

•Ama Dablam
22,494

•Pangboche

| 0 | 1 | 2 | 3 | 4 | 5 Miles |
| 0 | | 2 | 4 | 6 | 8 Km |

15. The Himalaya: Mount Everest and the neighbouring peaks
of Lhotse, Nuptse, Khartaphu, Makalu, Baruntse, and Ama
Dablam.

16. U.S.S.R.: the Pamirs, with Peak Lenin.

A view from the south of Machapuchare (22,956 feet) and Annapurna II (26,041 feet).

Climbing the ice ridge above Camp IV on Machapuchare.

Manaslu (26,760 feet), which was climbed by the Japanese in 1956.

later (M. Harada and H. Tanabe, H. Miyashita and K. Nakazawa).

The little-explored Kutang Himal and the Ganesh Himal are defined by the Buriganga and Trisuli Gandaki Rivers, both passable by animals and trade routes to Dzongka and the Tsangpo Valley in Tibet. The highest peak in the Ganesh Himal (24,299 feet) was reconnoitred by New Zealand and Japanese parties in 1953 and 1954, and climbed by R. Lambert's Swiss expedition in 1955 (E. Gauchat, Mme C. Kogan, R. Lambert).

Kosi Section

The peaks approached up the Kosi tributaries include the highest in the world. Rainfall is heavy here, torrents can be difficult of passage, and almost all carrying has to be done by porters.

Drained by the Sun and Bhote Kosi tributaries are the Langtrang and Jugal Himal, first explored by Tilman in 1949. In 1955, Mrs M. Jackson's party climbed in the Jugal Himal, the highest peak of which, Lönpo Gang (23,239 feet), was climbed by the Japanese in 1962. The Langtrang Himal contains a number of fine peaks, including Gangchhen Ledrub (23,771 feet), a difficult and dangerous mountain on which two Japanese climbers, K. Morimoto and K. Oshima, and the Sherpa Gyaltsen Norbu, were killed in an avalanche in 1961. In 1963 two members of an Italian expedition lost their lives on the mountain, and the following year an Australian party withdrew in the face of deteriorating weather.

North of the Langtrang and Jugal Himal is the massive peak of Shisha Pangma or Gosainthan (26,291 feet), which, because of its position in Tibet, is inaccessible to western mountaineers. It was climbed by a Chinese party in 1964. South-west of this area lies Gosainkund, the sacred lake in which Siva sleeps.

East of the Bhote Kosi lies the Rolwaling Himal, whose principal summits, Gaurisankar (23,440 feet) and Menlungtse (23,555 feet), are of formidable aspect. Shipton was first to penetrate this area during the 1951 Everest reconnaissance, and in 1955 A. Gregory's party mapped extensively and climbed a number of peaks. Although Gaurisankar has been attempted by Swiss (1954), Japanese (1959), and British (1964) parties, it remains, like its neighbour Menlungtse, unclimbed.

The Dudh Kosi, now a highway for expeditions, drains the Everest group while its western tributary, another Bhote Kosi, descends from the direction of the 19,000-foot Nangpa La, over which goes the high trade route from the Sherpa country of Sola Khumbu to Tibet. The story of climbing in this area centres round Everest (29,028 feet), with which we should first deal.

The first seven expeditions approached the mountain from

The northern approaches to Everest from Base Camp on the Rongbuk Glacier. The early attempts to climb the mountain were made by way of the north-east ridge, the upper part of which is visible to the left of the summit.

(*Above*) The successful 1953 Everest party and (*below*) the
1921 Reconnaissance party.

Everest (29,028 feet), Lhotse (27,923 feet), and Nuptse (25,726 feet) from the west. Behind and to the right is Makalu (27,824 feet), and in the distance the Kangchenjunga massif.

Pumori (23,442 feet) from the Khumbu Icefall. The summit of Gyachung Kang (25,990 feet) can be seen over the north-east ridge.

Tibet. On this side the Everest pyramid is a great sweep of rock slabs. Above the snowy North Col, at times dangerous, these lead easily to the final steep section 1,000 feet below the summit. C. K. Howard-Bury's 1921 reconnaissance was followed by Bruce's expeditions of 1922 and 1924; on the first, G. I. Finch used oxygen; on the second, E. F. Norton, with T. H. Somervell, reached over 28,000 feet. Later G. H. L. Mallory, spearhead of all three parties, disappeared high up with A. C. Irvine. In 1933 three of Ruttledge's party reached a point about 900 feet from the summit, but the expeditions of 1935, 1936, and 1938 were not so successful.

After the war Tibet closed and Nepal opened its doors. Shipton, in 1951, found a route up the difficult Khumbu ice-fall on the south side, and in 1952 the Swiss gained access to the west cwm and climbed over the Geneva Spur to the South Col (26,201 feet). From this point R. Lambert and Tenzing Norkey climbed high on the south-east ridge. Sir John Hunt's party completed the route in 1953 when Sir Edmund Hillary and Tenzing reached the summit.

Since its ascent Everest has been visited by no fewer than six expeditions, including one from Communist China in 1960 which claims to have reached the summit from the north. A. Eggler's Swiss party climbed both Everest and Lhotse (27,923 feet) in 1956. After two unsuccessful expeditions in 1960 and 1962, an Indian party reached the top in 1965. Perhaps the most amazing *tour de force* was that of

N. G. Dyhrenfurth's American expedition, which, in 1963, made the first traverse of the summit; ascending by the difficult west ridge and descending by the south-east ridge (J. W. Whittaker, Nawang Gombu; W. Unsoeld, T. Hornbein; B. Bishop, L. Jerstad).

Completing the Everest trinity is Nuptse (25,726 feet), which lies on the serrated ridge extending west from Lhotse. More a ridge feature than a separate mountain, it was climbed by J. Walmsley's party in 1961.

In the preparations for Everest many minor peaks around have been climbed, particularly on the Tibetan side by Shipton's 1935 party. Cho Oyu (26,750 feet), reconnoitred by the British in 1952, and attempted by Lambert in 1954, was climbed that same year by a small Austrian party, the summit being reached by H. Tichy, J. Jochler, and Pasang Dawa Lama. It has since been climbed by an Indian party, and in 1959 was the scene of an avalanche disaster to an all-women's party.

Meanwhile, in 1954, both New Zealand and American parties reconnoitred Makalu (27,824 feet) from the south. The latter, which explored extensively in the Barun and adjacent valleys, climbed, among other peaks, Baruntse (23,688 feet) (C. Todd, G. Harrow, G. Lowe, W. Beaven). In the autumn of that year the French found the best route up Makalu, on the northern flank, and climbed Kangchungtse (25,120 feet). Next year, again led by J. Franco, they ascended

Cho Oyu (26,750 feet).

Makalu in classically competent manner. Using oxygen, seven members reached the summit in perfect conditions. To complete this remarkable *tour de force* they also made the first ascent of Chomolönzo (25,640 feet).

In 1960/1 Hillary led a scientific expedition to the Barun region. A hut was constructed at a height of 19,000 feet with the help of aircraft, and some members spent the winter here. As early as March, M. P. Ward, W. Romanes, B. Bishop, and M. Gill climbed the dramatic Ama Dablam (22,494 feet), near the top of which M. J. Harris and G. Fraser disappeared in 1959. An attempt was then made to climb Makalu without oxygen for scientific purposes. Bad weather and illness defeated the party and P. Mulgrew, who with T. Nevison and Annullu reached 500 feet below the summit, was badly frostbitten.

Other notable achievements in the Mahalungur Himal, as the range from Cho Oyu to Makalu is called, have been the ascents of Pumori (23,442 feet) in 1962 and Gyachung Kang (25,990 feet) in 1964, both of which lie on the main crest to the west of Everest. Erwin Schneider's survey expeditions have produced excellent large-scale maps of the Khumbu and Rolwaling areas and Hillary's 'Schoolhouse' expeditions have built schools for the Sherpas of Sola Khumbu.

Before leaving eastern Nepal we must say a word of the Sherpas. The 1921 Everest expedition engaged them from the hill station of Darjeeling, since many have emigrated there. Sola Khumbu was not visited by westerners till 1950. Since then it has become familiar to expeditions, while Sherpa customs have been ably described by C. von Fürer-Haimendorf.

Originally the Sherpas come from Tibet, and their customs, which include polyandry, are Tibetan in character. They are Buddhist, and the monastery of Thyangboche has strong kinship with that of Rongbuk on the north side of Everest. Mani walls and the sacred words 'Om mani padme hum' are seen everywhere. In winter the Sherpas are found at levels below that of Namche Bazar (11,000 feet). In spring they move up and in summer graze yaks and sheep above 16,000 feet. Since they started to carry for expeditions, many Sherpas have become fine mountaineers. Outstanding are Ang Tharkay, Lewa, Tenzing, Pasang Dawa Lama, Ang Nyima, Tashi, Dawa Tenzing, Annullu, and several Gyaldgzens. They now take full part in expeditions as members, not just as porters.

Tribute should finally be paid to the Sherpanis, or Sherpa women, often the real heads of the family, to whose fine carrying powers many parties have cause to be grateful.

Sikkim Himalaya

Kangchenjunga (28,208 feet) is so dominant a feature of Sikkim that it must be considered with it, though it was finally climbed from Nepal. The western valleys have much in common with that of the Tista, which drains Sikkim. Having a rainfall even greater than Nepal's, the low gorge of the Tista is a hothouse of sub-tropical plants and insects, steep jungles alive with leeches and, after the rains, scarred by landslides. Yet

Kangchenjunga is not far off, and climbing towards Lachen or Lachung, whichever path he chooses, the traveller finds himself among brambles and wild roses and delicious apples. Further north again, over the 18,000-foot Donkya La or up the Lachen Chu, he is in Tibetan country and among Tibetans. Gentians and edelweiss peep shyly from a waste of boulders.

Sikkim is administered from Gangtok and ruled through a Maharajah. It is predominantly Buddhist and has fine temples. Indian, Tibetan, and Sherpa mingle in the stock, but the aboriginal Lepchas, a shy little race with its own religious practices, are also to be seen. The easiest route to Tibet crosses the Natu or Jelep La (14,390 feet) to the Chumbi Valley. Into Sikkim, of recent years, Tibetan refugees from Chinese Communist rule have fled, crowding Kalimpong and patiently awaiting resettlement.

The problem of quick change of climate and heavy precipitation is faced by all expeditions here. Surveyed in the last century by Captain Harman, H. C. B. Tanner, and others, the mountains particularly attracted Kellas, who climbed east and north of Kangchenjunga, very often with Sherpas only. Among his ascents shortly before the First World War were Langpo Peak (22,800 feet), Kangchenjau (22,700 feet),

Dense rain forest in the Tista Valley. It was by way of the Tista that most of the early expeditions approached Tibet and the north side of Everest. It is important today as a trade route between Sikkim and Tibet.

The Kangchenjunga group from above Darjeeling.

Chomiomo (22,430 feet), which lies to the north-east of
Kangchenjunga at the head of the Lachen Chu. It was
climbed in 1911 by Dr A. M. Kellas.

An easterly satellite of Kangchenjunga, Siniolchu (22,600 feet).

7a. The Everest group and Ama Dablam from the Imja Khola.

7b. The Kangchenjunga massif from the west.

Chomiomo (22,430 feet), and Pauhunri (23,180 feet). He also explored the Zemu basin.

Kangchenjunga has been reconnoitred from all sides. A French party attempted the south-west flank as early as 1905. G. O. Dyhrenfurth led an international expedition to the north-west quadrant in 1930, but judged there to be no safe route after the death of one Sherpa. The most determined attacks were those of Paul Bauer's Bavarian parties, from the Zemu. In 1929 and 1931 these ascended the great North-East Spur, even tunnelling through it at times. In 1931 they reached 25,260 feet; but one climber and a porter were killed. These two expeditions are classics of grim resolution. After 1947, when Sikkim became difficult of entry, J. Kempe returned to the neglected south-west Yalung face and found a possible route. A year later, in 1955, a strong British 'reconnaissance' party under R. C. Evans climbed the mountain, using oxygen. J. Brown and G. C. Band were followed next day by Streather and N. Hardie. Both parties stopped at a point twenty feet below the summit, out of deference to the wishes of the Maharajah.

Kangchenjunga covers an enormous area and is ringed with satellites. Conspicuous from Darjeeling is the square-topped Kabru (24,002 feet). Graham made a vigorous attempt in 1883, and two Norwegians reached almost 24,000 feet in 1907. C. R. Cooke completed the climb in November 1935, the first post-monsoon ascent of a peak over 24,000 feet. Meanwhile Dyhrenfurth's party had consoled itself with more northerly summits: the south-west summit of Nepal Peak (23,442 feet), climbed by E. Schneider, Jongsong Peak (24,340 feet) and Dodang Nyima (22,720 feet), climbed by Schneider and H. Hoerlin, and Ramthang Peak (21,982 feet), which Schneider climbed with Smythe.

Much strenuous exploration of the Zemu area followed, this being the nearest one of all to civilization. Pallis came here in 1936, and in the same year K. Wien and A. Göttner, members of another Bauer party, reached the wonderful fluted ice-pyramid of Siniolchu (22,600 feet)–perhaps the finest ice climb done in the Himalaya before the Second World War. Its neighbour, Simvu (22,360 feet), also yielded. The same year Shipton and E. G. H. Kempson, returning from Everest, climbed Gordamah Peak (22,200 feet). Cooke and Hunt reconnoitred the approaches to Kangchenjunga after the monsoon of 1937, and in 1939 L. Schmaderer, H. Paidar, and E. Grob, after a remarkable campaign, climbed the much-sought-after Tent Peak (24,089 feet), along the ridge from Nepal Peak (23,560 feet), which they also climbed.

During these years tea planters and other inhabitants of Darjeeling did important journeys themselves, and also, through the Himalayan Club, helped expeditions. The club selected and recommended porters, provided equipment, held meetings, and published an important journal. Since Partition access to Sikkim has become very problematical; at the same time many of the club's functions are taken over by the

A camp near the Sebu-La, with peaks of the Sikkim-Tibet border behind.

8a. Morning light on K2.

8b. A Tibetan Buddhist lama with dagger and thunderbolt emblem performs family rites in a Garhwal village.

Himalayan Society and the Sherpas' Society, through which porters are now recruited.

Kangchenjunga's magnificent western outlier Jannu (25,294 feet) was reconnoitred by the French in 1957. A route from the south-east was attempted in 1958, but danger from avalanche became too great and the party withdrew. In 1962 the mountain was climbed by an expedition led by L. Terray. Facing Jannu across the Yalung Glacier is Talung Peak (24,112 feet), which was ascended by a German expedition in 1964.

North Bhutan: looking south-east from the summit of Yak Peak (18,000 feet) towards Rinchita.

Eastern Himalaya

Comparatively little is known of the mountain districts of the Eastern Himalaya. The western peaks are on the undemarcated frontier between Bhutan and Tibet, the eastern stand above the unadministered forest tracts of Assam, which merge into Tibet along the disputed McMahon Line. There has been no very accurate survey.

The western area is drained by the Amo Chu, known as the Chumbi Valley in its upper reaches, and by two other rivers; eastern Bhutan by tributaries of the Manas. Through northern Assam, inhabited by Aka, Dafla, Miri, and Abor tribes, comes the Subansiri, tributary of the Brahmaputra. The little-known state of Bhutan, now crowded with Tibetan refugees, is cut by north–south flowing rivers, each valley having its own administrative centre, the capital of the state being Punakha.

East of Pauhunri, Tibet thrusts a tongue of land southwards down the Chumbi Valley, which has for long provided
the main route to Lhasa. Standing on the border of Tibet and
Bhutan, east of the Lhasa road, is Chomolhari (23,997 feet),
a mountain sacred to the Tibetans which was first climbed by
F. S. Chapman and the Sherpa Pasang.

A few political officers and botanical experts penetrated the
country east of Chomolhari around the turn of the century. In
1906 C. White crossed the difficult Mon La Kar Chung Pass
(17,442 feet) and explored the area round Kulha Kangri
(24,784 feet), one of two groups on the Great Himalayan crest
near the source of the Bumtang Chu. The other, lying to the
south-west, contains a number of peaks in the region of 24,000
feet.

North-west of Punakha, among the mountains drained by

the Mo Chu, lies the Lingshi group with the peaks of Masagang
(23,507 feet) and Kangchita (22,441 feet), while to the north-
east, surrounding the Pho Chu, are the peaks of the Kangla
Ka Chu La and Lunana groups.

For largely political reasons, the Bhutan Himal has been
much neglected, though recent visits have been made by
scientific parties. A. Gansser made geological explorations in
1963 and M. P. Ward and F. S. Jackson have visited areas
north-east and north-west of Punakha. Although they were
primarily concerned with medical research, they added much
to the knowledge of this remote area.

East of Kulha Kangri, the elevation of the Himalayan crest
is considerably lower, and although the naturalists F. Ludlow,
G. Sherriff, and Kingdon Ward made journeys to eastern
Bhutan in the 1930s, the country is very little known. Equally

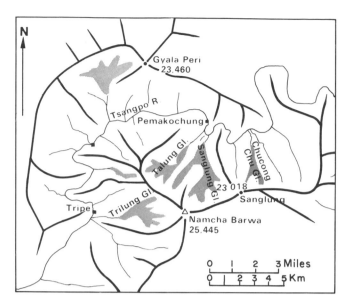

unknown are the 150 miles between Bhutan and the great peak of Namcha Barwa, just on the Tibet side of the Tibet–Assam border. Namcha Barwa (25,445 feet), which marks the extreme east end of the Great Himalaya, was first discovered by survey officers in 1912. The area was visited again in 1913 by F. M. Bailey and H. T. Morshead, who mapped the course of the Tsangpo, which cleaves an immense gorge between Namcha Barwa and its sister peak Gyala Peri (23,460 feet). Gyala Peri, however, is outside the Himalayan compass.

Wilfrid Noyce

The Himalaya: Namcha Barwa and Gyala Peri.

Eastern Himalaya: Namcha Barwa (25,445 feet), the eastern cornerstone of the Himalaya, from Tri pe on the Tsangpo River.

(*Above*) Eastern Himalaya: the south-eastern aspect of Gyala Peri (23,460 feet).

(*Below*) North Bhutan: unclimbed peaks on the Bhutan–Tibet border.

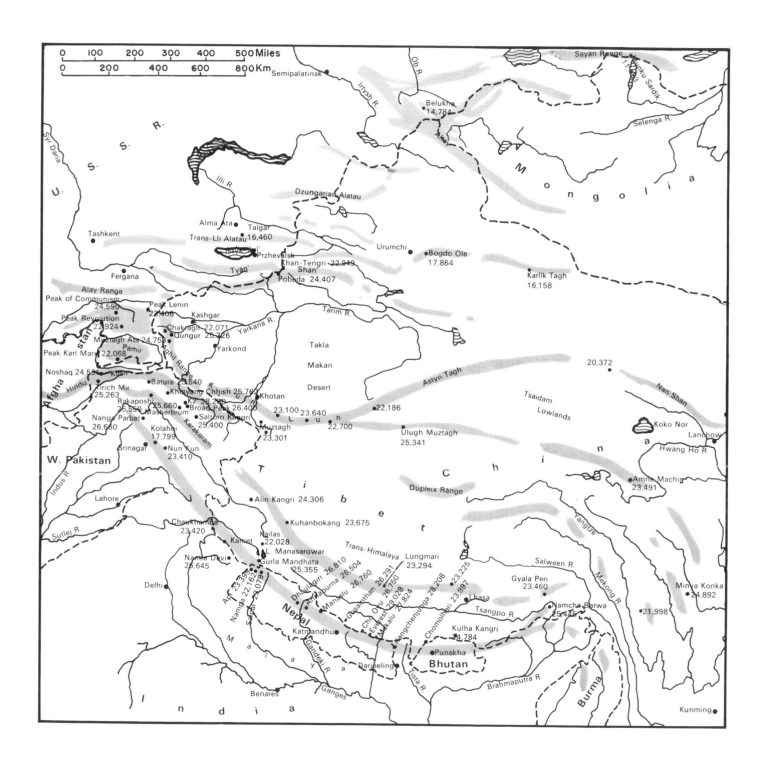

The ranges of Central Asia.

The U.S.S.R.

The Pamirs

Introduction

In the south-east corner of the Tadzhik S.S.R., occupying an area roughly 150 miles square, is the great complex of the Pamir, the Bam-i-dunya or 'Roof of the World' of Persian writers. From this central knot sprawl the great chains of Asia – the Hindu Kush, Tyan' Shan', Kun Lun, Karakoram, and Himalaya. The name 'Pamir' derives from the broad valleys of the southern and eastern areas, but has since come to include all the mountains between the Alay Range and the Ab-i-Panja or Oxus River.

This unique mountain cluster is made up, for the most part, of roughly east–west trending ranges between which are lakes such as Karakul', Yashil'kul, and Sarezskoye which punctuate briefly the overwhelming bleakness of the terrain. The Pamirs are, in effect, a high altitude desert, for although heavy snowfalls at a high level nourish some of the largest glaciers in the world outside the Polar regions (the Fedchenko Glacier, for example, is forty-five miles in length and, with its tributary streams, embraces an area of over 600 square miles) below the snow-line precipitation is slight, summer temperatures are high, winds tend to be violent, and the soil is generally very poor. Insignificant and scanty growth of grass and shrubs bears witness to this aridity of climate in which the scattered Kirgiz rear their flocks of yak, cattle, and sheep. In the western and northern valleys the more sedentary Tadzhiks have provided artificial irrigation for their crops of wheat, millet, and melons and extensive fruit orchards.

Animal life abounds in the Pamirs and includes bear, wolf, snow leopard, and the fine mountain sheep, *Ovis poli*.

Historical

Paradoxically, the Pamirs were far from being a barrier between East and West. Standing, as it were, at the heart of Central Asia, they formed a pivot between the ancient empires of China in the east and Persia and Rome in the west, and from the first century B.C. they carried the arteries which allowed the cultures of east and west to flow freely and to mingle. They became a link in the great 'Silk Road', and there was a continuous through-traffic of embassies, travelling monks, and merchant caravans until the sea route to India and further east was opened up by Vasco da Gama and, from the opposite direction, by Magellan.

These thoroughfares across the Pamirs naturally followed the principal east–west valleys: those of the Alay or Kysylsu in the north and the Wakhan or Panja in the south. The latter was traversed by the Buddhist monk Hsüan Tsang in about A.D. 642, and, much later in the thirteenth century, by Marco Polo, who travelled up the Panja (Pyandzh) and Pamir Rivers and thence to Yarkand.

Because of their great strategic value the Pamirs were, not surprisingly, the scene of much conflict. Persian and Chinese empires both made attempts to gain control of the vital trade routes which were later to carry the tide of Islam into Kashgaria and even into parts of Tibet. Russian expansion southwards during the latter half of the nineteenth century brought her up against the British, who were reaching out from north-west India, and much exploration, mostly with a military eye, was done by officers on both sides. By an agreement in 1896 the bone of contention, the Wakhan, was given to Afghanistan, thus providing a buffer between the major powers. A great deal of knowledge of the area was added by Sir Aurel Stein and the British consuls-general at Kashgar, and by Sven Hedin, who, in 1894, attempted to climb Muztagh Ata in the Kashgar Range. But by and large the detailed exploration of the Pamirs fell to the Russians.

In the years following the annexation of Tadzhikistan, two geographers were particularly active: A. P. Fedchenko and N. L. Korzhenevsky. Fedchenko's work in the Trans-Alay Range in 1871 enabled him to fix its highest peak, which was later named Peak Lenin, and his reconnaissance mapping with N. A. Severtsov in 1877–8 made it possible for Putyata and Benderskiy to begin a topographical survey in 1883.

Thirty years separated V. F. Oshanin's discovery, in 1878, of the immense glacier at the head of the Muksu – which he named after Fedchenko – and Korzhenevsky's explorations of the great peaks which feed it. In 1910 he discovered a fine peak of over 23,000 feet which he named after his wife and fellow worker, and in 1926 he found another high peak at the junction of the Peter the Great Range and the Academy of Sciences Range, which, at 24,590 feet, proved the highest in the Pamirs.

In the wake of the scientists came the mountaineers, and by 1933, when the Tadzhik Pamir Expedition was opening up vast tracts of hitherto unknown country, climbers had already been active for several years.

Mountaineering in the Pamirs

Peak Lenin (23,406 feet), the first 23,000-foot peak to be discovered in the Soviet Union, was also the first to succumb. The mountain stands in the Trans-Alay Range, where it is intersected by a short north–south spur, the Zulumart Range, and although generally an unimpressive peak, it throws a magnificent north face towards the broad Alay Valley. The southern slopes descend with rather less severity to the Saukdara Valley, which drains westerly to join the Muksu close to Altynmazar. It was from Altynmazar that the 1928 joint Soviet-German expedition, led by W. Rickmer Rickmers, approached Peak Lenin. Following the Greater Saukdara Glacier they gained a saddle at 19,095 feet on the east ridge, from which a long undulating crest took the summit party, K. Wien, E. Allwein, and E. Schneider, to the top. The following year, a second attempt, led by N. V. Krylenko, was abandoned only 1,000 feet from the summit owing to illness in the party.

The first Soviet ascent was made in 1934 and approached the mountain from the north. After establishing a base camp at 13,780 feet, the Lenin Glacier was followed to a snow dome and a terrace at 20,000 feet beneath the upper sections of the north face. By climbing a rock ridge, V. Abalakov, N. Chernukha, and I. Lukin reached the east ridge, which they followed to the summit. Subsequent attempts at a more direct route from the terrace were unsuccessful owing to the great danger from avalanches. The third ascent, in 1937, was significant in that, for the first time in the Pamirs, aircraft were used to drop supplies to the party on the mountain.

After the Second World War attempts on the mountain became more frequent and parties became larger. In 1952 a traverse was made under the leadership of V. A. Kovalev, and two years later the difficult north face was climbed for the first time. K. Kuzmin's ascent of the south ridge in 1955 included a traverse of Peak October (22,244 feet), and in 1958 a woman, E. Mamleyeva, reached the summit for the first time.

It was the north face, however, which attracted climbers

eager for difficult routes, and in 1960 two new ascents were made from this side. The V. P. Cheredova party climbed the east ridge from the Krylenko Pass, and a party led by Y. G. Arkin tackled the steep north face. At the same time two groups, a Georgian party under L. Akhvlediany and a Moscow party led by V. M. Abalakov, made traverses from east and west to meet on the summit. Peak Dzerzhinsky (22,025 feet), to the west of Peak Lenin, was also included in the traverse.

Accessibility and a benign disposition have made Lenin the most popular peak in the Pamirs, and, judging from the number of ascents it has had, the most frequently climbed high peak in the world.

South-west of the Trans-Alay Range is a complicated knot of ranges bordered on the north by the Muksu and on the east by the immense Fedchenko Glacier. Here the north–south Academy of Sciences Range unites the Peter the Great, Darvaz, Vanch, and Yazgulem Ranges in the highest, and certainly the most interesting, section of the Pamirs. The group is drained by a number of turbulent streams which have cleaved deep gorges in the western flanks, but these approaches were unknown in 1933 when a group from the Tadzhik Pamir Expedition first reconnoitred the supreme monarch, the Peak of Communism (24,590 feet). The group, which included V. M. Abalakov, D. Gushchin, N. A. Nikolayev, U. M. Shiyanov, and Dr V. I. Maslov, started out from Altynmazar and followed the Fedchenko, Bivachnyy, and Ordzhonikidze Glaciers, which brought them on the eastern flanks. Once on the mountain, the route, initially a gentle rib, soon became more severe. Six great rock *gendarmes* had to be traversed in order to reach a more gentle snow ridge, where a high camp was placed at a height of 22,638 feet. On 3 September, after five days of bad weather, Abalakov and N. Gorbunov set out for the summit. Gorbunov, however, succumbed to the effects of altitude only

Peak Lenin (23,406 feet) from a camp in the Achiktash, Pamirs.

a few hundred feet from the top, which Abalakov went on to reach alone.

The second ascent, in 1937, by Y. Beletsky, N. Gusak, V. Kirkorov, and O. Aristov, using the same route, was marred by the death of Aristov, one of the outstanding Russian climbers of that period, who fell from an ice slope only thirty feet below the summit.

So far the focus of attention had been on the northern and eastern flanks, but in 1955 a Georgian party under O. Gigineishvily and A. Ivanishvily put through a route from the south-west. From the upper reaches of the Garmo Glacier, which drains a vast basin on this side of the massif, the route followed the Belyayev Glacier to a high saddle to the south of Peak Pravda (21,018 feet). After turning Peak Pravda to the east, a camp was established at about 23,000 feet, from which four of the party, I. Kakhiany, D. Medzmariashvily, M. Khergiany, and L. Akhvlediany, were able to reach the summit. Two years later a party of ten, led by K. Kuzmin, made another ascent from the Garmo Basin. This time, however, the route took the west ridge and included a traverse of Peak Leningrad (21,349 feet). In the same year a strong Georgian party demonstrated the feasibility of making prolonged high-altitude traverses when they made a circuit of six peaks above 19,600 feet, including Peak Garmo (21,637 feet). Two further routes were made on the Peak of Communism in 1959 and 1961. The first, led by Kuzmin, took a difficult line from the Upper Belyayev Glacier and skirted the south face to gain the west ridge. The other, led by I. Tamm, tackled the east face from the Bivachnyy Glacier.

In 1962 a joint British-Soviet expedition, led by Sir John (now Lord) Hunt, visited the Garmo Glacier area, and climbed a number of peaks, including the Peak of Communism, Peak Patriot (c. 21,000 feet), and Peak Garmo. The success of this

A view from the north of the Peak of Communism (24,590 feet), the highest peak in the Pamirs.

The Pamirs: Peak of Communism and the Garmo Glacier.

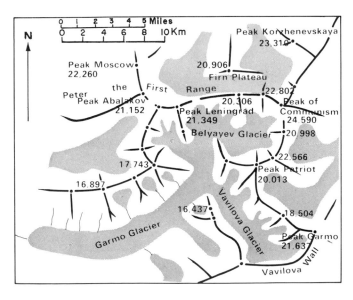

Krutoi Rog (Steep Horn), a fine peak in the upper cirque of Glacier No. 5, a tributary of the Fedchenko Glacier.

international venture was marred by the deaths of Wilfrid Noyce and Robin Smith, who, together with A. G. Ovchinnikov and A. Sevast'yanov, had reached the summit of Peak Garmo. While descending, however, one of the two slipped, pulling the other off his feet. They were unable to brake and fell 4,000 feet to the glacier below.

Peak Korzhenevskaya (23,310 feet), the third highest peak in the Pamirs, was first attempted in 1937 by D. Gushchin's party, which only reached the lower summit (22,671 feet). The higher summit was reached in 1953 by A. Ugarov's party, which approached the mountain from the Muksu Valley, along the Fortambek Glacier and through a gorge which led them on to the Korzhenevsky Glacier. From a col on the north ridge, the party forced their way past three rock *gendarmes* to the summit of the lower peak. After descending to the gap between the two peaks, a further 1,000 feet brought them on to the highest summit.

Peak Korzhenevskaya commands magnificent views. To the north-east lies the Trans-Alay Range and Peak Lenin, and, to the south, the Peak of Communism with its great snow plateau. To the west, stretching almost to Samarkand, can be seen the distant Gissar and Zeravshan Ranges. Peak Korzhenevskaya has had very few ascents and remains the least explored of the major peaks in the Soviet Union.

In the Yazgulem Range, surrounding the upper reaches of the Fedchenko Glacier, is another important knot of peaks, including Peak Revolution (22,924 feet) and Peak Fikker (22,041 feet). Although Schneider attempted Peak Revolution in 1928, the mountain remained inviolate until 1954 when A. Ugarov's party forced a way up the north-east ridge. In 1961 a Leningrad expedition under S. Savon traversed the peak, and the following year L. Myshlyayev climbed the north buttress. This last ascent marked the beginning of a new era in mountaineering in the Pamirs, an era characterized by extensive traverses and difficult face climbs.

South of the Yazgulem Range, the Rushan Range stretches eastwards, where it becomes the North Alichur Range before being lost amid the broad plateaux of the Eastern Pamirs. Straddling the Rushan Range is Peak Patkhor (19,856 feet), which can be approached from the south, where a motor road runs eastwards from Khorog. The first ascent was made in August 1946 by Abalakov, A. Sidorenko, and Y. Ivanov, who followed the Markovsky and Patkhor Glaciers to the west ridge. Three weeks later the same party made the first ascent of Peak Karl Marx (22,068 feet) in the Shakhdara Range. This range is the southernmost in the Pamirs and is separated only by the Panja Valley from the Hindu Kush.

In 1954 a Georgian party climbed Peak Karl Marx by a more difficult route, and subsequently a party under M. Gvarliani climbed Peak Engels (21,359 feet). The route followed a snow couloir in the south-west face giving on to steep rock which led to the summit dome. A traverse taking in both Marx and Engels peaks was made in 1964 by P. Budanov's Leningrad party, which also made the first ascent of the north face.

Looking south towards the upper reaches of the Fedchenko Glacier and Peak Revolution (22,924 feet), in the Pamirs.

The Tyan' Shan'
Introduction

The Tyan' Shan', or 'Celestial Mountains', consist of many roughly parallel east–west ranges which extend for over 1,000 miles, from the outskirts of Tashkent, where there are peaks over 14,500 feet in the Chatkal Range, to the town of Urumchi in the Sinkiang Province of China, beyond which they rise again in the Bogdo Ola Range. The northernmost of these ranges, the Trans-Ily Alatau, overlooks the town of Alma-Ata and reaches its highest point in Peak Talgar (16,460 feet), which, owing to its accessibility, is much visited by mountaineers. The mountains are continued westwards in the Kirgiz Range, which contains a number of summits over 15,000 feet. To the south lies the broad, slightly salt, Issyk-kul', and the town of Przheval'sk from which routes reach southeast through the Terskey-Alatau into the loftiest peaks of the Tyan' Shan', which are grouped close to the Chinese frontier.

The Tyan' Shan' are, on the whole, less arid than the Pamirs. Although desert vegetation is found in the foothills, the upper levels support forests of spruce, fir, and juniper, and above them are alpine pastures often strewn with gentians and saxifrage.

For most of their length the great arc of the Tyan' Shan'

A view from the north of the Sarydzhaz Mountains which lie to the north of, and parallel to, the ranges of the Central Tyan' Shan'.

forms the northern rim of the Tarim Basin, along the northern edge of which ran the Tyan' Shan' Nan Lu, one of the principal caravan routes. Their hazy outlines, reaching out from the sands of the Takla-Makan, must therefore have been familiar to many a traveller as his caravan, laden with silks from the eastern emporiums, trod the slow curve towards Kashgar and the west. Against the continuous backcloth of the Tyan' Shan' he would have measured his daily progress.

These southern fringes of the range were described in some detail by the Buddhist monk Hsüan Tsang, who travelled there in the seventh century B.C. In the early eighteenth century, Jesuit missionaries from Peking penetrated certain parts and supplied much of the information for d'Anville's *Atlas of China*, which was published in 1735.

The first to visit the northern fringes of the range was the Russian geographer P. P. Semënov (subsequently Semënov Tyan-Shansky), who in 1857 sighted Khan-Tengri, the 'Lord of the Sky'. It was while seeking routes to Khan-Tengri in 1902 that Dr G. Merzbacher realized the full complexity of this central part of the range. He found his way to Khan-Tengri from the north barred by the Sarydzhaz Range and the deep trough of the Northern Inylchek Glacier. Not easily put off, Merzbacher made attempts on two major peaks, Marmornaya Stena, the 'Marble Wall', and Peak Semënov before skirting west the following year to reach the snout of the Inylchek Glacier, which led him into the heart of the Tyan' Shan'. Here, as Merzbacher's explorations revealed, a short north–south spur, the Meridional Range, unites three east–west ranges, the

The upper reaches of the Inylchek Glacier and the peaks of the Meridional Range.

Sarydzhaz, Tengri Tag, and Kokshaal-Tau Ranges, in the form of a reversed letter 'E', between whose limbs flow the two branches of the Inylchek Glacier.

Mountaineering in the Tyan' Shan'

Khan-Tengri (22,949 feet), centrally situated on Tengri Tag, was for a long time thought to be the highest peak in the range, and it was to climb it that the first purely mountaineering expedition visited the Tyan' Shan' in 1931. The expedition, led by M. T. Pogrebetsky, followed the Northern Inylchek Glacier to a point beneath the north face. From here a steep rib took them on to easier ground from which the summit was reached without too much difficulty. Two subsequent ascents were made in 1936, in quick succession, and following the same route as used on the first ascent. A party from Alma-Ata reached the summit on 24 August and they were followed, on 5 September, by a party consisting of V. Abalakov, L. Gutman,

M. Dadiomov, and L. Saladin. As if in a fit of malignant rage at having yielded too readily in 1931, the 'Lord of the Sky' stooped to visit retribution on this second party. They were overtaken by bad weather on the descent and were all badly frost-bitten. One of the Russians fell several hundred feet and Saladin died of blood poisoning. It was a costly victory.

Since then a number of new routes have been put through on the peak. In 1964 the B. Romanov party climbed the south-west buttress from the Southern Inylchek Glacier and a party led by K. Kuzmin tackled a new approach from the north. Also on Tengri Tag, to the west of Khan-Tengri, is Peak Chapayev (20,899 feet), which was first climbed from the north-east by a party led by I. Tyuntyunpikov in 1937.

By climbing the 'Marble Wall' (21,051 feet), Merzbacher had hoped to clarify the structure of the ranges further south, and this he undoubtedly would have done had the peak, which stands at the junction of the Sarydzhaz and Meridional Ranges, been more easily accessible. Forty-four years, however, were to pass before the peak was climbed and, in order to reach the summit, the party led by A. Letavet, had to make

Peak Pobeda (24,407 feet), the highest summit in the Tyan' Shan', and Peak 22,704 feet from the Diky Glacier.

a long traverse over Peak Uzlovaya (16,634 feet) and Peak Pogranichnik (17,225 feet). As Merzbacher had hoped, the summit afforded fine views of the Kokshaal-Tau Range and a series of panoramic photographs were taken which were to prove important in the further study of the Tyan' Shan' and particularly in the identification of Peak Pobeda, the highest in the range.

The Kokshaal-Tau Range, the southernmost in this central knot, contains a magnificent line of peaks, a number of which exceed 22,000 feet. The possibility that one of these peaks might be higher than Khan-Tengri was suggested as early as 1932 when a group of Kharkov mountaineers, climbing near the Vysoky Pass, looked across at the great peak which stands at the head of the Zvëzdochka Glacier. Two years later a geodetic survey party from Tashkent established that one of the peaks on the long crest rose to 24,407 feet, but they were uncertain which. The uncertainty continued for a

number of years, during which time Professor Letavet reconnoitred the approaches from the upper Inylchek Glacier. During this expedition three members of his party, L. Gutman, A. Sidorenko, and Y. Ivanov, climbed a high peak on the main ridge, which they named Peak Komsomol.

Letavet's photographs from the 'Marble Wall' in 1946 settled the disagreement, and between 1952 and 1955 a number of parties made reconnaissance explorations and abortive attempts from the east along the crest of the Kokshaal-Tau Range, and from the north where Peak Pobeda throws an immense face into the head of the Zvëzdochka Glacier.

It was from the Zvëzdochka Glacier that the first ascent was made in 1956. From the glacier the route led through an icefall to the western slopes of the Aktau Ridge and thence gained the great north-east spur. Camps were set up in ice caves between 17,400 and 23,000 feet which enabled the party to sit out the frequent spells of bad weather. The route was long and difficult, traversing rock towers and threading through numerous icefalls. Finally, on 30 August, V. Abalakov, N. Gusak, V. Kizel, and ten others emerged from the steep

(*Above*) Russian mountaineers in a camp beneath the north
face of Peak Pobeda, Tyan' Shan'.

(*Above*) A Russian camp at 18,000 feet on the upper Zvëzdochka Glacier, Tyan' Shan'.

(*Below*) Aktau (20,279 feet) and Khan-Tengri (22,949 feet) from the slopes of Peak Pobeda, Tyan' Shan'.

A massive avalanche on the north face of Peak Pobeda (24,407 feet).

final ice field on to the summit of Peak Pobeda. Two years later, I. Yerokhin's party made the second ascent by a route which approached from the east.

A number of accidents in recent years have confirmed that this remote and difficult peak calls for the most careful preparation. An unsuccessful attempt in 1960 cost a number of lives, and the following year disaster struck a Georgian party, three of whose members died from exhaustion on the descent.

The Altay Mountains

The Altay is a complex mountain group running roughly north-west to south-east, astride the Sino-Soviet frontier some 600 miles north-east of the Tyan' Shan'. Within the U.S.S.R. are the Northern and Southern Chu Ranges, with peaks up to 13,691 feet, and, to the west, the twin-peaked Belukha massif, whose eastern peak reaches 14,784 feet. Belukha contains a number of small glaciers which were visited by F. Gebler in 1835. The first ascent of the eastern summit was made in 1914 by the well-known explorers of the Altay, the brothers B. V. and M. V. Tronov, along a route which has remained popular to the present day. Approaching from the south, along the Katun' Glacier, the route ascends a ridge between the middle and eastern branches of the glacier to gain a col, and thereafter follows steep snow and ice slopes to

the summit. In 1933 a party under the leadership of V. M. Abalakov and including V. P. Cheredova and Y. A. Kazakova chose a more difficult route from the north, from the Akkemsky Glacier to the narrow north-east ridge and across Mont Delone to the eastern summit. In 1937 Y. A. Alekseyev climbed the western peak (14,567 feet) from the Chërnyy Glacier.

Other Ranges

There are a number of other ranges in the U.S.S.R. worth mentioning. The Sayan Range, with the peak of Munku-Sardik (11,453 feet), presents no serious problems to the mountaineer and is remotely situated to the west of Lake Baykal. In the extreme north-east of Siberia is the Chersky Range, which boasts a few large glaciers that have only recently been discovered, and the peak Pobeda (10,325 feet). This is a region almost totally unexplored by mountaineers, and although it lies close to the Siberian 'Pole of Cold', it experiences relatively warm summer weather.

The Arctic Urals, with their fairly easy peaks of about 6,000 feet, such as Narodnaya (6,214 feet), are similarly of only limited interest to the mountaineer.

Alexander Khrguian

Tibet and China

The mountains of Tibet and China belong to many different chains and are spread over vast areas of Asia. They are, to the Western climber, among the least accessible in the world, not so much owing to their physical remoteness as to political restrictions. During the present century Central Asia and western China have been reasonably accessible for only a very few years. Russian climbers have been active since the late 1920s and recently Chinese expeditions have started exploring the remoter parts of their vast domain, but only a handful of Western explorers have managed to make use of brief clearances in the turbulent political skies. Among these were Sven Hedin and Sir Aurel Stein before the First World War, and, between the wars, Eric Shipton, H. W. Tilman, Kingdon Ward, and R. Burdsall and his companions, to mention but a few of the best known.

A certain order can be brought about in this sea of hills and valleys if we consider the Central Asian mountains as belonging to a series of chains fanning out from the great knot of the Pamirs and including in their branches vast, elevated drainless basins such as the Takla-Makan, Tarim, and Tsaidam. The Takla-Makan is closed in to the north and west by the Tyan' Shan' and their continuation, the Bogdo Ola range and the Pamirs, and to the south by the Kun Lun and the Astyn Tagh. Beyond the Tarim Basin rise the Nan Shan mountains and the imposing Amne Machin group. The vast Tibetan plateau is hemmed in by the Kun Lun mountains to the north and is criss-crossed by a number of chains of which very little is known. One authority, P. Gourou, in his book L'Asie, claims that there are thirty-six different mountain ranges in Tibet alone. There is, however, little unity in this ocean of 'peaks, passes and glaciers', and certainly nothing to compare with the serrated succession of peaks in the Alps, Andes, or Himalaya. In this vast area, of which something like 270,000 square miles are higher than Mont Blanc, entire chains are mapped vaguely, if at all, and many high mountains are barely known to 'exist'. Of these untrodden ranges Eric Shipton has said: 'there are those who imagine that the number of unexplored and unclimbed mountains is fast running out. . . . But I defy even the most pessimistic mountaineer to travel far in the highlands of Central Asia and still hold that view.' Such an idea is heartening despite the fact that today frontier-posts are proving tougher obstacles than the mountains.

Perhaps the best known, or ought one to say the least unknown, of the Central Asian mountains are the lofty massifs which rise to the south-west of Kashgar, in what Shipton has called the 'Kashgar Range': Muztagh Ata (24,758 feet),

Qungur I (24,918 feet), Qungur II (25,326 feet), and Chakragil (22,071 feet). Most of the important ancient trade routes crossing Asia pass near these mountains, such as the Oxus–Sarikol Kashgar route followed by the monk Hsüan Tsang in 644 B.C. and the Polos in A.D. 1273.

Sven Hedin, though hardly equipped for high altitude mountaineering, and composedly riding a yak, made four attempts on Muztagh Ata and twice reached an altitude of about 20,600 feet. Bearing in mind the early date, 1894, this was no small achievement. He was followed by Sir Aurel Stein, who attempted the mountain in 1900. Eric Shipton and H. W. Tilman, with the Sherpa Gyalzen, came close to success in 1947, and the mountain was finally climbed in 1956 by a large party of Russians and Chinese led by E. A. Beleckij. It was climbed again three years later by a party of thirty-three Chinese, eight of whom were women. Qungur I was also climbed in 1956 by a mixed Russian-Chinese party led by K. Kuzmin.

Further north, the Tyan' Shan' divide Russian territory from China before turning eastwards and entering fully into Sinkiang. The Russian part of this chain has already been considered (see pages 123–8).

North of the Takla-Makan and east of the city of Urumchi, the Tyan' Shan' rise again to form the Bogdo Ola group, a compact massif of moderate height by Asian standards, but otherwise quite formidable. The height of Bogdo Ola has been variously estimated. Grober puts it at 21,366 feet, and Hedin at 18,045. This latter height was considered by Shipton to be more acceptable. Shipton and Tilman visited the group in 1948, and although they failed on Bogdo Ola they did climb an important secondary peak of about 17,000 feet. Further east, the chain disappears into the sands of the Gobi Desert.

South of the Takla-Makan the Tibetan plateau rises abruptly from parched sandy plains to form a formidable wall which can be considered a sort of counter-Himalaya hemming in the Tibetan land mass on the northern side. The chain is known partly as the Kun Lun and partly as the Astyn Tagh. There appear to be a number of peaks in excess of 23,000 feet, but heights are very uncertain. Ulugh Muztagh, known also as Ustun Tagh, may be anything between 23,490 and 25,340 feet. Another Muztagh, known also as K5, may be 23,890 or merely 22,100 feet. Few of the peaks have names and the only climbs recorded appear to be those of W. H. Johnson, who in 1865 – a remarkably early date – reached peaks designated as E57 (21,768 feet) and E58 (21,972 feet). He also claimed a peak E61 (23,892 feet), but this has been much disputed and it is

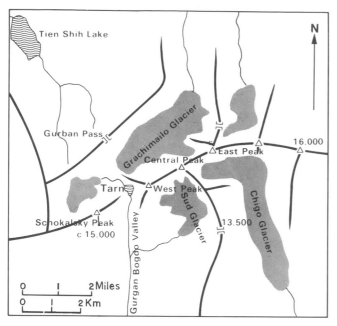

Eastern Tyan' Shan': the Bogdo Ola group.

supposed that he really climbed Zogputaran (22,638 feet).

Much that has been said about the Kun Lun and the Astyn Tagh could be repeated about the mountains of Tibet. Little is known, for instance, about the truly mysterious Dupleix Mountains shown on most maps about 300 miles north of Lhasa, and which are said to reach the very considerable height of 24,600 feet. Other important mountains are scattered over the Tibetan plateau; the Aghil range in the west, the Trans-Himalaya in the south. Kailas (22,028 feet), explored by H. Ruttledge and T. S. Blakeney, is by far the most famous. One of the great sacred mountains of the world, it is visited by both Hindu and Buddhist pilgrims, who consider it to be the throne of Shiva and the centre of the world. From its snows, so the faithful say, flow the great rivers of India and Tibet. Near by, not far from Lake Manasarowar, rise two high mountains, Kuhanbokang (23,675 feet) and an unnamed peak (23,163 feet). Further east, Lungma-ri (23,294 feet) should be mentioned, and two peaks of *c.* 23,000 feet near Lhasa.

Eastern Tibet boasts two of the most alluring and inacces-

The summit of Qungur II (25,326 feet) (*centre*), with the lower peak of Qungur I (24,918 feet) to the left.

sible mountains in Asia: Namcha Barwa (25,445 feet) and Gyala Peri (23,460 feet). These mountains, which were first explored in 1913 by F. M. Bailey and H. T. Morshead, stand like pillars on either side of the Tsang-po River where it turns southwards to break its way along deep gorges to the Indian plain. The parallel with Nanga Parbat at the other end of the Himalaya round which the Indus bends is most striking.

On the Tibetan side of the Himalaya there are a number of important mountains such as Gurla Mandhata (25,355 feet) and Shisha Pangma or Gosainthan (26,291 feet). These peaks, though belonging politically to Tibet, are structurally part of the Himalaya chain and are considered separately in the Himalaya section (see pages 101–6).

According to some authorities, the mountains of China's

Muztagh Ata Range: Qungur and Chakragil.

On the east ridge of Bogdo Ola, Eastern Tyan' Shan'. Both the east ridge (in the foreground) and the north-east arête (on the right) were attempted unsuccessfully by Shipman and Tilman in 1949.

Kailas (22,028 feet), a mountain sacred to both Hindus and Buddhists, who believe it to be the throne of Shiva and the centre of the world. True devotees will circumambulate the mountain by repeatedly measuring their length lying flat on the ground.

(*Below*) The city of Gyantse. Thick walls of mud separate the holy city from the houses of the lay population.

Chomolhari (23,997 feet) dominates the Tibetan plain near the village of Tuna on the main caravan route between India and Tibet.

The south-west aspect of Minya Konka (24,892 feet), Szechwan Province.

western provinces are an extension of the great ranges of Central Asia. To others, they are much older and have an entirely different origin. Practically, however, they form a continuous, if not always contiguous, mass with the mountains of Central Asia, the main topographical difference being that the ridges tend to run from north to south rather than from east to west.

The Nan Shan range culminates in a peak of 20,372 feet. Further south rises the important Amne Machin group, about which many wild speculations have been made. At one time it was thought to be the mysterious giant, higher than Everest, which was repeatedly seen by pilots flying over the 'hump' between India and China during the Second World War. Later it was reduced to a mere 16,400 feet. A recent Chinese expedition led by Pai Chin-hsiao ascertained a height of 23,491 feet for the highest peak, but there seem to be over a dozen minor peaks between 20,000 and 23,000 feet.

Typical scenery on the Tibetan plateau.

The best-known and highest of the Chinese mountains is Minya Konka, or Minya Kangkar (24,892 feet), whose summit was reached in 1932 by T. Moore and R. L. Burdsall. The ascent of this peak was one of the major achievements of the time. Kamet had been climbed barely a year before, and although the technical difficulties may have been inferior to the ones encountered on a Himalayan peak of comparable height, much exploration had to be undertaken by the small American party before a feasible route was found. Minya Konka was climbed again in 1957 by a Chinese expedition led by Shih Chan-chun. On this expedition four of the members were lost.

Little is known of Chinese mountaineering activities in recent years, although they must have explored many of the mountains in their vast territory. It is known that a peak of 17,109 feet in the Kilian Range was climbed in 1958. Peak Lenin in the Pamirs was climbed by a Chinese party and a very determined group of eight women are said to have made a winter ascent of a peak of 20,266 feet in the Tangla Range in Tibet.

Fosco Maraini

Japan

Introduction

The Japanese islands form part of the system of island arcs that sweeps in broad curves down the western side of the Pacific Ocean. Bordered in part on the Pacific side by the great ocean trench descending to depths of 35,000 feet, and to the west by the Japanese sea which exceeds 10,000 feet in depth, the Japanese mountains, some sixteen of which exceed 10,000 feet in height, are the visible part of a great mountain system whose greater part lies below sea level. The mountains are part of the Alpine fold system and are still being actively built up. This is witnessed by the frequent earthquakes (often over 1,500 a year), which are occasionally of catastrophic proportions, by many hot springs, and by the sixty volcanoes known to have been active in historic times. Altogether Japan has more than 500 volcanoes, including its highest mountain, Fuji-san. Not all the mountains are volcanic, however, and the main climbing areas are in the strongly faulted and folded regions composed chiefly of granite and older sedimentary rocks, especially in central Honshu, where three arcuate belts of mountains meet in the region known as the Japanese Alps.

The mountainous character of three quarters of Japan, coupled with high precipitation over most of the country, has resulted in intense erosion of the uplands, which are characterized by deeply slashed gorges cut by rapidly flowing rivers. On emerging from the mountains, these rivers have deposited much material as numerous small plains, on which the bulk of Japan's dense population is concentrated.

In general

Mountaineering in Japan made a late start and owes much to the Rev. W. Weston (who first applied the word 'Alps') at the end of the last century. The sport caught on, hunters becoming the first guides, until now large and numerous parties climb both for pleasure and on pilgrimage to the shrines which adorn some of the peaks.

The first Japanese Alpine Club handbook appeared in 1930, at a time when W. H. Murray Walton was continuing Weston's impetus. Numerous huts were built, guide books (in Japanese) were written, and Japanese climbers became increasingly active in the Himalaya and elsewhere. Members of the Imperial Family, notably Prince Chichibu, have become expert mountaineers.

The Japanese Alps: the Hodaka group from the east. From left to right they are Mae-Hodaka (10,138 feet), Oku-Hodaka (10,466 feet), and Kita-Hodaka (10,181 feet).

The Japanese Alps: the fine pyramid of Yariga dake (10,433 feet) from the east. On the left is the high ridge which extends for three miles to the Hodaka group and which provides an interesting traverse.

The Japanese Alps: winter conditions on Tsurugi dake (9,853 feet). This photograph from the north shows the fine ridges which give routes of a high standard.

Northern Alps

This is the range best known to mountaineers. It runs for over sixty miles southwards from the Sea of Japan, about 120 miles west from Tokyo, and includes still active volcanoes. The flora is varied and interesting, with fine cypresses, giant birches, beeches and oaks, and many varieties of Alpine flowers.

The ridge is easily accessible from the east, where Matsumoto and Omachi are the principal centres. Within the range hot springs like Nakabusa and Kamikochi form tempting starting-points, and there are a number of Japanese Alpine Club huts.

In the northern group stands Tsurugi dake (9,853 feet), one of the most 'Alpine' peaks with a variety of rock and snow routes. A few miles south, overlooking the Kurobe Gorge, which bites deeply into the range, is the sacred peak of Tateyama (9,891 feet), whose summit shrine is visited by pilgrims every summer. The ridge southwards bears some fine summits, but undoubtedly the finest stretch is between Yarigadake (10,433 feet) and Oku-Hodaka (10,466 feet). The traverse of this with intervening peaks was first made by Yuko Maki in 1917. The rock pinnacle of Ko Yari deserves mention for its climbs; and sounder rock than most is to be found on the buttresses of the Hodaka group.

South again stands the volcano of Yake dake (8,062 feet); but the finest of these volcanoes is Ontake (10,051 feet), south of the River Soda. Ontake was climbed towards the end of the eighteenth century by Fukan Reijin, who, it is said, was guided to the summit by a ptarmigan. The mountain is easily climbed by a pilgrim route from Fukushima. All the way up this most sacred mountain are shrines, traditional scenes of ritual practices by pilgrim bands. It is of interest that at the top of almost every Japanese mountain is the emblem of some Shinto deity.

Central and Southern Alps

The Central Alps comprise one main ridge running parallel, to the west rather than north of the Southern Alps. The high point is West Komagadake (9,708 feet), but the ridge has many almost equal summits, beginning with the more spectacular rock peak of Kengamine (9,623 feet).

These Central and Southern Alps are less visited than the Northern, and are less rewarding. The most northerly height, East Komagadake, can be approached from the east up a path dominated by Byobu iwa, which has fine granite for climbing. The ridge passes south, Japan's second highest summit, Kita dake (10,474 feet), standing off the watershed and looking across, to the north-east, at the twin granite monoliths of Hoozan which give difficult climbing. Kita dake itself gives a long scramble through undergrowth, forest trees, and the obnoxious 'creeping pine'.

South from Kita dake, and beginning with Aionodake (10,464 feet), the ridge stretches over many 10,000-foot summits, accessible easily from the Tenryu Valley to the west.

Fuji-san

Standing isolated and unique, east from the Southern Alps and fifty miles west of Yokohama, is Fuji-san (12,390 feet), which, though not a mountaineer's peak, compels the attention of mountaineers. An extinct volcano, it can be ascended from different sides or traversed, the conditions varying according to season. Although no record exists, it is said that a Buddhist monk climbed the mountain in about the seventh century. The best time is spring, when snow lies and the views are superlative. In winter Fuji has become popular with skiers, and, like Ontake, the mountain is the goal of pilgrim bands of all description.

Wilfrid Noyce

(*Left*) The Japanese Alps: the Ushiro-Tateyama range, whose highest point is Tateyama (9,891 feet).

The summit of Fuji-san from the north-west.

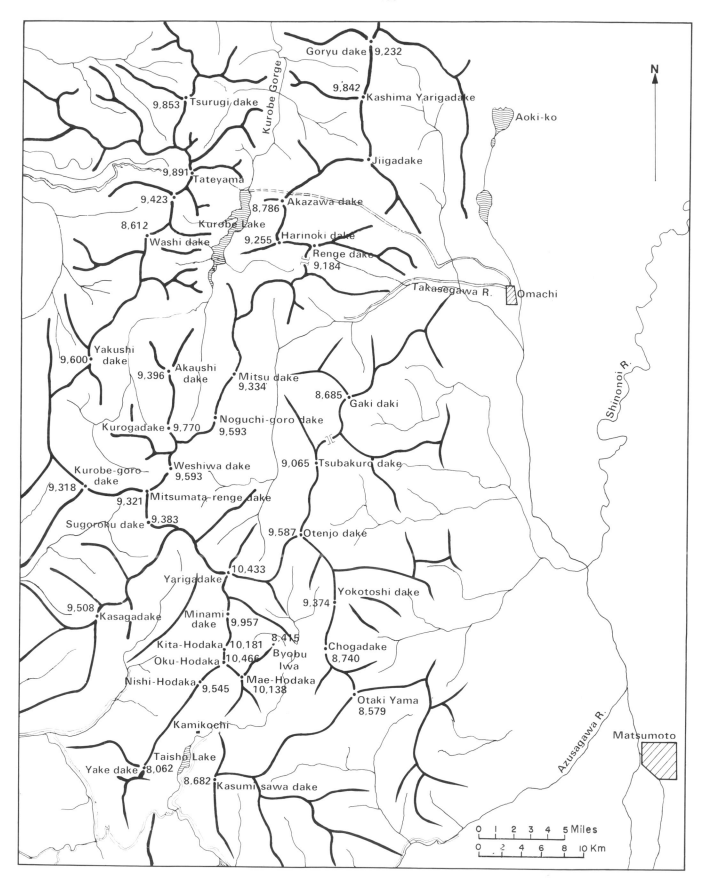

Goryu dake 9,232

9,842

Kashima Yarigadake

Aoki-ko

N

9,853 Tsurugi dake

Kurobe Gorge

Jiigadake

9,891 Tateyama

9,423

Akazawa dake

8,612

8,786

Kurobe Lake

Washi dake

9,255 Harinoki dake

Renge dake
9,184

Takasegawa R. Omachi

Yakushi
dake

9,600

9,396 Akaushi
dake

Mitsu dake
9,334

Shinonoi R.

8,685 Gaki daki

Noguchi-goro dake
9,593

Kurogadake 9,770

9,065 Tsubakuro dake

Kurobe-goro-
dake

Weshiwa dake
9,593

9,318

9,321 Mitsumata-renge dake

Sugoroku dake 9,383

9,587 Otenjo dake

Yarigadake 10,433

Yokotoshi dake
9,374

9,508 Kasagadake

Minami
dake 9,957

Kita-Hodaka 10,181
Oku-Hodaka 10,466

8,415
Byobu
Iwa

Chogadake
8,740

Nishi-Hodaka
9,545

Mae-Hodaka
10,138

Otaki Yama
8,579

Kamikochi

Matsumoto

Taisho Lake
Yake dake 8,062

8,682 Kasumi sawa dake

Azusagawa R.

0 1 2 3 4 5 Miles
0 2 4 6 8 10 Km

Formosa and Korea

Formosa

Formosa is an island, mountainous in the centre and north-east. After 1894 it became part of the Japanese Empire, but the inhabitants of the interior had not abandoned the custom of head-hunting, and such mountaineering as has been done has been done with a police escort and some trepidation.

A further complication to travel is the high tree-line, which, owing to the island's position astride the Tropic of Cancer and the high rainfall, is as far up as 12,000 feet. Niitaka (12,960 feet; but all heights are uncertain), in the centre of the island, was climbed in 1896 by S. Honda and Forestry officials. By the ordinary way it is easy; but it has four fine, if friable, rock buttresses, explored by T. Numai in 1930. Tsugitaka (12,897 feet), the second highest summit and dominating the north-east area, is climbed from the Pyanansha Police Post. A long traverse over Hapanorau (12,250 feet), climbed by Murray Walton in 1930, leads to Daihasenzan (11,720 feet), a remarkable 'Lost World' peak climbed in 1928 by T. Ikoma and T. Numai. From the same base Chusoenzan (12,190 feet), Nankotai (12,460 feet), and other eastern peaks can be climbed.

A feature of Formosa is the tremendous rock scenery of the east coast and the gorge of Takkiri, with its 4,000-foot walls.

At the time of writing, and with the Chinese Nationalist government in residence, new peaks and routes of Formosa are not likely to be explored for some little time to come.

Korea

The mountains of Korea, though politically inaccessible to most, deserve at least a mention. The highest peak, Hakutozan (approximately 9,000 feet), was climbed by Younghusband in 1886. The 'Diamond Mountains' rise along the central section of the north-east coast, and their 5,000-foot granite summits became popular with Japanese rock climbers before the war. Near Seoul the egg-shaped Insupong and other low but popular peaks offer difficult climbs.

Wilfrid Noyce

The Northern Japanese Alps.

3 The Mountains of Africa
East Africa

Historical: the Nile sources

The belief that the source of the Nile lay amongst snow-clad mountains in equatorial Africa can be traced as far back as the fifth century B.C., when Aeschylus, aware of the country's dependence upon the river, wrote of 'Egypt nourished by melting snow'. Aristotle, too, wrote of a mountain of silver lying to the south-west of the Nile. This belief seems to have been widely held at the time, and indeed there is evidence to suggest that Egypt had contact with the upper Nile from very early times; but Herodotus, in attempting to explain the annual Nile flooding, dismissed such views as worthless, thinking it unlikely that snow could exist in such obviously hot regions.

By the first century A.D. merchants from the Mediterranean world were trading extensively along the East African coast. One of these, a Greek named Diogenes, is reported to have travelled inland from Rhapta (which may be identified with modern Pangani) for twenty-five days, reaching two great lakes and 'the snowy range of mountains whence the Nile draws its twin sources'. Bearing in mind the distances involved, it is most unlikely that Diogenes reached the Ruwenzori and far more probable that he saw either Kilimanjaro or Mount Kenya. During the second century, Claudius Ptolemy produced his remarkable map, which was no doubt compiled from all available information and on which he depicted the Nile

flowing from two lakes which were fed by the waters from a range of mountains extending in an east–west direction. He named the mountains *Lunae Montes*. Ptolemy's map had enormous influence, and so far as the Nile source was concerned, it remained unchallenged for seventeen centuries.

The first substantial indication of equatorial snows came in 1848, when John Rebmann of the Church Missionary Society saw the dome of Kilimanjaro. A year later his colleague, J. L. Krapf, sighted Mount Kenya. News of these discoveries had a mixed reception in England, where some efforts were made to discredit Krapf and Rebmann. There followed, however, a general revival of speculation on the Nile sources, and it was in order to solve this perennial problem once and for all that Sir Richard Burton and J. H. Speke travelled to Africa in 1856. But although Speke briefly glimpsed the Virunga volcanoes in 1858, and later, with J. A. Grant, reached the source of the White Nile in Lake Victoria, the *Lunae Montes* eluded discovery. They were to remain elusive for a further quarter of a century until, in 1888, while camped some distance west of Lake Albert, two members of H. M. Stanley's expedition caught sight of a snowy range of mountains to the south-east. A month later Stanley too saw the mountains, to which he gave the name Ruwenzori.

It may have been premature to regard this discovery as the end of the great search. Dissenting voices were still heard. But the mountains appeared to fulfil, if not all, certainly most of the conditions laid down by Ptolemy. Surely here at last were the legendary Mountains of the Moon.

The southern aspect of Mount Baker from the slopes of Mount Luigi di Savoia. Below and to the left lie the Kitandara Lakes, with, behind, the Scott-Elliot Pass and Mount Speke. In the foreground is the Freshfield Pass.

(*Above*) The Kitandara Lakes, situated south-west of Mount Baker and in one of the most beautiful parts of the Ruwenzori.

(*Below*) Alexandra (16,703 feet) and Margherita (16,763 feet), the twin peaks of Mount Stanley from the Stanley plateau. In profile is the fine east ridge of Margherita, which was first climbed by Bernardzikiewics and Pawlowski, two members of a Polish expedition, in 1939.

Mount Stanley (16,763 feet), the highest summit in the Ruwenzori range.

Kilimanjaro, with the twin peaks of Mawenzi (16,890 feet) and Kibo (19,340 feet), from the north.

The Ruwenzori

Ptolemy's *Lunae Montes*, the Ruwenzori, though they are not so extensive as shown by the Greek geographer on his map, are worthy indeed of so mighty a river as the Nile. The mountains lie along the western border of Uganda, between the Rift Valley lakes of Edward and Albert. Ruwenzori, the name given the mountains by Stanley, is probably a corruption of the Bakonjo '*Ru-enzururu*', meaning 'hill of snow'. They are a complex system, some sixty miles in length and thirty miles in width, at the centre of which are six massifs carrying glaciers.

Fittingly, the highest peaks bear the names of the men who so eagerly sought them, although it is not without some irony that the highest commemorates not the chief protagonists in the 'Nile duel', as Burton and Speke were at one time called, but the resourceful, iron-willed, and thoroughly professional explorer who first saw them.

Mount Stanley, with its twin summits, Margherita (16,763 feet) and Alexandra (16,703 feet), Mount Speke (16,042 feet), and Mount Baker (15,889 feet) are the three highest and form a compact triangle enclosing the upper Bujuku Valley. To the north lie Mounts Emin (15,740 feet) and Gessi (15,470 feet), while Mount Luigi (15,178 feet) dominates the Kuruguta and Nyamugasani Valleys at the southern end of the range.

Owing to their remoteness and structural complexity, the Ruwenzori were the last of the great East African mountains to be explored. Incessant bad weather, for which the mountains are renowned, prevented many of the early parties from penetrating beyond the forest belt, and it was not until 1900 that the glaciers were reached for the first time. Five years later, D. W. Freshfield and A. L. Mumm came to tackle the serious mountaineering problems, but with little success. In 1906 the Duke of the Abruzzi visited the mountains with a

well-equipped expedition, and with a characteristic thorough-ness climbed Margherita and many other peaks, and attempted the first scientific study of the range. In the same year a British Museum party, led by A. F. R. Wollaston, made a collection of plants and animals but did little climbing. During the course of seven expeditions between 1926 and 1932, Dr G. N. Humphreys contributed much to the exploration of the mountains, including the first east–west crossing of the range.

Although some of the earliest attempts were made from the west, including J. J. David's remarkable solo ascent to the Stanley ice plateau in 1904, the first ascents of the main peaks from the Congo were made by Count X. de Grunne's Belgian expedition in 1932. In the same year Eric Shipton and H. W. Tilman set a new standard by making, in addition to the third ascent of Margherita and a new route on Mount Speke, the first ascent of the difficult north face of Mount Baker, a route which has not yet been repeated. In the years following, the Ruwenzori became increasingly frequented. The lesser peaks were climbed and new routes were made on the major peaks, especially on Mount Stanley. Although most of them are mixed snow and rock routes of moderate standards, the north-east ridge of Albert, climbed by Smith and Fletcher in 1956, and the west ridge of Alexandra, climbed by Ghiglione, Mauri, and Ferrario in 1960, are particularly noteworthy. For the climber demanding greater challenge, there is the west face of Mount Baker, which has yet to be climbed.

Travel in the mountains today is made much easier by the huts owned and maintained by the Mountain Club of Uganda, which are conveniently situated on the approach route up the Mubuku Valley and at strategic points throughout the range.

In addition to their mountaineering attractions, the Ruwenzori are a naturalist's paradise. The lower slopes are clothed in montane forest, which gives way to bamboo at about 8,000 feet. The Alpine zone above 10,000 feet is dominated by giant forms of lobelia, heather, and groundsel. In the forest zone there is a wide variety of bird life, including a number of species peculiar to the range, such as the Ruwenzori Turaco. One may also see Colobus and Blue Monkeys, Hyrax, Red Duiker, and occasionally the Ruwenzori Leopard.

Kilimanjaro

Kilimanjaro, the highest mountain in Africa, is also one of the greatest volcanoes in the world. Its immensity is, at first sight, difficult to grasp, particularly when seen from across the arid Amboseli Plains which lie to the north-west. Measuring roughly forty miles from east to west and thirty from north to south, the mountain lifts a vast dome of ice to 19,340 feet, some 15,000 feet above the surrounding plains.

The mountain consists of three main peaks, all of which have been centres of volcanic activity at one time or another: Kibo (19,340 feet), Mawenzi (16,890 feet), and Shira (13,140 feet). Kibo is the most perfectly preserved, having a wide caldera and inner cone, while both Mawenzi and Shira are greatly eroded, the latter not being of much interest.

The ice-cap of Kibo and the glaciers which flow from it have shrunk greatly in the last eighty years so that none now reach below 15,500 feet, and on the north and east sides Kibo's silver crown may soon be only seasonal.

The first man to venture on to the mountain was the Baron von der Decken, in 1862, fourteen years after Rebmann had first seen the snows. Five years later, Charles New, a Methodist missionary, reached the Saddle between Kibo and Mawenzi. German interest in East Africa was growing, and it was a German, Hans Meyer, who, with L. Purtscheller in 1889, first reached the summit of Kibo, unfurled the German flag, and named the highest point in honour of Kaiser Wilhelm. German

imperialism in East Africa, like that of Britain, which succeeded it, was short lived, and after independence in 1961 the highest point was renamed Uhuru Peak. Mawenzi succumbed less readily, and it was not until 1912 that the summit was reached by E. Oehler and F. Klute.

The easy way up Kibo from the Saddle presents no obstacles apart from that of altitude, but on the south and south-western sides difficult ice routes have been made on some of the glaciers. Particularly worthy of mention is the Heim Glacier route, climbed by A. Nelson, H. J. Cooke, and D. N. Goodall in 1957, and the Kersten Glacier route, climbed by W. Welsch and L. Herncarek in 1962. Although the Heim Glacier route has been climbed solo in a day by M. Adams, these are serious routes generally necessitating bivouacs.

Mawenzi, on the other hand, cannot be ascended without rock-climbing and, depending upon conditions, some snow and ice pitches. Overlooking the Saddle is the 2,000-foot west face, which has a number of routes of varying standards, and for the more serious climber there is the north face route, climbed by M. Tremonti and M. Bianchi in 1958. The immense east face of Mawenzi has, as yet, only had one ascent, by Edwards and Thomson in 1964, and it is surely here that one must look for future new routes.

Mount Kenya

Mount Kenya is perhaps the most beautiful of the African mountains. Standing almost astride the Equator, it dominates the highlands lying to the north of Nairobi, resembling a vast inverted saucer, capped with a pyramid of snow-clad peaks. Like Kilimanjaro, Mount Kenya is an extinct volcano, and

The east face and summit of Mawenzi (16,890 feet). Behind is Kibo, whose highest point, Uhuru Peak, lies on the left-hand edge of the crater rim.

9. The Caucasus: Dongus-orun from the Baksan Valley.

10a. (*Overleaf*) The Tyan' Shan': Chapayev Peak (20,899 feet) and Khan-Tengri (22,949 feet) from a camp on the Zvëzdochka Glacier.

10b. (*Overleaf*) Mount Kenya from the west.

must have once been several thousand feet higher than it is at present, but the crater has been eroded away to expose a crystalline plug of syenite. It is this plug which forms the central peaks.

Batian (17,058 feet), the highest peak, is named after a famous Masai *laibon*, or medicine man, and it is separated from its twin, Nelion (17,022 feet), by a narrow gap, the Gate of the Mists. Radiating from the twin peaks is a complex system of ridges and pinnacles to delight the mountaineer and which provide some of the finest rock and ice climbing in Africa. The mountain is laced by a dozen or so glaciers varying in size from the Lewis Glacier, the largest, which descends from Point Lenana (16,355 feet), to the minute Diamond Glacier which clings to the south face below the Gate of the Mists.

The expedition made by Count Teleki and L. von Höhnel in 1887 began the thorough exploration of the mountain. Approaching from the south-west they reached a height of about 14,000 feet. In 1893 J. W. Gregory reached the Lewis Glacier and six years later Sir Halford Mackinder, with the

The central peaks of Mount Kenya from the Teleki Valley. From left to right they are: Point Pigott (16,265 feet), Batian (17,058 feet), Nelion (17,022 feet), and Lenana (16,355 feet). In front are Point John (16,020 feet) and Midget Peak (15,420 feet).

The north face of Mount Kenya. The climbs here are among the hardest on the mountain. Clearly visible on the left is the sheer east face of Nelion, which was first climbed in 1963 by H. Klier, S. Aeberli, and G. B. Cliff.

guides César Ollier and Joseph Brocherel, made the first
ascent of Batian. For thirty years the mountain withstood
further attacks, until, in 1929, Eric Shipton and P. Wynn-
Harris made the second ascent as well as the first ascent of
Nelion. Shipton returned the following year, with H. W.
Tilman, and together they made a complete traverse, from
west to east, of the twin peaks. The remarkable ascent of the
north face by Arthur Firmin and P. Hicks opened the post-
war period with a flourish. Firmin followed this with an ascent
of the south face of Batian with J. W. Howard. The difficult
west face was added by R. A. Caukwell and G. W. Rose in
1955. There followed an increasing number of routes on
Batian and Nelion as well as on surrounding peaks. The east
face of Nelion, which had for long been regarded as the last
major problem, was finally climbed in 1963 by H. Klier,
S. Aeberli, and G. B. Cliff. A few days earlier, Cliff, with
D. Rutowitz, had made an ascent of the north-east pillar of
Nelion. In 1964 R. Baillie and T. P. Philips made the grand
traverse of the mountain, from Point Pigott (16,265 feet) to
Point John (16,020 feet), following it up with a fierce route on
the north face of Point John.

Although bivouacs may be necessary on some of the more
serious routes, most of the major peaks can be approached
from huts built by the Mountain Club of Kenya, which has
also published an excellent guidebook to both Kilimanjaro
and Mount Kenya.

Both Kilimanjaro and Mount Kenya support vegetation of
a unique kind. On each mountain a forest belt extends to
between 9,000 and 11,000 feet. On the drier northern slopes,
the forest belts are considerably narrower and less luxuriant.
Above the forest are moorlands with giant heath which give
way to the giant lobelias and groundsel of the alpine zone,
which extends to about 14,500 feet. Above this altitude little
vegetation is to be found.

The Virunga volcanoes

The eight Virunga volcanoes, sometimes known as Bufumbiro,
meaning 'that which cooks', lie across the western Rift Valley
between Lakes Edward and Kivu, straddling the borders of
the Congo, Uganda, and Ruanda. The two western, active,
cones, Nyiragongo (11,350 feet) and Nyamulagira (10,050
feet), which lie wholly within the Congo, have intermittently
erupted streams of lava which have extended as far south as
Lake Kivu. The central group contains the highest peaks,
Karisimbi (14,783 feet) and Mikeno (14,553 feet) as well as
the much lower Vissoke (12,174 feet). Sabinio (11,960 feet),
Mgahinga (11,435 feet), and Muhavura (13,542 feet) comprise
the eastern group on the Congo–Ruanda border.

The first to visit the mountains was a German officer, Graf
Götzen, in 1894. After the First World War the Belgians ex-
pressed an interest in the mountains and a number of parties
visited them, such as that of Father van Hoef, who first
climbed Mikeno in 1927. However, it was to the naturalist

The Virunga Volcanoes: Nyiragongo (11,350 feet). Behind
is the crater of Nyamulagira.

that the mountains issued their strongest appeal: they attracted
men like Carl Akeley, whose strenuous efforts resulted in the
creation, by the Belgians, of the Albert National Park which
embraces the volcanoes and which ensures the protection of
perhaps their most interesting inhabitant, the rare mountain
gorilla.

Ethiopia

Ethopia contains the greatest area of high mountains on the
African continent. This mountain fastness fostered the
Axumite kingdom during the early Christian era and later
protected Ethiopic Christianity from the tide of Islam. The
country retained a mystic seclusion until well into the eighteenth century, when James Bruce travelled from the source
of the Blue Nile at Lake Tana to its confluence with the White
Nile at Khartoum.

The mountains may be divided into nine major groups, of
which the Amaro, Guge, Batu, and Chilalo ranges all lie south
of the natural moat formed by the Rift Valley. Of these, perhaps the Batu, with summits of 14,000 feet, and the Chilalo
range, visited by the Duke of the Abruzzi in 1928–9, offer the
best climbing possibilities. North of the Rift are the Chokke
and Guna Highlands, the two groups which border the arid
coastal lowlands, and the Simien mountains, which hold the
highest peak, Ras Dashan (15,159 feet). To the rock climber
the high summits of the Simien group are less interesting than
the surrounding isolated spires, all of which are probably unclimbed. Since the Second World War most of the ranges have
been visited, notably by Dr Hugh Scott, but the mountains
are still very little known.

Ian McMorrin

Southern Africa

The mountains of Southern Africa form an almost continuous arcuate rim, enclosing the interior plateau and extending from the Cape to the River Zambezi. The three roughly parallel ranges of the Cape fold-mountains outline the southern coast-line, while the eastern rim is formed by the Drakensberg, which culminates in the great wall of mountain lying along the Natal–Lesotho border. Further north are the Chimanimani and Inyanga Mountains of Rhodesia and Mlanje in southern Malawi.

Although the Portuguese navigators visited the southern tip of Africa during the fifteenth century, it was the Dutch who first established a station there, and their hardy descendants, the Boers, who, in 1838, shook off the yoke of the British government at the Cape and journeyed north through the mountains to the highveld beyond. The 'Great Trek' was the first exodus from the fast-growing civilization of the coast. Faced with a hostile country, the Boers had little time for aesthetic diversions and it is not difficult to see why a pursuit such as mountaineering was slow to evolve.

Perhaps the true birth of mountaineering in South Africa

The Drakensberg: the Column and Pyramid from Cleft Peak. Across the cloud-filled Umlambonja Valley are the Chessmen, Inner and Outer Horns, the Bell, and Cathedral Peak.

(*Above left*) The Drakensberg: the Eastern Buttress, Devil's Tooth, and Inner Tower from the Sentinel. After resisting a number of attempts, Devil's Tooth was first climbed in 1950.

The Inner and Outer Mnweni Pinnacles at the head of the Mnweni Valley in one of the most remote and beautiful parts of the Drakensberg.

The Drakensberg: the north face of Monks Cowl, a peak with a reputation for difficult routes.

Table Mountain: a feature of Table Mountain is the vertical cliffs which provide first-rate rock climbing. With the slopes of Devil's Peak in the background, the climber is at the end of the 'Catwalk' on the Catwalk Route.

was in 1884, when Gustav Nefdt climbed the western pinnacle of Toverkop. Seven years later, in 1891, a small group of enthusiasts, headed by Dr R. Marloth, founded the Mountain Club of South Africa, which thus became the third British mountaineering club, after the Alpine Club and the New Zealand Alpine Club, which was also founded in 1891. In the years following the Boer War of 1899–1902, mountaineering became increasingly popular. The scope was unlimited. The great sandstone crags of Table Mountain overlooking the city of Cape Town offered a rich harvest of difficult climbs. Further afield were the Cedarberg, the Hex River Mountains, du Toit's Kloof Mountains, and the immense walls of the Drakensberg.

Up until the Second World War the leaders in the field were such figures as G. F. Travers-Jackson, W. T. Cobern, K. Cameron, O. B. Godbold, J. Langmore, and George Londt. The climbs were the classic ones: Africa Face on Table Mountain, the Klein Winterhoek frontal route first climbed by Londt in 1921, and routes in the Transvaal Magaliesberg. In the Drakensberg most of the major peaks were climbed: the Sentinel, Cathedral Peak, and the Giants and Champagne Castles (11,077 feet). There remained only

The north-west face of Du Toit's Peak, which was first climbed by Mamacos and Butler in 1949. Their route, a Grade VI, is still regarded as one of the finest in the country.

Table Mountain: negotiating a pitch on Barrier Sandwich Route. Exceptionally severe, the route is one of many on this famous buttress.

isolated spires, such as the Column, Mponjwane, the Injasuti Triplets, the Mnweni Pinnacles, and the Devil's Tooth. The advent of the 'iron age' and the high standard of climbing which accompanied it accounted for many of these last problems. Table Mountain became the nursery for 'tigers' and the difficulty of its routes increased accordingly. Touch and Go, Postern Crest, Fingertip Face, and Fernwood Precipice all rated Grade VI. Difficult routes were made also among the 'country' mountains: the Witteberg, Molenaarsberg, and du Toit's Peak whose north-west face, climbed by M. Mamacos and C. C. Butler in 1949, is still regarded as amongst the most arduous in the country. Further north, in Rhodesia, a growing number visit the 8,000-foot Chimanimani Mountains each year, and difficult climbs have been made on the granite inselbergs scattered about the high plateau.

The climber in Southern Africa is doubly fortunate. Although his mountains are, for the most part, small in stature, there is an abundance of them and they experience a benevolent climate which is, to some extent, predictable.

Ian McMorrin

North Africa

The Hoggar and Tibesti

Contained within the vastness of the Sahara desert lie two of Africa's perhaps most unique mountain groups: the Hoggar and Tibesti.

The Hoggar (or Ahaggar) is situated in southern Algeria, some 900 miles from the North African coast. Formed as a result of volcanic extrusions through fissures in the ancient plateau, the Hoggar present a chaotic world of jagged pinnacles and broad shallow valleys, or *wadis*, almost completely devoid of vegetation.

Before the end of the nineteenth century the Hoggar was almost totally unknown. Missionaries attempting to penetrate the area were invariably massacred by the warlike Toureg. When, however, in 1902, France achieved at least a partial supremacy over the Toureg, access was finally gained to the land that the French explorer and writer Duveyrier had described as 'the country of fear'. Perhaps the most important figure in the early exploration of the Hoggar was Charles de Foucauld, who, in the ten years preceding his assassination at Tamanrasset in 1916, conducted a systematic investigation of the mountains. Following the geological expedition by Lombard and Perret in 1932, the European world became increasingly interested in these remote mountains, and climbers, for the most part French, soon followed in the footsteps of the scientists. The magnificent spire of Ilamane (9,050 feet) fell in 1953 to Bossard and Hauser, and a few months later Coche and Frison-Roche made the first ascent of Iharen (5,847 feet) and the Garet-el-Djenoun (7,600 feet). The Martin–Pierre–Syda expedition of 1951 accounted for Aukenet (8,200 feet) and Issekrar (6,220 feet), which was climbed by the south pillar, a route involving the use of artificial techniques. With the exception of the Garet-el-Djenoun, which lies in the Tefedest, all the previously mentioned peaks are situated in the central Hoggar, an area of roughly 1,000 square miles known as the Koudia, which contains the highest summit, Tahat (9,870 feet).

Six hundred miles of barren desert, inhabited only by the nomadic Touareg, separate the Hoggar from the Tibesti to the east. Although the German explorer, Nachtigal, reached Bardai on the northern slopes of the Tibesti as early as 1869, it was not until the turn of the century that much was known about the mountains. Jean Tilho did much to put the Tibesti on the map, and between the wars a few scientific parties visited the range. These culminated in Thesiger's remarkable camel journey from the Sudan in 1939.

The Hoggar: the basalt columns of Ihaven (5,847 feet), situated in the Tamanrasset plain.

Ilamane (9,050 feet), perhaps the best-known peak in the Hoggar.

The Hoggar: the barren Koudia with the peaks of the Tidjamayène massif, north and south Tezoulag.

Atlas Mountains: Jebel Toubkal (13,665 feet), the highest summit in North Africa, from Aksoual (12,828 feet).

Atlas Mountains: Ouanoukrim (13,270 feet) from Tazarhart.

The extinct volcanoes of Tousside (10,700 feet), Emi-Koussi (11,204 feet), and Tieroko (10,430 feet) are the highest in the Tibesti, but although they are of great interest to the geologist, they offer little to the rock climber. Since 1945, however, a number of parties have made the best of what there is. More interesting are the numerous volcanic spires which surround the main peaks and a number of routes have been made, notably on the Aiguilles Sisse to the west.

The Atlas Mountains

The Atlas Mountains extend a total distance of 1,200 miles from Tunisia to western Morocco. They comprise six groups: the Rif, Middle Atlas, High Atlas, Anti-Atlas, Tellien, and Saharan Atlas, the first four being in Morocco and the last two extending over part of Algeria. Peaks of the Anti-Atlas and Middle Atlas reach over 11,000 feet, and in Algeria the Djurdjura have long been popular. For the mountaineer, however, the important group remains the High Atlas, penetrated by Charles de Foucauld in 1883. Even in this range, extending over 200 miles, comparatively little climbing has been done outside the Toubkal massif and one or two isolated summits like the dramatic 'Cathedral', accessible from Marrakesh. The French, who occupied Morocco early in the century, were the chief pioneers. Huts were built in the Toubkal massif and by 1938 a guidebook was produced. The first notable explorers, L. Gentil and the Marquis de Segonzac, were followed by the de Lépineys, L. Neltner, M. de Prandières, and A. Stofer, as well as the British climber, B. Beetham. Good snow conditions encouraged the development of skiing, but both skiing and climbing activity decreased after the departure of the French some years ago.

Perhaps the best seasons for climbing are spring and early autumn, although for the serious winter climber the Atlas has great possibilities. In spring snow and rock climbing alternate, while in September the peaks are dry, travel whether on foot or by mule is easy, and from huts or camps in the high corries it is possible to traverse several peaks in the day. The rock is variable and usually best along the ridges. Thus the traverses of tower and pinnacle give the most attractive climbing. The arêtes of Toubkal (13,665 feet) are deservedly famous, as is the ridge of Ouanoukrim (13,270 feet) and the sharp pinnacle of Tadaft (12,796 feet). But for the seeker of novelty, there are still unclimbed buttresses leading to the rock-girt Tazahrhat plateau and on the flanks of Aksoual (12,828 feet), Angour (11,745 feet), and Anrhemer (12,773 feet) further east. Owing largely to easier travel facilities, in recent years interest in the Atlas has quickened and the number of parties visiting the mountains increases yearly. Particularly important have been H. M. Brown's winter expeditions of 1965 and 1966, which resulted in a number of excellent ascents, notably the 6,000-foot north ridge of Aksoual and some fine routes on the south face of Angour.

Apart from climbing, the traveller in the Atlas is charmed by the valley terraces of maize, the ochre and red hillsides, the different vegetation of the richer northern slopes, and the arid Saharan landscape. He will enjoy meetings with the Berbers, a proud and independent people who resisted the French up to 1934 and who wrest a hard living from an exacting environment. His valleys will be as important as his peaks.

Ian McMorrin

A camel caravan crossing the Tizi n'Techka in the high Atlas.

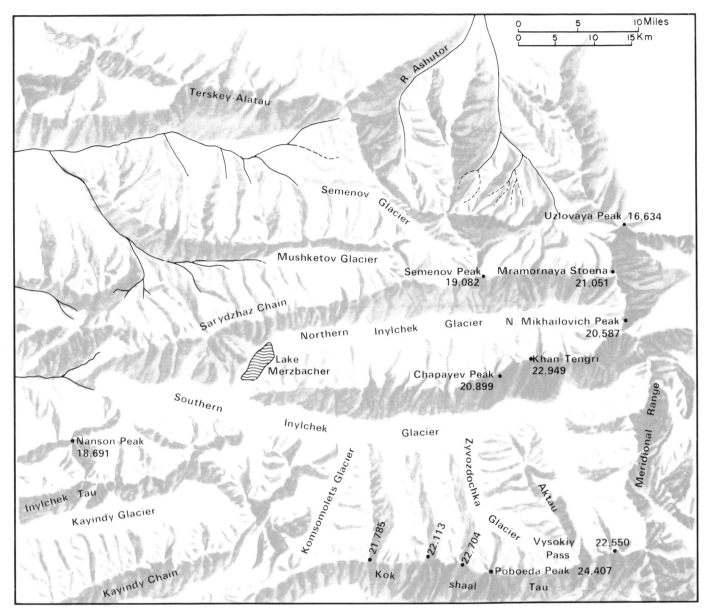

17. U.S.S.R.: the Central Tyan' Shan'.

Kraepelin
15,720
Mount Emin
Bottego
15,418
Umberto
Mount Gessi

Iolanda
15,470

Kihuma
14,405

Ensonga
Mount Speke
(Duwoni)
Vittorio Emanuele
16,042

Middle Portal
14,337
Portal
Peaks

Margherita
16,763

R. Bujuku

Mount
Stanley
Moebius
16,134
L. Bujuku

Scott Elliot
Pass 14,345

Kinyangoma
14,536

Mount Baker

Edward
15,889

R. Mubulu

Sella
15,179

Mount Luigi di Savoia
Weismann
15,157
R. Kuruguta

Okusoma
15,021

0   1   2   3 Miles
0   1   2   3   4   5 Km

18. East Africa: the Ruwenzori with the central peaks including Mounts Stanley, Speke, and Baker.

19. East Africa: Kilimanjaro with Kibo and the neighbouring
peak of Mawenzi.

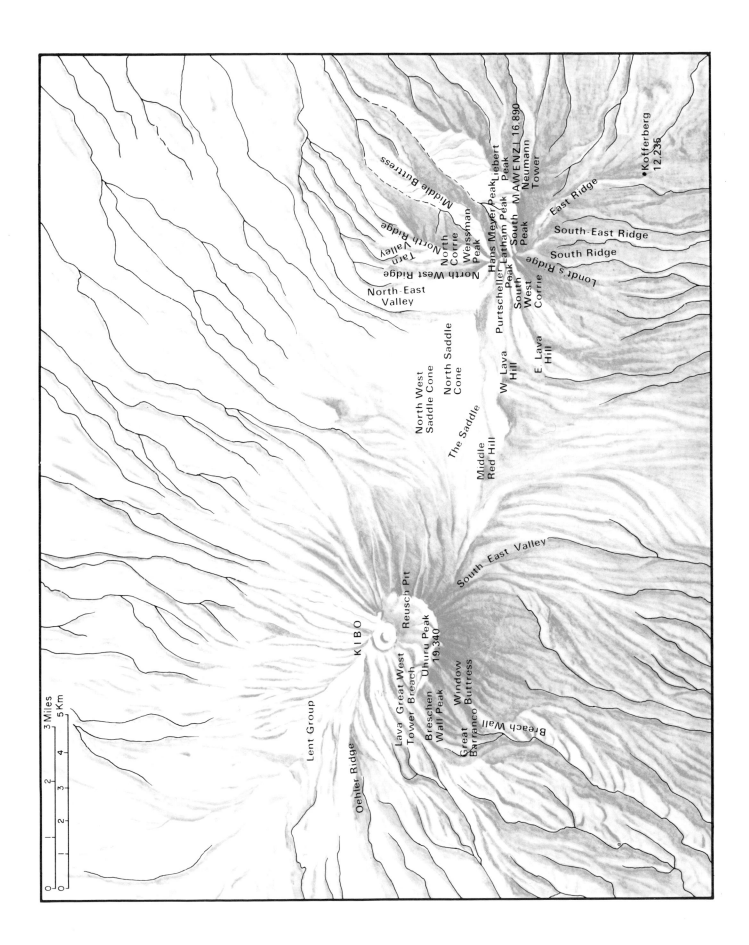

Kofferberg
12,235

MAWENZI 16,890
Neumann
Tower
Liebert
Peak
South
Peak
East Ridge
South-East Ridge
South Ridge
Latham Peak
Londt's Ridge
Hans Meyer Peak
Weissman
Peak
Purtscheller
Peak
South
West
Corrie
North
Corrie
North West Ridge
North Ridge
Tarn
North
Valley
Middle Buttress
North-East
Valley
E. Lava
Hill
W. Lava
Hill
North West
Saddle Cone
North Saddle
Cone
The Saddle
Middle
Red Hill

South-East Valley

Reusch Pit

KIBO
Uhuru Peak
19,340
Great West
Breach
Lava
Tower Breach
Breschen
Wall Peak
Window
Buttress
Great
Barranco Wall
Breach Wall

Lent Group

Oehler Ridge

3 Miles
5 Km
0   1   2   3   4
0   1   2   3

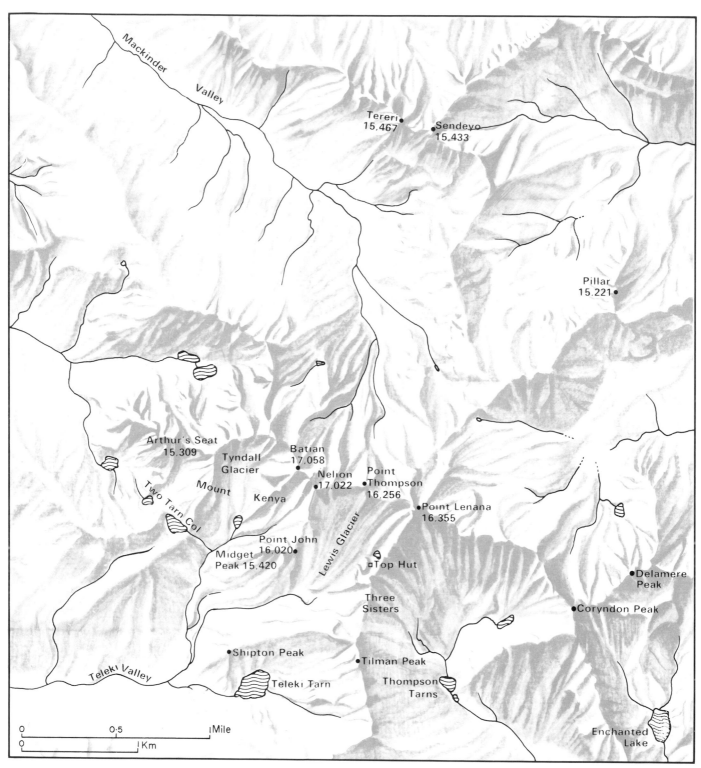

20. East Africa: Mount Kenya with the twin peaks of Batian and Nelion.

4 The Mountains of Australasia
New Zealand

History of Climbing in New Zealand
Early Records

During the 500 years of Maori occupation, the mountains of New Zealand were left unvisited, except for some mountain valleys of the South Island, which were the source of jade called greenstone, highly prized for weapons and ornaments. No reliable records exist, however, of any attempt to climb above the forest level.

The mountains were first seen by Abel Tasman in 1642, and again by James Cook in 1770, who recorded the existence of glaciers, but did not know them by that name when he wrote, '. . . of prodigious height, the mountains and some of the valleys being wholly covered with snow'. Mount Cook was named in 1851 during a survey of the coast and harbours by H.M.S. *Acheron*, and ten years later land-hungry sheep farmers began to explore the upper reaches of the mountain valleys. One of them was Samuel Butler, author of *Erewhon* and *The Way of All Flesh*, who saw Mount Cook and wrote: 'though it is hazardous to say this of any mountain, I do not think that any human will reach its top; but I am forgetting myself into admiring a mountain which is of no use to sheep'.

The climbers of the last century

Apart from the ascents in 1839 (remarkable for their early date) of the two North Island volcanoes: Mount Egmont (8,260 feet) by Dr Diffenbach and Mount Ngauruhoe (7,515 feet) by J. C. Bidwell, an Australian botanist, mountaineering began in 1882 when the Rev. W. S. Green made a determined effort to climb Mount Cook. Green's expedition and his very near success stimulated interest in New Zealand and England.

Mount Cook and Mount Tasman from the east. The triple summits of Mount Cook rise over 8,000 feet above the glacier. The long east ridge to the middle peak was climbed by Mahan and Bryant in 1935. The east face, directly below the high peak, was climbed in 1962. Mount Tasman, the ice peak to the right of the centre, rises above the Grand Plateau. The first ascent was made in 1895 by Zurbriggen, Fitzgerald, and Clark over the Silberhorn, the snow peak just to the left of the high summit.

G. E. Mannering and M. J. Dixon made attempts on Mount
Cook over several years. In 1894 E. A. Fitzgerald came from
England with Matthias Zurbriggen with the loudly declared
intention of climbing the highest mountain and was bitterly
disappointed when three young New Zealanders, G. Graham,
T. Fyfe, and J. Clark (the latter just seventeen years old)
climbed Mount Cook on Christmas Day 1894. Fitzgerald and
Zurbriggen made several first ascents, including Mount
Tasman (with J. Clark) and Mount Sefton by the great east
ridge. Clark became a guide and went on to make the first
ascent of many of New Zealand's finest summits, while Fyfe
made a solo first ascent of Mount Malte Brun, about which he
wrote a most laconic account: 'played a lone hand with Malte
Brun—and won'.

About this time, with the Alpine Club of Great Britain as
their pattern, the New Zealand Alpine Club was formed and
has flourished ever since.

Fifty years of another Golden Age

At the turn of the century mountaineering was flourishing,
with a small corps of professional guides led by J. Clark and
two outstanding brothers, Peter and Alec Graham. The
Graham brothers were self-taught mountaineers, born on the
West Coast, and the two of them dominated climbing for a
quarter of a century. Between them they climbed most of the
remaining giants and opened new routes and traverses on
Mounts Cook, Tasman, and Dampier. Peter Graham was

Mount Tutoko, the highest in Fiordland, is swept by wind
and snow for much of the time. Samuel Turner, with the
guide P. Graham, made the first ascent after eight attempts.
The glaciated south face showing in this picture has been
climbed.

Ice climbing has developed in New Zealand because this is
generally the easiest way to the summit. These three
climbers are just below the summit of Mount Lendenfeld.

guide during sixteen of the first twenty ascents of Mount Cook and always climbed without using crampons, having developed a legendary ability to cut steps with a huge ice-axe. His greatest climbs and traverses were made leading an Australian lady, Miss Freda du Faur. Alec Graham was joined for many seasons by Dr Teichelmann and Canon Newton, and they made many first ascents. Guideless amateurs like H. F. Wright and A. P. Harper were exploring and climbing in other parts of the range. These were followed later by H. E. L. Porter and M. Kurz, who brought crampons and pitons to New Zealand, but pitons have not been much used as the rock is shaley and friable. Porter climbed all but one of the named peaks over 10,000 feet and has written some of the best descriptions of climbing in the Southern Alps.

The Second World War almost put an end to new climbs, and after 1945 a new spate of first ascents completed all the untrodden summits and the main ridges of all the highest peaks, many of these going to another self-taught guide, H. Ayres.

In the outer ranges, Mount Aspiring was climbed in 1909 by Clark and A. Graham with Major B. Head. In Fiordland the great Mount Tutoko was attempted many times from 1897 onwards. In 1919 Samuel Turner began the first of his six expeditions, which he claimed cost him more than £2,000, until he finally succeeded with P. Graham, reaching the summit in rain and cloud. After two days in a tent they donned their wet clothes and repeated the ascent in fine weather.

Further north in Canterbury, the Canterbury Mountaineering Club was formed of students and artisans whose energetic groups explored and climbed the peaks of Mounts Whitcombe, Evans, and Arrowsmith, about which J. Pascoe has written so vividly in his book *Unclimbed New Zealand*.

The post-Everest era

It is difficult to state exactly when an era ends and a new one begins; by 1950 the major peaks and leading ridges had been climbed and the gentle tempo of New Zealand climbing which had been following some thirty years behind Europe quite suddenly changed. And today the race for the faces and new flanks is frankly on; the east faces of Cook and Tasman have been ascended direct. Until 1950 only thirty-odd ascents of Mount Tasman and seventy of Mount Cook had been made; both mountains were regarded with awe by guide and amateur, who looked upon the climbing of them as the climax of years of apprenticeship. Now the mystique has gone and the post-Everest era has brought karabiner, piton, and étrier and the diligent search for the 'last' problems.

Fording flooded streams is a constant hazard in the approach to the New Zealand peaks. Techniques using the rope as a safeguard are highly developed.

The North Island

The mountains of New Zealand extend through both the two large islands—the North Island and the South Island—and the smaller and southernmost island—Stewart Island. Much of the North Island is hilly and the highest mountains are volcanic. The geological origin of the North Island seems to be more recent than the more mountainous South Island, and has been romantically described according to Maori legend as a great fish brought to the surface by a magic fish-hook; great swellings arose where it was clubbed by the gods who caught it, and the still active volcanoes are the cooling death-twitches of the giant.

The highest mountain is Ruapehu (9,175 feet), a massive volcano rising in a series of ridges to an extensive plateau and a warm lake surrounded by ice. Ruapehu looks as if it has blown its top off, and if the volcanic cone had continued the mountain might have been over 15,000 feet. Two more volcanoes rise near by, Ngauruhoe (7,515 feet) and Tongariro (6,517 feet). Tongariro National Park, which contains these volcanoes, is a centre of skiing for North Island and very few mountaineers bother to go there. The Pinnacle Ridge and Girdlestone Peak of Ruapehu offer climbs of no great difficulty. West of them, near the coast, is another volcano, Mount Egmont (8,260 feet), whose extinct cone lies at the steepest angle of repose, and in winter, when sheathed in ice, it can be a hard ice climb. In summer mass ascents have been made—187 people once reached the summit in one day. It also has the highest death-roll of New Zealand's mountains.

The four volcanoes stand in isolation: the main mountain ranges extend in an almost continuous chain from East Cape south-westwards for 300 miles to Cook Strait, where the sea divides the islands. These mountains, all with peaks around 5,500 feet, include the Kaimanawa, Kaweka, and Raukumara Ranges in the north, and the Ruahine and Tararua Ranges further south. No mountaineering in the special sense of the word is done, but many climbers make long traverses of these areas as preparation for the long approach marches that have to be made in the South Island.

Three volcanoes rise in the centre of North Island. Tongariro, in the foreground, has several craters; Ngauruhoe is the active cone in the middle distance; Ruapehu, at the top of the photograph, is the highest peak and provides the best climbing and skiing in North Island.

Ngauruhoe erupts violently from time to time. This photograph was taken at night by the light of the eruption.

The South Island

The South Island is about 500 miles long with a clearly defined mountain backbone. The unimaginative name 'Southern Alps' is used for the mountain chain between Arthur's Pass and Haast Pass. The Alps reach their greatest height in Mount Cook (12,349 feet), Mount Tasman (11,475 feet), and Mount Dampier (11,287 feet) in the Navigator Range, where there are some fifteen other peaks over 10,000 feet.

Other high ranges continue to form the backbone of the South Island. In Nelson and Marlborough Provinces are the Tasman and Douglas Mountains, around 5,000 feet, the St Arnaud and Spencer Mountains, where the highest are

Mount Travers (7,671 feet) and Mount Una (7,550 feet); and the Inland Kaikoura and Seaward Kaikoura, whose highest peaks are Tapuaenuku (9,465 feet) and Manakau (8,562 feet).

In Otago and Southland Provinces the chain continues as the Young Range, the Richardson, Forbes, and Humbolt Mountains; and 100 miles south of Mount Cook, one of the island's most attractive mountains stands as a perfect glaciated horn, Mount Aspiring (9,959 feet). The Haast range, in addition to Aspiring, contains some of the most delectable names: Stargazer, Moonraker, Skyscraper, Rolling Pin, and Spike, all named after the highest top-sails of a square-rigged ship.

And lastly, Fiordland, a block of steep mountains embayed by glaciated fjords containing Olivine, Murchison, Stuart, Franklin, and Darran Mountains. The highest peak in Fiordland is Mount Tutoko (9,042 feet) in the Darran Range.

The Tasman Glacier in the Mount Cook National Park is the largest and longest, nearly nineteen miles long; the Murchison and Godley Glaciers are each around eleven miles long. These and other glaciers flow down the eastern side of the Alps to melt into skeiny broad streams which flow across the high tussock-covered plains about 2,000 feet above sea-level. The Southern Alps are generally steeper on their western side, and the glaciers there flow more rapidly and descend almost to sea-level. The Fox and Franz Josef Glaciers cascade for eight miles from 10,000 feet to 600 feet above sea-level, with their main streams flowing through rain forest.

The highest peaks all stand inside the National Park, accessible by road and by light plane with a few hotels and many mountain huts. Over 8,000 feet above Tasman Glacier rises the massif of Mount Cook with its three summits and a summit ridge over a mile in length. To climb all the routes on the massif would involve many years of mountaineering. The most used route to Mount Cook's highest summit is from the Haast Ridge hut over the Grand Plateau and via the Linda Glacier leading directly up the north face. The east face of the mountain is very steep and was climbed direct for the first time in 1962. From the Hooker Valley the west face of the mountain offers various routes leading up to rock buttresses mostly consisting of slatey greywacke. In good weather the 'Grand Traverse' of all three peaks is still one of the finest climbs in New Zealand.

A little over two miles to the north of Mount Cook stands Mount Tasman surrounded by her satellite peaks: 'From every direction it stands out in unique majesty draped in a bridal robe of shimmering white, through which the rocky framework peeps out here and there to reassure one that the vision is not merely a creation of fantasy' (H. E. L. Porter). No route to the summit is easy and all involve long and steep ice climbing. The first west ridge traverse from Mount Torres has recently been made, and more recently still two Austrian guides climbed the east face direct.

Of the other great peaks it is only possible to mention some

Mount Aspiring lies 100 miles to the south of the Mount Cook area. The first ascent, in 1912, was made across the Bonar Glacier in the foreground and by the north-east ridge (facing the camera). The south-west ridge to the right provides a harder alternative.

Mount Torres, and Mount Tasman from the west. Routes from this side are very difficult, requiring long approach marches through forest. The peaks have mostly been attempted from a bivouac in a snow cave.

Grey Peak, on the left, and the ridge leading to Mount Haidinger. The rock tower is seldom climbed since much of the rock in New Zealand is friable and loose.

Mount Green and, to the left, the Minarets. The usual route up Mount Green follows the ice-route directly up the face.

names: Sefton (10,359 feet), La Perouse (10,101 feet), Hicks (10,443 feet), Dampier (11,287 feet), Haast (10,295 feet), Haidinger (10,059 feet), Douglas (10,107 feet), The Minarets (10,022 feet), Elie de Beaumont (10,200 feet), Malte Brun (10,421 feet), and refer the would-be-climber to the records in the *New Zealand Alpine Journal* and the *Canterbury Mountaineer*. These peaks are among the highest and easiest of access. Many hundreds slightly less high and more difficult of access occupy the enthusiasts who seek the remote and enjoy exploration.

The Southern Alps: weather and fauna

The Southern Alps lie between latitude 40°S. and 45°S., which is similar to the northern latitude of the Pyrenees and Caucasus. Their axis lies across the prevailing winds which sweep across the Pacific bringing deluges of snow or rain. The summer snow-line is around 6,000 feet and in winter 3,000 feet. The summer season for climbing starts in December and continues through January and February, and has long had an unfair reputation for very evil weather. Storms do strike suddenly and last for several days, but most seasons also have clear, calm climbing days, and weather records show both a high rainfall and a high number of sunshine hours. Winds, particularly the 'North-wester', can be very strong indeed,

and because of their ferocity climbs taking more than twenty-fours hours are rarely attempted, and attempting climbs which need high bivouacs can put climbers in some very desperate circumstances.

Today the mountain valleys which are not covered with dense forest are used for sheep and cattle grazing since, compared with the European Alps, or even the Himalaya, the valleys are less fertile and much less populated. No mountain villages exist; only the isolated farm buildings consisting of a homestead and, standing apart, cattle or sheep pens, some horses or even a Landrover for mustering, and perhaps a small aeroplane sheltering with a motor-car.

Before the arrival of European settlers, New Zealand had no animals such as deer, bear, or cats (large or small), nor any snakes; it was unique in having only wild bird life. Now all types of mountain animal have been introduced and have become pests: pigs, wild cattle, red deer, Canadian moose, European chamois, and Himalayan thar. Most of the bird life still exists, particularly the hardy mountain parrot–the kea; whereas the flightless weka and takahe are being killed out by weasels and dogs.

There are many varieties of indigenous alpine flora, which are mostly white in colour. The most common are the giant mountain daisy (*celemesia*) and the Mount Cook lily (*ranunculus*).

George Lowe

Australia

Australia has no high mountains; for a continent nearly as large as Europe this is unique. The Great Dividing Range, extending for over 2,000 miles in length and consisting of eroded plateaux ranging from 3,000 feet to 5,000 feet, reaches its highest point in Mount Kosciusko (7,328 feet) in the State of New South Wales. It is a rolling, ragged range of old rocks covered in thorny vegetation and hardy snow-gum trees and there are about fifteen peaks over 5,000 feet. In winter the precipitation of snow is heavy down to 4,000 feet. Skiing is popular with relatively few Australians. Hiking clubs have been formed in the cities and are called 'bush walking' clubs. Rock climbing as a sport has not yet developed.

In South Australia the Flinders Range runs for 400 miles with a maximum height of 3,900 feet. It is a fold range consisting of a curious landscape of mounds and basins which are encircled by ridges of hard quartzite.

The mountains of Western Australia are mainly a series of low, barren sandstone ridges emerging from the desert wasteland. There are a few massifs with bluffs and pinnacles sculpted by the wind. Rocky streambeds and usually dry lakes are found in this forbidding landscape. Mount Bruce (4,014 feet), in the Hammersky Range, is the highest point and lies north of the Tropic of Capricorn.

In the centre of the continent lie the Macdonnell Range, with Mount Ziel (4,955 feet), and the Musgrave Range, with Mount Woodroffe (4,970 feet).

Tasmania

The island of Tasmania, which forms the smallest state, contains the most interesting mountains in Australia. Although only 5,000 feet high, they stand up with crests of considerable character, surrounded by a luxuriant native flora. Four small national parks contain the most attractive areas: Stacks Bluff (5,010 feet), Cradle Mountain (5,069 feet), Mount Ossa (5,305 feet), Frenchman's Cap (4,756 feet), and Mount Field West (4,721 feet). In the south-west of the island lies Federation Peak, which has only recently been climbed and explored.

George Lowe

'Narrowneck', a climbing area in the Blue Mountains, New South Wales. The sandstone cliffs of the Blue Mountains have been the scene of much recent development by a growing fraternity of Australian climbers.

Belougeries Spire in the Warrenbungle Mountains, New South Wales. This 1,100-foot 'plug' of trachyte affords routes of a high standard.

Placing a bolt on 'The Mantleshelf', a Grade V route on the Three Sisters, Katoomba.

11. Mount Cook from the south.

12. The north face of the Grand Teton, Wyoming.

On the first ascent of Ball's Pyramid, a gigantic pinnacle which towers 1,843 feet above the Pacific Ocean some 430 miles north-east of Sydney. After resisting eight expeditions, the Pyramid finally succumbed in February 1965 to a strong party of Sydney climbers. The summit was reached by B. Allen, D. Witham, J. Davis, and J. Pettigrew.

New Guinea

The island of New Guinea lies close to the equator, just north of Australia. Rising above the jungles and swamp lands is the highest island mountain chain in the world, extending about 1,100 miles from west to east. In the Nassau Range in the west of the island stands the Carstensz Pyramide or Carstensz Toppen (16,500 feet), Ngga Poloe (16,400 feet), and Mount Idenburg (15,750 feet). These mountains form a great horseshoe with a large glacier in the centre enclosed by gigantic cliffs up to 10,000 feet high.

Further west in the Oranje Range are the peaks Wilhelmina Top (15,585 feet) and Juliana Top (15,420 feet). West again, in Australia Trust territory in the Bismarck Range, is Mount Hagen (15,400 feet), and, at the far eastern end of New Guinea, is the Owen Stanley Range with the highest point, Mount Victoria (13,363 feet).

The mountains of New Guinea still comprise one of the least-known areas of the world and much of the glaciated area around Carstensz Pyramide remains unexplored. The snow peaks were first discovered in 1623 by Jan Carstensz, but no attempt was made to climb them until 1911, when a British expedition, including Dr A. F. R. Wollaston, set out to reach them. They struggled for a year with rain and the jungle and were defeated after only a fleeting glimpse at the mountains. In 1913 Wollaston returned and reached the snow and ice on the south wall. The south wall defences of Carstensz Pyramide have proved to be the crux of the approach, and this was breached in 1936, after an air reconnaissance by a Dutch expedition led by Dr A. H. Colijn. The party climbed the glaciers and reached the snow peak of Ngga Poloe (16,400 feet), but were defeated by the rocky ridges of Carstensz Pyramide. In 1961 a party of New Zealanders tried to reach the peak from the north and were defeated. Returning a year later, one of the party, P. Temple, joined with Heinrich Harrer and made the first ascent of the mountain.

George Lowe

The Carstensz Pyramide (16,500 feet) is an imposing rock without the easy snow route found on most other peaks in the Carstensz area. It is worthy indeed of being the highest mountain in New Guinea, and in fact the whole Pacific Basin. It was climbed on 13 February 1962 by Harrer, Temple, Kippax, and Huizenga.

Sunday Peak (left) and Ngga Poloe (both *c*. 16,000 feet) here form the crest of the Noordwand. This wall stretches almost unbroken for five miles to the west, and access through it is possible with ease at only two or three points. In the foreground is Lake Larsen (*c*. 12,000 feet). Ngga Poloe was the only peak climbed by the Dutch in 1936 after their approach from the south.

A view from New Zealand Pass of the Basins of Ijomba and the great plateau from which the northern approach to the Carstensz Pyramide is made. The plateau was entirely ice covered in the last ice age and moraines can be traced in the moss forest to a height of 6,000 feet.

A section of the Carstensz Noordwand west of New Zealand Pass, showing its typical formation of easy terrace surmounted by severe face. The ice cap fringes the Noordwand throughout, except in the vicinity of New Zealand Pass.

5
The Mountains of North America

General Introduction

The major summits of North America lie close to the arc of a
great circle which can be drawn from Orizaba, in Mexico, at
the south-eastern end, to Mount McKinley in Alaska, nearly
4,000 miles distant to the north-west. A few hundred miles
east of such an arc are the Colorado Rockies, the Tetons, the
Canadian Rockies and Selkirks, while slightly further to the
western side lie the Sierra Nevada of California and the
Cascades of Oregon and Washington. The great boundary
peaks between Alaska and Canada, including Mount St Elias,
are arrayed along this arc.

In considering so lengthy a system of mountains, which
extends over more than 45° of latitude, it is natural to find
that most mountaineering variables take on a full spectrum of
values. Thus, at the southern end, timber grows above 13,000
feet, permanent snowfields are rare, and mild temperatures
prevail even at midwinter, while at the northern end, trees can
scarcely survive at sea level, heavy snowfalls nourish some of
the world's greatest glaciers, and sub-zero temperatures
should be expected on the high peaks at midsummer. All kinds
of rock are to be found, from the volcanic ash of Mexican and
Cascade volcanoes, the sedimentary strata of the Canadian
Rockies, to the unexcelled granite of the Sierra Nevada, Wind
River Mountains, and Bugaboos. The cliffs of Yosemite can
be reached in an hour's scramble from the highway, while,
on the other hand, countless peaks in Canada and Alaska are
so remote that they have only been approached by aircraft
landing on the near-by glaciers or lakes. Thus North American
mountains cannot be described in general and must be taken
up region by region. We shall begin at the southern end of the
North American Cordillera–in Mexico, where the recorded
history of North American mountaineering had a birth so
separated from its main existence as to scarcely constitute
even a previous incarnation.

Mexico and Popocatepetl

In Mexico the mountains of North America begin nobly with
three great volcanoes which, while not technical mountaineering problems, are of interest in the annals of mountaineering
by virtue of their substantial altitudes and curious histories.
Most easterly and lofty of the three is Pico de Orizaba, or
Citlaltepetl (18,700 feet), the third highest peak in North
America. One hundred miles to the west lie the sister summits
of Ixtaccihuatl (17,000 feet) and Popocatepetl (17,888 feet),
easily reached and visible from Mexico City.

The first ascent of Popocatepetl by the conquistadores of

Popocatepetl, Mexico. First climbed by the conquistadores
of Cortés, when the volcano was still active.

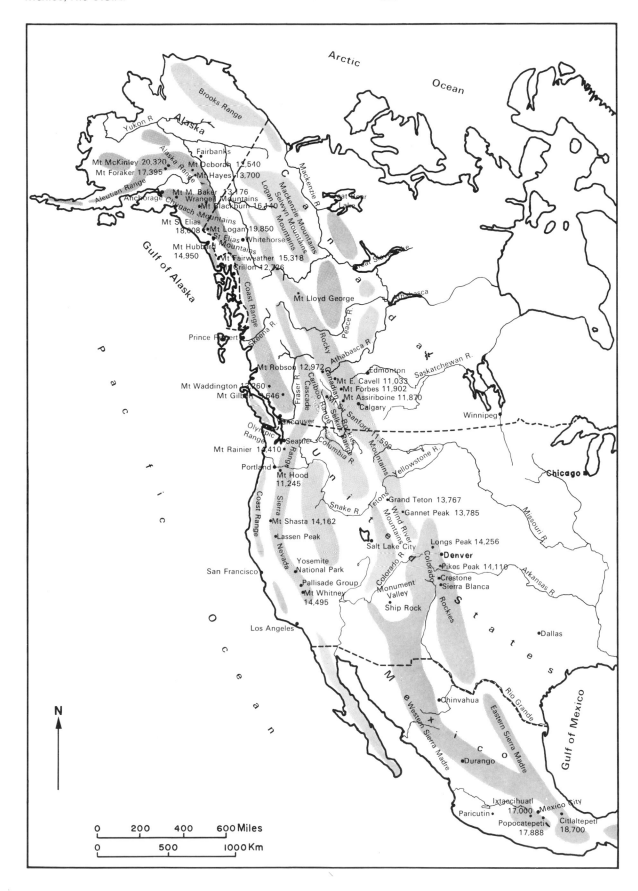

Arctic
Ocean

Brooks Range

Alaska

Yukon R.

C

Mackenzie R.

Fairbanks

Mt McKinley 20,320
Mt Foraker 17,395

Alaska Range

Mt Deborah 12,540
Mt Hayes 13,700

Aleutian Range

Anchorage

Chugach Mountains

Mt M. Baker 13,176
Wrangell Mountains
Mt Blackburn 16,140

Logan Mountains

Selwyn Mountains

Mt S. Elias
18,008

Mt Logan 19,850

St. Elias
Mountains

Whitehorse

a

n

a

d

a

Great Bear
Lake

Gulf of Alaska

Mt Hubbard
14,950

Mt Fairweather 15,318

Mt Crillon 12,726

Mt Lloyd George

Mackenzie Mountains

Great Slave
Lake

Athabasca

Coast Range

Steena R.

Prince Rupert

Rocky

Peace R.

Athabasca R.

Saskatchewan R.

P

a

c

i

f

i

c

Mt Robson 12,972

Mt Waddington 13,260
Mt Gilbert 13,646

Fraser R.

Cariboo
Range
Cascade

Canadian

Selkirk
Rockies

Range

Edmonton

Mt E. Cavell 11,033
Mt Forbes 11,902
Mt Assiriboine 11,870

Calgary

Winnipeg

Vancouver

Olympic
Range
Seattle

Columbia R.

Mt Sanford 11,598

Mt Rainier 14,410

U

n

i

Yellowstone R.

Chicago

Portland

Mt Hood
11,245

Range

Snake R.

Tetons

Grand Teton 13,767
Gannet Peak 13,785

Wind River
Mountains

Missouri R.

t

Sierra

Mt Shasta 14,162

Lassen Peak

Salt Lake City

Longs Peak 14,256

Denver

San Francisco

Nevada

Yosemite
National Park

Pallisade Group

Mt Whitney
14,495

Colorado R.

Colorado R.

Monument
Valley

Ship Rock

Pikes Peak 14,110

Crestone
Sierra Blanca

Rockies

Arkansas R.

a

t

e

s

Dallas

Los Angeles

Coast Range

O

c

e

a

n

M

e

Western Sierra Madre

Chinvahua

Eastern Sierra Madre

Rio Grande

Gulf of Mexico

x

i

c

o

N

Durango

Ixtaccihuatl
17,000

Mexico City

Paricutin

Popocatepetl
17,888

Citlaltepetl
18,700

| 0 | 200 | 400 | 600 Miles |
| 0 | | 500 | 1000 Km |

Cortés is surely a unique landmark in early mountaineering history, but it seems almost natural when viewed amidst the many exploits of these men. It was in 1519, just after the army of Cortés had arrived at Tlaxcala, that one of the captains, Diego de Ordáz, asked to be permitted to investigate the origin of a vast plume of smoke given off by the snow cone of Popocatepetl, then in active eruption. Receiving the approval of Cortés, Diego de Ordáz set out with nine soldiers and some Indian guides. Their afflictions on the mountain were great, as ashes of the eruption rained down on them repeatedly and they reported that at one time smoke began to rush out of the crater with such noise and violence that the whole mountain seemed about to disintegrate. Whether they reached the summit itself is disputed, but we may imagine that they were not greatly concerned with locating precisely the highest point on the crater rim, for indeed the whole mountain seemed then to possess little permanence.

Better authenticated is the exploit of Francisco Montaño in descending into the crater in 1522 to obtain sulphur from the fiery pit. The mountain was still in eruption, and twice during the ascent Montaño and his three men took cover against a bombardment of hot ashes and boulders. Upon reaching the rim, Montaño was lowered a hundred feet down the steep walls, where he found plenty of sulphur. The expedition was a success and carried 300 pounds of sulphur back down the mountain – falling into various crevasses *en route* – to receive a hero's welcome from Indians and Spaniards alike.

After the ascent of Montaño it was judged easier and far safer to obtain sulphur from Spain than from the crater of Popocatepetl and there was no further recorded mountaineering on the continent for more than three centuries. Popocatepetl also slept, active no longer. The mountain was next ascended in 1827, and since then many thousands have climbed to the crater. In 1918 sulphur exploitation began again, but was suspended in 1919 after a disastrous accident. A mass ascent of Popocatepetl is now made each October with nearly a thousand people reaching the crater, and during the season (October–February) ascents are frequent. The Francisco Montaños of today must look to other mountains.

Present-day Mexican climbers have, of course, sought out their sheer crags of sound rock to sharpen technical skills. Near Mexico City, popular rock climbing centres are Las Monjas, Las Ventanas, and Frailes Crag. Further north, longer climbs have been made on the granitic rocks of Peñon Blanco in the Province of Durango while the 1,000-foot cliffs of the Cañon Basaceachic in Chihuahua are still untouched by the climber's piton.

Notable in its own right is also the infant volcano of Paricutín, which sprang from the cornfield of a Michoacan farmer in February 1943.

Eastern United States

Turning now to the United States we must pass over the eastern two thirds in a paragraph. There are no summits in this area which cannot be reached by walking, but several fine cliffs, ranging in height from 200 to 800 feet, offer excellent rock climbing. Particularly popular are the Schwangunks, near New York City, Seneca Rock, near Washington, D.C., and Cathedral and Whitehorse Ledges and Cannon Mountain in New Hampshire. Less well known are the ice climbing and winter mountaineering, especially in Huntington Ravine on Mount Washington. Here steep water-ice and savage weather can combine to stop the most determined climber. On the summit of Mount Washington (6,288 feet) a wind velocity of 231 m.p.h. has been recorded and sub-zero (Fahrenheit) winds of hurricane velocity are common from December to March.

The American South-west: Shiprock

Let us now return to follow the main North American cordillera north from the Mexican border. In the south-western United States the highest peaks are easily ascended, and far more challenging are the numerous vertical spires formed by erosion of jointed sedimentary rock or remnants of volcanic cores. Since the most notable can be scaled only with artificial techniques, usually including expansion bolts, these spires have only recently become of interest to American

Shiprock, New Mexico. Rising 1,600 feet from its base, the summit is the right-hand one of the two. The route is up the back to the large notch to the right of the summit.

climbers. Most of the first ascents have been made only in the last two decades and by climbers trained on such vertical walls as those of Yosemite.

The most prominent of these spires is Shiprock, a castelated tower of rhyolite rising some 1,600 feet above the arid Navajo Indian Reservation in the north-west corner of New Mexico. After many unsuccessful attempts, it was first ascended in 1939 when a group of California climbers pioneered a complicated route through its defences. After two days of preparation, they completed the route with one bivouac. Though Shiprock has now been climbed several hundred times, the original route, now liberally studded with pitons and expansion bolts, has been followed by most parties – albeit with numerous variations. Present parties usually complete the climb without a bivouac, but those forced to spend the night on the rock may be bemused by the throb of Navajo drums rising over the desert. In recent years, some new routes involving extensive artificial climbing have been forced to the summit.

Sandstone towers of Monument Valley and other monoliths of the American south-west are now challenging the modern rock engineer. Many have been ascended, but virgin summits remain in this land of coloured sand and rock and clear air – a land once thought unproductive and largely granted to the Indians, but now yielding oil, gas, and uranium.

It is gratifying to find that the original Americans are profiting from their unexpected wealth, as newly-paved roads, schools, hospitals, and even tribal motels will attest. Visiting mountaineers may note that the region is somewhat warm in summer and climbing most pleasant during spring and early autumn.

The Rockies
The Colorado Rockies
Moving north from New Mexico, we come to the Colorado Rockies, a range of high rock peaks having occasional mountaineering interest. Here are more than forty summits exceeding 14,000 feet, with not one as much as 500 feet higher:

Wind River Mountains, Wyoming. The snow summit to the left is Gannet Peak, and in front lies the Titcomb Lake Valley, with Mounts Helen, Sacajawea, and Fremont to its right. The lakes are at about 10,500 feet, while Gannet Peak rises to 13,785.

this uniform elevation indicating that they are the surviving high-points of a plateau which has been gradually worn away. Most of the summits are easily reached, but a number of the major peaks have steep sides which offer interesting climbs up to 2,000 feet long. Ascents are primarily rock, although pleasant snow routes can be made in spring or early summer.

Best known is the grey granite east face of Longs Peak, which has yielded a variety of routes ranging from the early but rather advanced ascent of the brothers Stettner in 1927 to recent artificial routes on 'the Diamond', a 1,000-foot vertical portion of the face. Good rock climbing has been found on other '14ers', as the 14,000-foot peaks of Colorado are known, notably on the east side of Crestone Needle and Peak, the north face of Sierra Blanca, and north-west face of Capitol Peak. The San Juan Needles of south-western Colorado form an interesting group of narrow arêtes and steep faces, of which many are unclimbed. This region is best approached by a narrow-gauge railway, once used to supply the mines in remote and high valleys and now maintained as a tourist attraction. Not only in the San Juans but throughout the Rockies of Colorado are found mute witnesses to the mining fever which gripped the area from the discovery of gold and silver in the 1860s until largely terminated in the silver crash of 1893. Abandoned mine shafts, deserted cabins, ruined mills, cableways, and ghost towns seem almost a part of the mountains. Some few mines are still actively worked, but the great majority are quiet.

In addition to climbs done on the high Colorado peaks, fine routes have been worked out on the walls of several of the deep river canyons which were cut into the plateau as gradual uplifting took place. The longest climbs are found in the Black Canyon of the Gunnison and the canyon of the Brazos River in northern New Mexico, both of which offer countless routes of 2,000 feet or more on exceptionally sound rock.

The Wind River Mountains
Some 300 miles north and slightly west of the Colorado Rockies we find one of the most delightful ranges in the United States, the Wind River Mountains of Wyoming. The

Maroon Bells, near Aspen, Colorado. The Bells are easily reached from a road up Maroon Creek. The rock is red and rather loose.

Wind Rivers have been formed by the glacial erosion of a great granite batholith roughly seventy-five miles long and twenty miles wide. At its northern end the range reaches its greatest height in Gannett Peak (13,785 feet), and on the flanks of Gannett and its satellites lie the largest glaciers of the American Rocky Mountains. It is likely that Gannett was first climbed by Captain Bonneville in 1833, while in 1842 General Fremont ascended a nearby high peak.

Most peaks of the Wind Rivers are about twenty miles from the nearest road, but once in the high country it is easy and delightful to move about from one group of peaks to the next. The U-shaped valleys, high and open, are dotted with countless lakes, and everywhere the firm granite beckons.

Perhaps the most pleasant month I have ever spent in the mountains was one in the Wind Rivers with two fine companions. Starting at the northern end of the range we worked our way to the southern end, climbing on the way numerous fair summits that caught our fancy. Though this was in 1949, we were able to make first ascents of some good peaks and even to name several of them. It was a trip on which everything went well, even our ten-dollar airdrop of food was successful, the weather was perfect and cracks were found whenever needed; it was, in short, a time of perfect harmony between men and mountains.

The Tetons

A hundred miles further to the north and west, the Tetons rise in one majestic sweep from the sage flats of Jackson Hole. Geologically, the Tetons form a classical example of a tilted fault block, some forty miles long, fifteen miles wide, and at least two miles thick, tilted upwards to the east. The spectacular eastern face of the Teton range thus represents a deeply eroded fault escarpment, while to the west the range falls off much more gradually. In the heart of the range, sound crystalline rock, especially gneiss and schist, offers the climber a vast diversity of holds and piton cracks.

Controversy attends the first ascent of the Grand Teton (13,766 feet). An ascent was surely made by Spaulding and Owen in 1898 following the present Owen route. It is likewise certain that Langford and Stevenson climbed to within 300 feet of the summit in 1872 and possible that they reached the summit as Langford claimed and Owen denied. On the other hand, perhaps the peak was first climbed by a Lieutenant Kieffer and two soldiers in 1893. But whatever the priority of ascent, there is no question that the Grand Teton is now the most popular rock summit in North America. About twenty routes and numerous variations have been identified on the mountain ranging from the sunny and popular Exum Route (the upper south ridge), and the long (4,000 feet) but

The Tetons, Wyoming. Looking across the Snake River and Jackson Hole we view the Tetons from the east. The summit of the Grand Teton is in clouds and the snow cover is typical of that found in June.

21. North Africa: Jebel Toubkal in the Atlas Mountains.

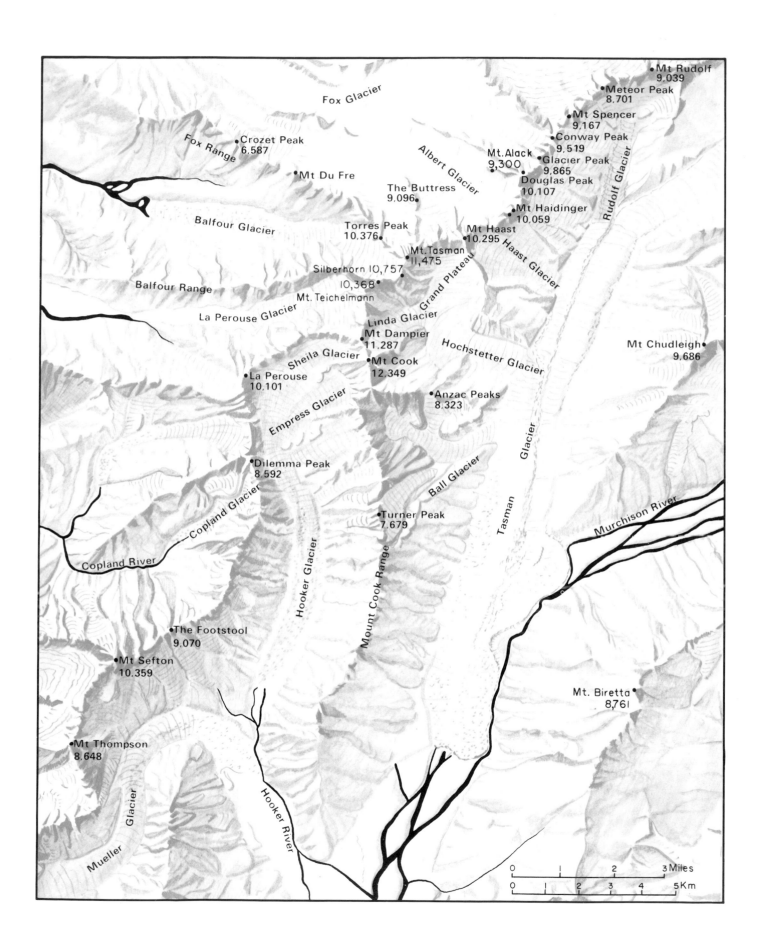

Fox Glacier

•Mt Rudolf
9,039

•Meteor Peak
8,701

Fox Range

•Crozet Peak
6,587

•Mt Spencer
9,167

Albert Glacier

Conway Peak
9,519

•Mt Du Fre

Mt.Alack
9,300•

•Glacier Peak
9,865

The Buttress
9,096•

Douglas Peak
10,107

Balfour Glacier

•Mt Haidinger
10,059

Rudolf Glacier

Torres Peak
10,376•

Mt Haast
•10,295

•Mt.Tasman
11,475

Haast Glacier

Silberhorn 10,757•

Balfour Range

10,368•

Grand Plateau

La Perouse Glacier

Mt. Teichelmann

Linda Glacier

•Mt Chudleigh
9,686

Mt Dampier
•11,287

Sheila Glacier

Hochstetter Glacier

•La Perouse
10,101

•Mt Cook
12,349

Empress Glacier

•Anzac Peaks
8,323

•Dilemma Peak
8,592

Ball Glacier

Copland Glacier

Murchison River

Copland River

•Turner Peak
7,679

Hooker Glacier

Tasman

Glacier

Mount Cook Range

•The Footstool
9,070

•Mt Sefton
10,359

•Mt. Biretta
8,761

•Mt Thompson
8,648

Glacier

Mueller

Hooker River

0   1   2   3 Miles
0   1   2   3   4   5 Km

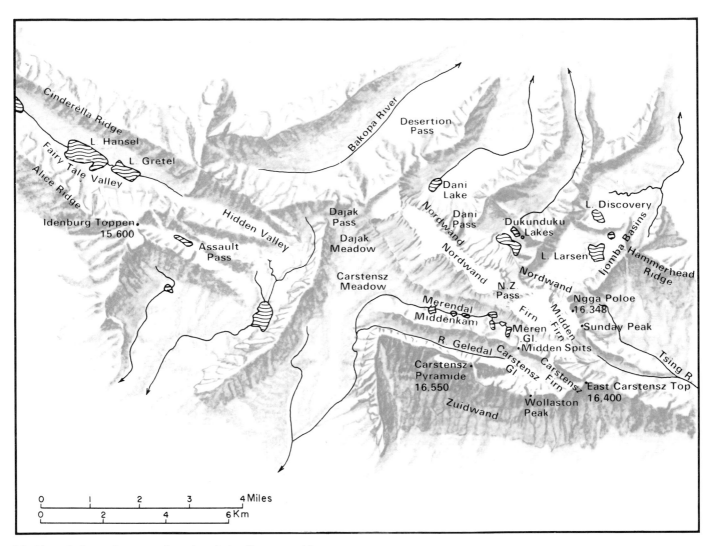

Cinderella Ridge

L. Hansel

Fairy Tale Valley

Alice Ridge

L. Gretel

Idenburg Toppen. 15,600

Assault Pass

Hidden Valley

Dajak Pass

Dajak Meadow

Carstensz Meadow

Bakopa River

Desertion Pass

Dani Lake

Dani Pass

Nordwand

Nordwand

Nordwand

L. Discovery

Dukunduku Lakes

L. Larsen

Ijomba Basins

Hammerhead Ridge

N.Z Pass

Ngga Poloe .16,348

Sunday Peak

Merendal

Middenkam

Meren Gl.

Midden Spits

Midden Firn

Firn

Carstensz Firn

Tsing R.

R. Geledal

Carstensz Gl.

Carstensz Pyramide 16,550

East Carstensz Top 16,400

Zuidwand

Wollaston Peak

0 1 2 3 4 Miles
0   2   4   6 Km

23. New Guinea: the central peaks of the Carstensz Mountains, West New Guinea.

22. New Zealand: the Southern Alps with Mounts Cook and Tasman.

24. North America: the Tetons and the neighbouring peaks including Mounts Owen and Moran.

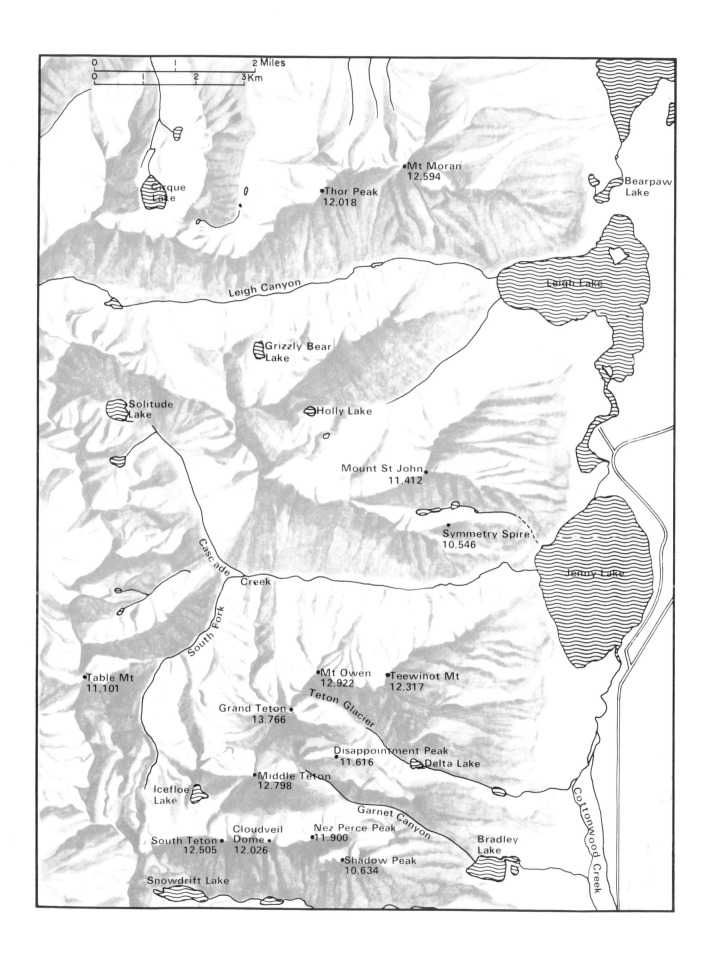

0   1   2 Miles
0   1   2   3 Km

Cirque Lake

•Mt Moran
12,594

•Thor Peak
12,018

Bearpaw Lake

Leigh Canyon

Leigh Lake

Grizzly Bear Lake

Solitude Lake

•Holly Lake

Mount St John•
11,412

Symmetry Spire•
10,546

Cascade

Creek

Jenny Lake

South Fork

•Table Mt
11,101

•Mt Owen
12,922

•Teewinot Mt
12,317

Teton Glacier

Grand Teton•
13,766

Disappointment Peak
•11,616

•Delta Lake

•Middle Teton
12,798

Icefloe Lake

Garnet Canyon

Cottonwood Creek

South Teton
12,505

Cloudveil Dome•
12,026

Nez Perce Peak
•11,900

Bradley Lake

•Shadow Peak
10,634

Snowdrift Lake

moderate east ridge, to the often icy north ridge (first climbed by R. L. M. Underhill and F. Fryxell in 1931) and the dark precipices of the north face (overcome by the famous Teton guide, P. Petzold, in 1936 with J. Durrance).

Of the major Teton summits, Mount Owen is the most difficult. It was not gained until 1930, by Underhill, K. Henderson, Fryxell, and P. Smith—a strong party of Teton pioneers. Worthy also is bulky Mount Moran with its 'frightening to look at but easy to climb' C.M.C. route, and the difficult south ridge, which, rising over 5,000 feet, provides one of the longest roped climbs in the United States. Finally, petite Symmetry Spire (10,546 feet) ranks, after the Grand Teton, as the most popular climb in the Tetons, offering several convenient and interesting rock routes on its south face.

The Teton range lies within Grand Teton National Park and the park officials have established regulations with which mountaineers in the area must comply. In particular, climbers must register for each intended ascent and must then report their return within some designated time. In compensation for these sometimes galling constraints, climbers should note that the park maintains a staff of experienced climbing rangers who each summer rescue injured mountaineers from some of the peaks.

The Tetons are one of the few mountain areas in North America where professional guides are regularly available during the season, including in recent years W. Unsoeld, L. Ortenburger, and D. Pownall. The only other areas which feature guided climbing are Mount Rainier, Washington (likewise in a National Park), and the Banff–Lake Louise region of the Canadian Rockies. Not only are there almost no guides in North America, but there are few huts or facilities catering for climbers. The best hut system is that of the Appalachian Mountain Club in the White Mountains of New Hampshire, a range of little interest to mountaineers. There are a few huts in the Sierra Nevada of California and the Cascades of Washington, and some facilities in the Canadian Rockies. But, as a general rule, American climbers are accustomed to carrying their own camping and sleeping equipment into the mountains and serving as their own guides.

North of the Tetons is Yellowstone National Park—a high timbered plateau, famous for its geysers and bears, best visited during June or September to avoid the peak concentration of tourists. Further north there are few challenging summits until one approaches the Canadian borders in Glacier Park. These peaks, however, are best treated as the southern extension of the Canadian Rockies, which will be described later. Instead, let us turn our attention to those summits closer to the Pacific Coast of the United States—the Sierra Nevada with Yosemite, and the Cascades.

Sierra Nevada and Yosemite

The Sierra Nevada is a massive continuous range in California, overall roughly 400 miles in length and forty miles wide. The peaks of primary interest are found in the southern third, from Mount Whitney in the south to somewhat north of Yosemite National Park. Only a few small glaciers remain in the Sierra, but the landscape shows evidence of heavy glacial erosion with steep cirques, U-valleys, and myriad lakes. The range is tipped slightly upwards to the east so that the highest peaks lie near its sharp eastern edge. From Owens Valley, which borders the Eastern Sierra for eighty miles, the mountains rise as a broken wall up to 10,000 feet high.

Many Sierra summits were reached for the first time on solitary ascents by such rugged individualists as J. Muir, C. King, and more recently Norman Clyde, veteran of some thousand Sierra ascents.

The High Sierra attracts climbers because of its sound granite, beautiful valleys, and stable summer weather. Among the most popular ascents are several routes on the east face of Mount Whitney, which at 14,495 feet is the highest mountain in the non-Alaskan United States, but unfortunately has a horse trail to its summit. More Alpine climbing is found in the Palisades group, which includes a number of straggling glaciers and five summits over 14,000 feet. Further north, the Minarets offer good climbs on metamorphic rock and the scenic delight of graceful spires reflected in calm water.

But it is on the sheer walls of Yosemite Valley, carved from primordial granite by glaciers long since gone, that American climbers have gained a deserved reputation for severe and sustained rock ascents. It might be questioned whether, in a discussion of mountaineering, such climbs of canyon walls deserve emphasis. However, in recent years the 'Valley climbs', as they are familiarly known, have established a new standard of excellence for American technical rock climbing which can be scarcely ignored. The unique character of Yosemite climbs arises from the structure of the rock—glacier polished, exfoliated, devoid of horizontal cracks and handholds; all ascents must follow vertical crack systems—chimneys, jam cracks, vertical piton cracks, and where no cracks appear the Valley climbers must drill holes in the hard granite and place expansion bolts. The superb rock plus dependable weather conditions combine to make the most difficult ascents almost devoid of objective danger.

Californians were first introduced to technical rock climbing by R. L. M. Underhill in 1931. Their technique advanced rapidly, and during the 1930s routes were established on the more reasonable looking Yosemite walls and towers. By the 1940s Yosemite climbers were applying their skills in such first ascents as those of Shiprock and Snowpatch in the Bugaboos, Canada. Finally, by the late 1940s, they were ready to attempt the sheer 2,000- to 3,000-foot faces. The first such ascent was made by J. Salathe and A. Nelson in 1947 with the direct five-day climb of the Lost Arrow from the valley floor. Similar faces were scaled during the next ten years, culminating in the ascent in 1958 of the direct south face of El Capitan, a 3,000-foot vertical to overhanging buttress of sheer granite.

(*Above*) The 10,000-foot eastern face of the Sierra Nevada from Owens Valley. On the right, Mount Whitney (14,495 feet).

(*Below*) Yosemite: Looking straight down the nose of El Capitan on Camp VI with the ground 2,500 feet below.

(*Above*) Sky, granite, and man. Approaching the summit overhangs on the nose of El Capitan.

(*Below*) Yvon Chouinard leading the difficult pendulum pitch on Mount Watkins, Yosemite.

The ascent, by W. Harding, G. Whitmore, and W. Merry, required forty-five days of effort, spread over a period of a year and a half. Three thousand feet of fixed rope, 675 pitons, and 125 expansion bolts were placed.

Several similar ascents have been made more recently in Yosemite, but more and more Valley climbers, such as Royal Robbins, Tom Frost, and Yvon Chouinard, are travelling to employ their formidable technique on such challenging North American rock problems as the south-western pinnacles (e.g. the Totem Pole), Bugaboo faces, the Logan Mountains, and other walls further afield.

The Cascades

Moving northwards from Yosemite, we would encounter such high volcanic peaks as Mount Shasta (14,162 feet) in northern California and Mount Hood, near Portland, Oregon. Highest and most interesting of the Pacific volcanoes is Mount Rainier, which at 14,410 feet is frequently seen dominating the horizon from Puget Sound. Rainier is a huge dormant volcano and steam vents are active at the summit crater. It supports twenty-eight glaciers on its flanks, including the six-mile-long Emmons Glacier, the largest in the United States (outside Alaska). While many of the glacier routes are comparatively easy, others, such as the Nisqually icefall, comprise difficult and dangerous ice ascents. The rock is generally so friable that rock routes are unpleasant or hazardous.

Northwards from Mount Rainier to the Canadian border, a distance of some 150 miles, lie many interesting summits of the Cascades range. These peaks, though seldom over 10,000 feet, receive heavy snowfall which sustains hundreds of small glaciers, and they afford the best ice and snow climbing in the United States (again excepting Alaska). Frequently the rock is also sound, so that a variety of fine mountaineering routes has been worked out in the Cascades. The deep narrow valleys, particularly on the western coastward side, are choked with rain forest, but roads and trails approach many of the best peaks, such as those around Cascade Pass, also Mounts Shuksan and Stuart. Other peaks, such as the Picketts in the North-Cascade Primitive Area, are difficult to approach and seldom visited. The Cascades form a splendid playground for the many mountaineers of the Seattle–Tacoma area, a region which has produced more all-round mountaineers, competent both on steep snow and rock, than any other in North America. Among them we must mention F. Beckey, the indefatigable seeker out of difficult first ascents and new routes throughout North America with hundreds to his credit, and P. Schoening, the superb expedition climber.

Across Puget Sound from Seattle the Olympic Peninsula is crowned by the compact Olympic Range. The Olympics

(*Right*) Climbing the fourth pitch of the North American wall, one of the most difficult routes on El Capitan.

boast heavy precipitation and extensive glaciers, but most of the summits are not difficult to climb.

Mountains of Southern Canada

Turning now to the mountains of southern Canada, namely those lying within about 300 miles of the United States–Canada border, we find that they may be divided into three main groups. Near the Pacific Coast we have the Coast Range of British Columbia, while some 300 miles east and parallel to the coast are the Selkirks and Purcells, with, separated from these by the great Rocky Mountain Trench, the Canadian Rockies. Each of these three regions must be described at some length. We shall start with the Selkirks, for there mountaineering in Canada had its beginning; indeed, there began mountaineering in the Alpine sense in North America.

Selkirks and Purcells

The Selkirks and Purcells, together with the Monashee and Cariboo Ranges, are known as the Interior Ranges of British Columbia to distinguish them from the Coast Range. On the east they are bounded by the Rocky Mountain Trench, one of the great geological features of North America. Extending some 800 miles north-north-west from Flathead Lake in northern Montana, the Trench contains in turn several major rivers, including the Kootenay, Columbia, Canoe, and Fraser. The several Interior Ranges are separated from one another by other valleys which need not concern us here.

Major summits of the Interior Ranges are 10,000 or 11,000 feet in height, glaciers reach down to about 5,000 feet, and the lower valleys, particularly in the northern portions of the ranges, are trackless with large streams and rain forest, tortuous slopes of slide alder rendering access to many of the finest summits uncertain and difficult. It is a paradise for the grizzly bear, still virtually unmolested by man.

The Selkirks presented a great barrier to westward travel in Canada, but when the Canadian Pacific Railway was finally completed to cross the Selkirks through Rogers Pass in 1885, that region became for a time the centre of mountaineering in North America. A hotel, Glacier House, was constructed by the railway at Glacier (4,100 feet) just west of the pass, and near by rose some of the most tempting peaks of the southern Selkirks. The spectacular quartzite pyramid of Mount Sir Donald (10,818 feet) rose nearly 7,000 feet above the hotel, while slightly further south lay the snowy Dawson and Purity groups–both over 11,000 feet. Substantial glaciers lent an Alpine foreground to the peaks. Indeed, the Illicillewaet Glacier was then a prominent spectacle from the railway, and from Glacier House, although it has since receded from view.

In 1888, the Rev. W. S. Green of the Alpine Club made several ascents and began a survey of many of the peaks. By 1890 Selkirk mountaineering was off to a lusty start; that year saw the ascent of Sir Donald by E. Huber and C. Sulzer of the Swiss Alpine Club, and H. Cooper, and the ascent of Mount Purity. During the next few years several first ascents were made by Professor C. Fay and associates from the Appalachian Mountain Club. In 1899 the first Swiss guides were installed at Glacier House, E. Feuz Sr and C. Hasler, and a new era of climbing began in the Selkirks. The Swiss guides played a prominent part in the subsequent climbing both in the Interior Ranges and the Canadian Rockies.

The peaks near Glacier remain the most popular in the Selkirks, perhaps primarily because they are the only ones that are easy to get to. While Glacier House, having twice burnt down, was abandoned in 1928, and the Canadian Pacific no longer maintains tourist facilities near Rogers Pass, the opening of a highway across the pass in 1962 with a camping-ground at Glacier recently further stimulated climbing in the Southern Selkirks. The most popular route is the classic north-west arête of Sir Donald, a narrow crest of sound quartzite which rises 2,700 feet from the Uto–Sir Donald Col.

Some thirty miles north-north-west of Glacier, the Selkirks culminate in massive Mount Sir Sanford (11,590 feet). Even today, Sir Sanford is difficult to reach. Three days of arduous back-packing, much through dense, mosquito-infested bush, is roughly a minimum (unless a helicopter is used): while, when Howard Palmer made his five expeditions to the mountain (1908–12), a canoe journey on the Colombia River preceded and followed the back-packing. The peak itself is a great domed block of limestone which carries a glacier on its north-west flank that was used as the dangerous first ascent route by Palmer and Holway, together with the guides R. Aemmer and E. Feuz Jr. That route, with variations which greatly enhance its safety by avoiding a long traverse below ice cliffs, has been used by most succeeding parties.

Of even more interest to mountaineers is the immediately adjacent Adamant massif, a heavily glaciated granitic intrusion into the heart of the Selkirks. Slightly more accessible than Sir Sanford, the Adamants offer a great variety of fine routes on firm rock and snow. Parties organized by S. Hendricks and W. Putnam were accomplishing first ascents there as recently as 1953. The area is now generally reached by helicopter.

Turning now to the Purcell Range we must concentrate our attention on the Bugaboos. Boasting superb crystalline granite, the Bugaboos provide some of the finest rock climbing in North America. The first ascent of Bugaboo Spire in 1916 was made by the great guide C. Kain, together with A. H. MacCarthy, Mrs MacCarthy, and J. Vincent. While not a severe climb by modern standards, some difficulties are encountered in surmounting the sheer 'great gendarme'. It has become customary to relate that here Kain jammed his ice axe in a crack overhead, which he then used as an essential hold, but upon reading Kain's own account we find that the ice axe, far from being essential, was a great nuisance.

Two major Bugaboos, namely Snowpatch Spire and the South Tower of Howser, yielded only in 1940 and 1941 respectively to the efforts of climbers versed in the employment

Mount Rainier, Washington. The massive and heavily glaciated character of this volcanic peak is here evident.

Mount Fury, Washington. This shows the north face of the East Peak, first climbed in 1938. Mount Fury (8,288 feet) is one of the principal peaks of the Pickett Range in the Northern Cascades.

Mount Olympus, Washington. This shows the west and highest summit of Mount Olympus (7,954 feet). The Olympic Mountains, lying across the storm paths of the prevailing westerly winds, receive some of the heaviest precipitation in North America.

Adamant Massif, Selkirks, British Columbia. The central peak is Mount Adamant, and at the right is Mount Austerity. The north face is here shown. Adamant was first climbed from the south by Howard Palmer's party in 1912.

Bugaboos, Purcell Range, British Columbia. The approach by logging road and trail leads up the lateral moraine to 'Boulder Camp' in the highest timber. In the centre of the picture is Snowpatch Spire, and, joined to it on the right, Bugaboo Spire. Behind and between is Howser Spire with the South Tower to the left.

13a. Bugaboo and Snowpatch Spires in the Purcell Range, British Columbia.

13b. The south-east face of Mount Hunter, Alaska.

Valley of the Ten Peaks, Canadian Rockies. Moraine Lake is easily reached by road from Lake Louise.

Mount Robson, Canadian Rockies. The north face, rising from Berg Lake, was first climbed in 1963.

14a. Popocatepetl (17,888 feet) seen from the lower slopes of its sister peak Ixtaccihuatl.

14b. Typical vegetation of the Sierra de Santa Marta with tall 'frailejon' (*Spelethia glossophilla*) and the peaks of El Guardian and La Reina from above the Mamancanaca Valley.

Mount Robson, Canadian Rockies. The highest peak in the Canadian Rockies, Robson (12,972 feet) was first climbed by this, the east face. The prominent snow slopes were followed with much step cutting.

of ironware. In the past few years, Yosemite-like routes have been established on many of the steepest Bugaboo faces.

The Canadian Rockies

The Canadian Rockies, which, as we have noted, lie just east of the Interior Ranges and are separated from them by the Rocky Mountain Trench, form an extended line of sedimentary peaks with some fifty summits above 11,000 feet and the highest, Mount Robson, at 12,972. Broad valleys, frequently containing beautiful lakes, with sheer stratified walls combine to create spectacular scenery of block-shaped, massive peaks rising from a flattish foreground. Most of the major summits, from Assiniboine in the south-east to Robson, over 200 miles north-west, are located in the Canadian National Park system, and some of the finest are easily reached from highways. It is generally easier to travel about in the valleys of the Rockies than those of the Selkirks, at least on the eastern side of the Rockies, in as much as the valleys are broader and the vegetation far less heavy. The summer weather, while sometimes fair for long periods, is, as in the Selkirks, more commonly described as unsettled.

As in the Selkirks, shortly after the completion of the Canadian Pacific Railway, European climbers began to visit the Canadian Rockies. Together with Swiss guides, they effected many first ascents in the early 1900s, of which, as an outstanding example, we may mention the ascent of Mount Assiniboine in 1901 by Sir James Outram with the guides Bohren and C. Hasler. By 1905, American climbers were actively seeking out ascents in the Rockies. Gradually the Canadian Pacific Railway transferred its efforts from Glacier to Lake Louise as a guided climbing centre.

Mount Robson was the object of various attempts from 1908. The ascent was finally made in 1913 by A. H. MacCarthy

Waddington Massif, Coast Range, British Columbia. From left to right on the skyline are Mount Waddington (13,260 feet) and Mounts Combatant, Tiedemann, Asperity, and the five summits of Mount Serra. The most popular current route on Waddington comes almost directly towards the camera.

and W. W. Foster with Kain via the east face and south-east ridge, a difficult and dangerous route which has seldom been repeated. Indeed, during many seasons Robson is not climbed at all because of adverse snow conditions, and the same can be said of many of the major snow ascents in the Canadian Rockies.

A unique first ascent was that of Mount Alberta in 1925 by six Japanese climbers together with three Swiss guides. Their record on the summit: 'on 21st July 7.35 PM, after sixteen hours strenuous climbing, we nine got the top of Mt Alberta. Guides Mr H. Fuhrer, Mr H. Kohrer, as their kind helper Mr J. Weber (SAC), these three gentlemen so kindly helped us. Our party six in number Y. Maki, S. Hashimoto, T. Hayakawa, Y. Miti, N. Okase, M. Hatano (JAC), We came from Japan called so far by this charming great mountain.'

Many of the major peaks of the Canadian Rockies are climbed only infrequently and numerous fine routes have yet to be done. A general reputation for unsound rock and treacherous snow combined to discourage many after the first ascents had been made. More recently, however, good rock climbs have been found, such as on the north face of the Tower of Babel and east faces of the Ramparts. Difficult new routes are also being made on major peaks, including the 'Wishbone Arête' and 'Emperor Ridge' on Mount Robson and the north face of Mount Edith Cavell. The Rockies thus still provide worthy challenges to the ambitious modern climber.

The Coast Range of British Columbia

The Coast Range of British Columbia comprises a wilderness of peaks stretching some 200 miles north-west from Vancouver. The coast is here deeply indented by a number of fjord-like inlets. Heavy precipitation leads to a dense rain forest abounding with the noxious thorny devil's club. The rivers are large also and it is hard to move about in the country – except on the glaciers. Until the use of aeroplanes, each trip into the Coast Range was a veritable expedition.

The Coast Range culminates in a splendid group of granite mountains around Mount Waddington, a group which in many ways resembles the Mont Blanc massif. While Waddington itself is but 13,260 feet in height, the massif nourishes at least five valley glaciers over ten miles long, which terminate below 3,000 feet. The relief is thus substantial and the range boasts unclimbed 5,000-foot faces.

The exploration of the Waddington area began only in 1926 when D. and P. Munday organized the first of several expeditions to penetrate the Coast Range from the sea, and in 1928 they succeeded in reaching the north-west summit of Waddington. In 1933 they joined forces with H. Hall Jr for an overland approach down the Homathko River, and once again they reached the north-west summit–only about 100 feet lower than the main summit, but connected by an 'impossible arête'.

Waddington was finally climbed in July 1936 by F. Wiessner and W. House. First they had to contend with the usual difficult back-packing approach from Knight Inlet, eight miles through the rain forest to the snout of the Franklin Glacier at 500 feet and then twenty miles up the glacier to the south face. Here they worked out a complex route, exposed to considerable rockfall.

In 1952, a Sierra Club party flew into the Coast Range, landing on Dumbell Lake near the snout of the Tellot Glacier, and they established a new route on Waddington from the north-east. This approach and route have been followed by most subsequent groups to Waddington.

In visiting the Waddington area, one is struck by its similarities to the massif of Mont Blanc as regards the structure and character of the mountains; but how dissimilar these regions are in facilities for mountaineering. The Coast Range has neither trails, huts, nor guides, and is visited even now by only a score or so climbers each year. Innumerable superb unclimbed routes, and even a virgin summit or two, remain in the Coast Range–one of North America's finest climbing areas.

Logan Mountains

Before turning to the major peaks of the Canada–Alaska border, reference must be made to a small range in central western Canada, the Logan Mountains. These are a range of the Selwyn Mountains lying along the border between the Yukon and North-West Territories. First visited by mountaineers in 1952, the range proved to be predominantly sound and vertical granite. Though the summits do not exceed 10,000 feet, they nevertheless offer long and difficult climbs. In 1963 a strong party of American rock experts forced a route, thereby completing what they authoritatively characterized as the 'most difficult Alpine climb yet done in North America'. This promised to be the first among many such ascents.

Alaska and the Yukon

We turn now to the mountains of Alaska and those of the Canadian Yukon near the border with Alaska. Indeed, a number of the important summits must be said to lie both in Canada and Alaska, since between about latitude 56° and 60° 20′ N. the boundary is defined by drawing straight lines between major summits, including Mounts Fairweather, Vancouver, and St Elias. Major peaks are surrounded by great glacier systems, and in the St Elias Mountains are some of the world's largest glaciers outside the Polar regions, including the eighty-mile-long Hubbard Glacier. Summits having the greatest importance for mountaineers are found in the Alaska Range, culminating in Mount McKinley (20,320 feet); and the St Elias Mountains, crowned by mighty Mount Logan (at 19,850 feet the second highest peak in North America), and including the rugged Fairweather Range at its south-eastern end. Also of interest to mountaineers are the Alaska Coast Range (along the lower Alaska–British Columbia border) and the Chugach Range, while fine climbs have also been made in the Wrangell Mountains and the Brooks Range in the north. While all the highest peaks are well known and have been climbed, most have been done by only a few routes, usually the easiest, and many smaller peaks offering worthy challenges to the modern mountaineer remain even to be explored.

In the history of Alaskan and Yukon mountaineering, the early expeditions to the giants St Elias, McKinley, and Logan stand apart and merit first consideration.

Mount St Elias

The 18,008-foot summit of Mount St Elias lies but thirty-five miles from the sea. Hence this beautiful pyramid was the first of the giants to be discovered by western explorers and the first to be ascended. Observed and named by the Russian navigator Vitus Bering in 1741, Mount St Elias was attempted by mountaineers in the 1880s. On the second of two expeditions, in 1891, Professor I. C. Russell attained an altitude of about 14,500 feet on the north-east ridge, which rises from Russell Col. Then, in 1897, the Duke of the Abruzzi led his powerful expedition to the summit. The Duke followed essentially the same route as that pioneered by Russell on his first expedition. Crossing the Malaspina, Seward, and Agassiz Glaciers, the Duke's party then ascended the heavily crevassed Newton Glacier from the east of St Elias and climbed to Russell Col at the end of the north-east ridge. From the col, at about 12,300 feet, they made the long snow ascent to the summit in a single day without technical difficulty. The expedition occupied a fifty-day round trip from the coast–mostly spent in bad weather, carrying or hauling loads in deep snow across and up the glaciers.

The second ascent of Mount St Elias was made in 1946 by a Harvard Mountaineering Club party, including Putnam, Miller, Mr and Mrs Kauffman, Latady, Ferris, and the brothers Molenaar. They landed at Icy Bay and climbed the south-west ridge, which proved somewhat more difficult than the Duke's route, but shorter and more direct. A number of air drops of food enabled all members of the party to concentrate on climbing the mountain. Nevertheless, nearly a month was consumed in the long ascent to the summit. For St Elias, like the other giants of the St Elias Mountains and the Alaska Range, is a peak of Himalayan proportions. While the problems of altitude are only slight, incessant bad weather and heavy snowfalls add difficulties peculiar to the Alaskan mountains. As a most extreme example of this, in 1958 a climber on St Elias suffocated in a tent which had been buried by a blizzard. It may be added that severe earthquakes are frequent in Alaska and while the author is not aware of any mountaineering fatalities attributed to the earthquakes, a number of routes have been drastically altered by such shock activity and a number of exceedingly narrow escapes have occurred. The third and fourth ascents of Mount St Elias were made in 1964 and 1965; the latter followed the fine northwest ridge.

Mount McKinley

When it became generally known around the end of the nineteenth century that Mount McKinley was the highest summit in North America, men of all kinds were, of course, attracted by the desire to be the *first* to climb it. Among those so motivated was Dr F. A. Cook, who claimed to have made the ascent accompanied by E. Barrille on 16 September 1906. While Cook no doubt carried out some difficult explorations, his 'ascent' is now generally regarded as pure fiction.

The famous 'Sourdough Expedition' of 1910 was partly an attempt to disprove the fictions of Dr Cook, but unfortunately the organizer, Lloyd, improvised a few of his own. At home in the Alaskan wilderness, the sourdoughs regarded their attempt on McKinley as simply a long mush. Carrying a wood-burning stove for cooking, they spent much time returning to the flats to hunt cariboo and moose and to obtain firewood. They used home-made ice axes and crampons. From a camp at 11,000 feet, below what is now known as Karstens Ridge, they prepared the ridge above, chopping and re-chopping steps into a tremendous 4,000-foot staircase. Finally, in one continuous 8,500-foot climb (slightly encumbered by a fourteen-foot spruce flagpole), two of the men, P. Anderson and W. Taylor, reached the North Summit (19,470 feet), near which they erected the flagpole, hoping that it would be seen by their friends in Fairbanks. Although the story was subsequently embroidered by Lloyd so that the whole exploit became suspect for a time, sighting of the flagpole by the 1913 first ascent party clearly authenticated the sourdoughs' amazing achievement.

In 1912 the South Summit (20,320 feet) was nearly reached by H. Parker, B. Browne, and M. LaVoy before they were forced to turn back in a furious storm. Their candour in clearly stating that they did not reach the summit, though perhaps but a few score feet below, seemed to restore the customary atmosphere of integrity to mountaineering on McKinley. Finally, in 1913, the highest point in North America was attained by H. P. Karstens, H. Stuck, W. Harper, and R. Tatum. Both of these parties followed a route including McGonagall Pass, Muldrow Glacier, and Karstens Ridge, and this route was followed by subsequent parties until 1951.

In 1947, Washburn published a series of his remarkable photographs in the *American Alpine Journal*, suggesting a variety of new routes on Mount McKinley's west and north sides. By now every one of these has been climbed and it is certainly appropriate that the first of these new routes, the West Buttress, was climbed by Washburn's party in 1951. This has proved to be the most popular route on the mountain. It is certainly the shortest, safest, and easiest. Further routes followed in quick succession.

In 1954 an important traverse of McKinley was made by Argus, Thayer, Viereck, and Wood. Profiting from unusually good weather, they ascended the lengthy South Buttress to reach the South Summit. During the descent on Karstens Ridge, the party fell several hundred feet. Thayer was killed and only after a major rescue operation was the injured Argus brought down. Also in 1954 a Wilson and Beckey party made the first ascent of the difficult west ridge of the North Peak – just north of the West Buttress.

In 1959 the western rib of McKinley's south face was ascended by four Teton guides, while in 1961 Riccardo Cassin led a powerful Italian party directly up the middle of the south face, a climb of over 10,000 feet at an average angle of nearly fifty degrees. Much of the technical climbing on the frozen granite which forms the core of the Alaska Range would have been a joy were it not for the McKinley weather. Also in 1961, a Canadian party completed the ascent of Pioneer Ridge, just west of the Muldrow Glacier. In 1962 the south-east spur was climbed, and in 1963 rather dangerous routes were pioneered on the East Buttress up the centre of the difficult Wickersham Wall, and at the western edge of the Wickersham Wall. In 1965 a Japanese party established a direct route up the South Buttress, while in 1967 American climbers completed a difficult and dangerous route up the centre of the south face. By 1964 at least a dozen quite distinct routes on McKinley had been climbed, and though all the great ridges have now been won, many challenging 'variants' and faces remain to tempt the experienced and hardy climber.

(*Above right*) Mount McKinley from the south-east. The great gorge of the Ruth Glacier is in the foreground. The South Buttress forms the skyline left of the South Peak, and from it the South-east Spur comes towards us.

(*Right*) Mount Huntington, Alaska Range. This exquisite 12,240-foot peak, just south of Mount McKinley, was first ascended by a French party under L. Terray in 1964 – an ascent made difficult and dangerous both by technical problems and bad weather.

North America's highest peak has been a rich source of mountaineering inspiration.

Mount Logan

The third of the giants, Mount Logan, lies thirty miles north-east of Mount St Elias. The largest mountain in North America, and one of the largest in the world, it rises to an immense plateau above 17,000 feet, over ten miles long and defended on most sides by gigantic cliffs around 10,000 feet high – an exciting playground for tomorrow's mountaineers.

The ascent of Mount Logan in 1925 was the most arduous feat of mountaineering to be undertaken in North America, a Himalayan effort without coolies or porters. Captain A. H. MacCarthy and H. F. Lambert were the leaders, and their party included Carpé, Foster, Read, A. Taylor, Hall, and Morgan. The attempt began in February 1925, when Taylor and MacCarthy, driving dog teams during the Yukon winter, began to lay out a chain of supplies towards the base of Logan. Early in May the rest of the climbers assembled at McCarthy, Alaska, for a long walk – first 100 miles with pack horses, then eighty miles further on up the Logan and Ogilvie Glaciers to King Col, and thence to the summit plateau. Mountaineering difficulties were few, but labours were great. Even above King Col, sixty- to seventy-pound packs were common. As the party approached the summit plateau, they became fully aware of the curse of its vastness. Blizzards threatened alternately to bury or to rip down their seven-foot tents, and the deep snow rendered advance or retreat equally painful. Finally, on 23 June, six reached the central and highest summit.

Their retreat across the summit plateau was a desperate ordeal. Half the party became lost and benighted in a snow storm, only by luck finding their high camp. Afflicted with frostbite and snowblindness, with supplies running out, they then abandoned the high camp to struggle across the plateau in a raging storm. Another night without shelter was passed before the safety of lower camps could be reached. Of such things are the satisfactions of mountaineering sometimes compounded.

Logan has now been climbed by several other and technically more challenging routes. The first of these was the long east ridge, ascended to the East Peak in 1957 by an American party. More recently, ridges have been ascended on several sides of Logan, including Independence Ridge on the north, Catenary Ridge from the north-east, Hubsew Ridge from the south-east, and the spectacular Hummingbird Ridge from the south. This great peak has become increasingly popular as the long overland approach can be avoided by landing ski-equipped aeroplanes on the lower glaciers.

Fairweather Range

At the southern end of the St Elias Mountains lies the rugged Fairweather Range, a region of steep peaks and extensive

Mount Logan, Yukon. Mighty cliffs bound most of the summit plateau, here seen from the north.

Mount Fairweather and Margerie Glacier from the north-east. Mount Quincy Adams is at the left.

glaciers close to the ocean, named by Captain James Cook in 1778. Though Cook may have found the climate there fair, most mountaineers would choose another title for this range, which customarily enjoys the foulest of weather. Mountaineering reconnaissance of Mount Fairweather itself (15,318 feet) began in 1926, and in 1931 the summit was reached by Carpé and Moore, following a steep ridge on the southern side. Other notable ascents in the range have been those of Crillon (12,726 feet) by Washburn, Carter and Holcombe in 1934, and a fine route on Mount Bertha (10,182 feet) by a Washburn party in 1940. The southernmost major summit, La Perouse

(10,728 feet), was reached by the United States Geological Survey in 1952, and Mounts Lituya (11,950 feet) and Quincy Adams (13,650 feet) were ascended in 1962. Though the peaks are not high, there remain many challenging virgin Fairweather summits, but the region is cursed by terrible weather and high potential earthquake danger.

Mount Lucania and other St Elias Mountains

In the St Elias Mountains, most of the major summits have now been reached. The ascent of Mount Lucania in 1937 by Washburn and R. Bates was peculiarly eventful. This was the first expedition where aircraft landings on a glacier were used successfully for bringing in climbers and their equipment at high altitude (8,750 feet). But shortly after Bates and Washburn had been landed on the Walsh Glacier, a prolonged and unseasonable rainstorm moved in to prevent the pilot's take-off. For five days and five nights the rain fell, so deteriorating the glacier surface that the pilot was barely able to get his plane off and could not bring in the rest of the expedition. So Bates and Washburn, stranded, albeit with fifty days' food and an abundance of equipment, decided that the best plan for walking out would be to attain a route followed by the Wood Yukon Expedition of 1935. But this could be done only by climbing to the summit of Mount Steele (16,644 feet), which had been ascended by the Wood party, and thus traversing the mountain. In heavy weather, Bates and Washburn advanced their camps towards a saddle between Mounts Lucania and Steele. Since trail-breaking in the snow, which fell freshly each day, was the hardest work, they adopted

the strategy of advancing camps only a short distance (typically two miles) so that several relays could be made each day on a somewhat packed trail. From the saddle they were able to take advantage of good weather to climb Lucania (17,147 feet) and then to traverse Steele, whence the Wood route was followed for over 100 miles to civilization at Burwash Landing.

Mount Bona (16,421 feet), at the northern end of the St Elias Mountains, was climbed by Carpé and Moore in 1930. A series of expeditions organized by W. A. Wood Jr, and under the auspices of the American Geographical Society and/or the Arctic Institute of North America, carried out a number of ascents including, in 1941, Mount Wood (15,885 feet) and Mount Walsh (14,780 feet), in 1949, Mount Vancouver (15,700 feet), and in 1951, Mount Hubbard (14,950 feet). Increasing advantage of air support was taken by these expeditions to reduce preliminary labour and expense.

Far greater technical climbing difficulties were found by two parties making the first and second ascents of King Peak adjacent to Mount Logan in 1952. Both a Thayer party, ascending the north face and west ridge, and a Schoening group on the east ridge encountered interesting problems.

Other major St Elias summits which have been climbed include Mounts Augusta, Bear, Cook, MacArthur Peak, and Natazhat.

Alaska Range

Mount Foraker (17,395 feet), second highest summit of the Alaska Range, was climbed in 1934 by C. S. Houston,

(*Right*) Mount Hayes, Alaska Range. The beautiful north ridge, coming towards us, was the route of ascent by the Washburn party.

Mount Foraker, Alaska Range. The ridge followed by the Houston party is that entering the photograph at the middle of the right side.

Unloading equipment from an aircraft in the Ruth Amphi-theatre, Alaska Range, a favourite starting-off point for expeditions, and becoming increasingly popular with airlifted skiers, who can use a small hut which has been built at one edge of the Amphitheatre. The pilot is Don Sheldon, whose skill at operating ski-planes in difficult situations is legendary.

A camp on the Tokositna Glacier during the approach to the south side of Mount Hunter (14,570 feet) by B. Biven and T. Smythe in 1968. Snowshoes are virtually essential on Alaskan glaciers.

Mount Deborah, Alaska Range. This is part of the spec-tacular Hayes group, 100 miles east of McKinley. The Beckey—Harrer route of 1954 followed in part the ridge left of the summit.

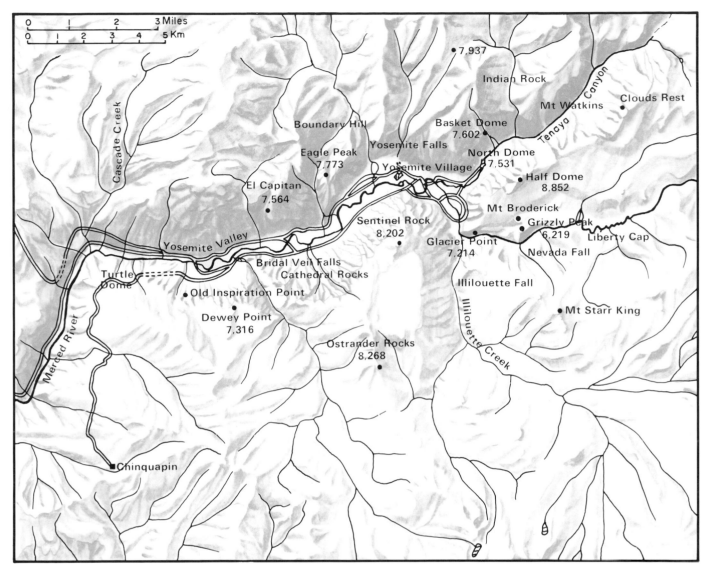

25. North America: the Sierra Nevada showing the Yosemite Valley.

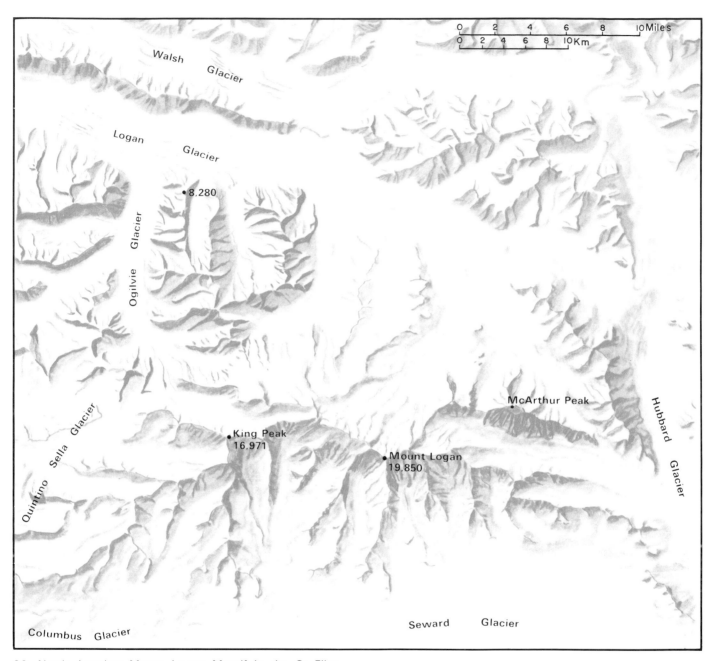

Walsh Glacier

Logan Glacier

•8,280

Ogilvie Glacier

Quintino Sella Glacier

McArthur Peak

King Peak
16,971

Mount Logan
19,850

Hubbard Glacier

Columbus Glacier

Seward Glacier

26. North America: Mount Logan Massif in the St Elias
Mountains.

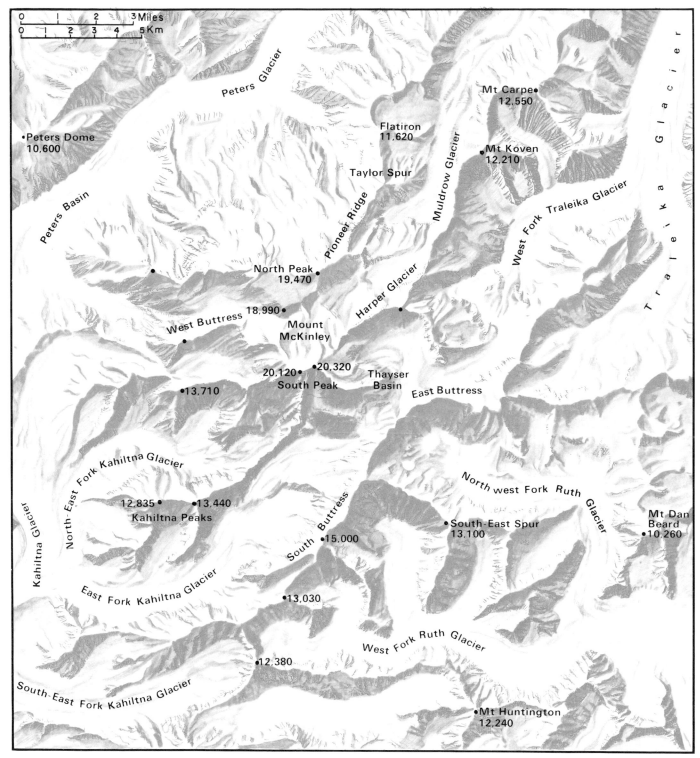

27. North America: the Mount McKinley massif in the Alaska
Range.

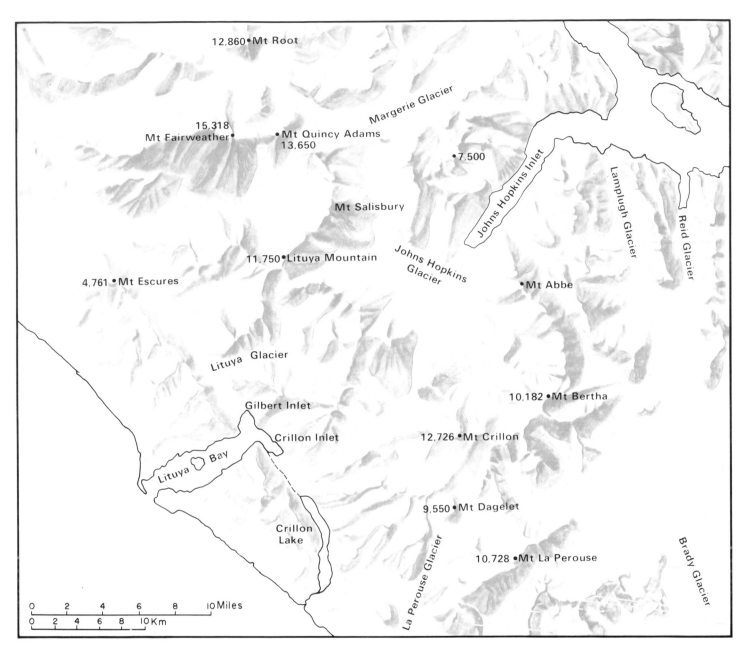

12,860•Mt Root

Margerie Glacier

15,318
Mt Fairweather•   •Mt Quincy Adams
                        13,650

•7,500

Johns Hopkins Inlet

Lamplugh Glacier

Reid Glacier

Mt Salisbury

11,750•Lituya Mountain

Johns Hopkins
Glacier

4,761 •Mt Escures

•Mt Abbe

Lituya Glacier

Gilbert Inlet

10,182 •Mt Bertha

Crillon Inlet

12,726 •Mt Crillon

Lituya Bay

9,550 •Mt Dagelet

Crillon
Lake

Brady Glacier

10,728 •Mt La Perouse

La Perouse Glacier

| 0 | 2 | 4 | 6 | 8 | 10 Miles |
| 0 | 2 | 4 | 6 | 8 | 10 Km |

28. North America: the Fairweather Range in the St Elias
Mountains including Mounts Quincy Adams and Crillon.

T. Graham Brown, and C. Waterston, following an interesting ridge on the north-west side. A second ascent and spectacular new route was completed only in 1963 by a party organized by A. Carter.

One hundred miles east of Mount McKinley, the Alaska Range rises to a series of beautiful summits culminating in Mount Hayes (13,700 feet). The north ridge of this elegant peak was attempted by an O. Houston party in 1937 and finally ascended by a party led by Washburn in 1941. Here, too, Mounts Hess and Deborah have also been climbed, the latter by F. Beckey, H. Harrer, and H. Meybohm in what the climbers characterized as the 'most sensational ice climb' they had ever made. The same party later made the first ascent of Mount Hunter (14,570 feet) near McKinley, following a steep and corniced ridge. In the same region, Mount Huntington (12,240 feet), a splendid and difficult peak, was first climbed by a French party under L. Terray in 1964, while a second route, via the west face, was ascended by a Harvard party in 1965.

Other Alaskan Ascents

Climbing in the Chugach Mountains was begun in 1938 when a Washburn party ascended the highest Chugach, now known as Mount Marcus Baker (13,250 feet). While technical difficulties were avoided on this ascent, as is frequently possible in the Chugach Mountains, there are plenty of problems for those seeking them. Unfortunately the beautiful Chugach

Devil's Thumb, Coast Mountains, Alaska-Canada. The first ascent of this difficult peak was made in 1946 by Beckey, Craig, and Schmidtke.

Mountains have the worst weather in Alaska–some of the worst in the world.

Highest of the Wrangell Mountains, Mount Sanford (16,208 feet) was also reached in 1938 by Washburn and Moore. They descended on skis as Wrangell summits are generally quite skiable. Much earlier Dora Keen and her husband-to-be, G. W. Hardy, made the first ascent of the beautiful Mount Blackburn (16,140 feet) in 1912.

The Coast Mountains, along the border between lower Alaska and British Columbia, have yielded a number of good ascents to Fred Beckey and others. Ascents of Kate's Needle (10,002 feet) and the Devil's Thumb (9,077 feet) by Beckey, Craig, and Schmidtke in 1946, and climbs of the Devil's Paw and Michael's Sword from the Juneau Icefield by a Beckey and Putnam party in 1951, may be mentioned as outstanding examples of Coastal ascents.

Thus the mountains of Alaska, some gigantic, some precipitous and several both huge and steep, have offered a variety of mountaineering challenges to climbers not only from North America but throughout the world. Although all the big peaks have now been climbed, many in the Alaska–Yukon region still remain to be pioneered.

George Bell

6
The Mountains of South America

Introduction

The Andes are the succession of ranges on the western side of South America stretching from latitude 11°N. to latitude 26°S. Covering 4,000 miles of latitude, the mountains offer striking differences, but, structurally like the Alps and the Himalaya, they are fold mountains. Unlike these areas, however, the Andes have been less intensely folded, and the resulting structures are less complicated. No large-scale thrusting seems to have occurred, like the nappes of the Alps, and where thrusting is present the horizontal displacement is relatively slight. The folding is usually symmetrical, and overfolding when it is present is more often found on the eastern limb of folds. The sedimentary rocks are mainly of lower Cretaceous age and consist of both argillaceous and arenaceous rocks largely of terrestial origin. In the Cordillera Blanca of Peru, the succession is closed by a fossiliferous marine limestone. The western sections are often obscured by recent alluvial deposits, but on the eastern flanks of the range there is evidence of Palaeozoic rocks.

Vulcanicity has apparently played an important role. The 6,600-foot south face of Huascarán, the highest mountain in Peru, is, for example, made up of a continuous succession of volcanic material. The products of vulcanicity offer a complete range of rock types: pyroclasts are represented by tuffs, ignimbrites, and agglomerates, while the lavas comprise dacites, andesites, and rhyolites as well as the more common basic types. Volcanoes are still active in three main regions: Ecuador and southern Colombia, southern Peru to the Atacama desert, and south of Tupungato to the interior of Patagonia.

The present geomorphology of the range is largely attributable to Quaternary glaciation. The glaciers and the snow-line generally seem to be retreating throughout South America, so the upper parts of the valleys are left rocky and barren and the mountains themselves are ringed with polished glaciated slabs.

The Andes of Venezuela

The Venezuelan Andes are arranged in three elevated chains. These are the Sierra de Norte and the Sierra de Santa Domingo, sometimes known collectively as the Central Highlands, and the Sierra Nevada de Merida. The Central Highlands support a cover of tropical forest up to a height of about 6,000 feet, and although they have no permanent snow cover, they do receive considerable amounts of snow during the rainy season. From the mountaineering point of view, those of the Sierra Merida

are much more attractive. The highest peak is Pico Bolívar (16,410 feet), and together with the other high peaks in the range, supports small glaciers and a permanent snow cover. The lower slopes up to 3,000 feet are known as the Tierra Caliente and are forested. The tropical forests give way to the Tierra Templada, where the main settlements are situated, and finally to the Tierra Fria, where only potatoes and wheat can be grown. Although the climbing in the Merida range has not attracted any large expeditions, the ease of access, particularly the *téléférique* from Merida to Pico Espejo, has made this a mountaineering playground for Venezuelan residents and for groups from the southern states of the U.S.A. Climbing was first introduced into the Sierra Merida by W. Sievers and F. Engel in 1885 and in 1887, but it was not until 1962 that El Vertigo (16,088 feet), the last of the unclimbed pinnacles of Pico Bolívar, was climbed by J. A. Vzcategui, D. Nott, and G. Band by a route of Grade V.

The Andes of Colombia

The Andes of Colombia are distributed in two parallel ranges running roughly north to south, called the Cordillera Central and the Cordillera Oriental. Besides these is the Sierra Nevada de Santa Marta, a somewhat isolated massif to the north of the main chains. A number of smaller isolated volcanic peaks exist at the southern end of the Cordilleras. The highest peaks compare quite favourably with the heights of other peaks throughout the Andes, and range from Pico Colón (18,947 feet) in the Santa Marta group, to Nevado Alto Ritacuba (17,926 feet) and Nevado del Ruíz (17,180 feet) of the Cordilleras Oriental and Central respectively. For the mountaineer, however, they are in many ways less attractive, and although access is good the snow-line, at about 16,000 feet, means that snow-caps and glaciers are relatively small. The climbing season is during the first three months of the year.

The history of climbing in Colombia does not date back as far as in other Andean regions, the first ascents being made in 1926 with the ascent of Nevado de Tolima (16,733 feet) in the Cordillera Central. German expeditions continued to take an interest in the area and were joined in 1939 by an American expedition. The Americans had been inspired by the reports of T. D. Cabot, who in 1930 had seen snow-covered peaks while on a Caribbean cruise. Both the German and American expeditions were satisfied by climbing the two highest peaks, both of equal height: the Germans climbed Pico Bolívar (18,947 feet) on 2 February and the Americans Pico Colón on 16 March. Since the Second World War most of the remaining peaks have been climbed by American, Italian, and German climbers.

The Andes of Ecuador

Like the Andes of Colombia, the ranges in Ecuador are arranged in two parallel chains running roughly north and south, the Cordilleras Oriental and Occidental. To the southwest of the latter is the lower range of Llanganate. The main chains are most famous for their two volcanoes, Chimborazo (20,563 feet), in the Cordillera Occidental, and Cotopaxi (19,350 feet), in the Cordillera Oriental. From 1745 to 1818 Chimborazo was regarded as the highest mountain in the world.

The climbing season is during the dry periods of June to September, but there is a secondary dry period during December; this is followed by the rainy season, which reaches its height in March and April and is accompanied by a prevailing easterly wind blowing from the moist Amazon plain.

As early as 1802 Alexander von Humboldt recorded an ascent of Pichincha (15,718 feet), but the earliest ascent recorded in Ecuador was that of a Spaniard, Toribio de Ortiguera, who in 1582 is credited with the ascent of Pichincha. Not surprisingly, the two large volcanoes attracted early expeditions. Between 1736 and 1744, Bouguer and C. de la Condamine climbed Corazón (15,718 feet) and Pichincha, and can justly lay claim to being the first great scientific expeditions to the high mountains. In 1802 Humboldt attempted Chimborazo, but it was left to Edward Whymper, with the guides J. and L. Carrel, to make the first ascent in 1880. Cotopaxi was climbed by A. Escobar and W. Reiss in 1872, but the highest point, an aiguille on the crater rim, was not climbed for certain until 1957. More technical rock climbs are now being undertaken on some of the larger south faces. The south face of Altar (17,450 feet) was climbed by the Italians F. Gaspard, M. Tremonti, and C. Zardini in 1963. This provided a Grade V climb and required the use of pitons. Although the Ecuadorian Andes are unlikely to attract large expeditions, there is undoubtedly much rock to be pioneered and it is likely that local climbers will be left with these pioneering problems.

The Andes of Peru

In spite of intensive climbing during the last two decades, Peru can still be regarded as the least well-explored of the Andean Cordilleras; there are several ranges not included on current maps. In the north is the Cordillera Blanca, closely followed to the south by the Cordillera Huayhuash and then the Raura–Guaico group. East of Lima there is an ill-surveyed region sometimes referred to as the Cordillera Central, which is composed of the Viuda, Huagaruncho, Nevados de Cochas, Huaytapallana, and Cerro de Pasco groups. Further south still, the main chain of the Cordilleras split to form two equally important continuations: the volcanic peaks of the Cordillera Occidental and the complex group around and to the south of Cuzco known as the Cordillera Oriental. The latter is made

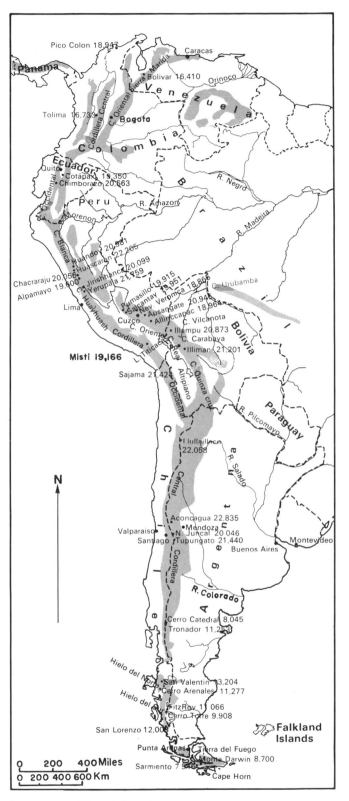

The ranges of South America.

up of a number of isolated *nudos*, or knots, of great beauty. These are the Vilcabamba, Urubamba, Vilcanota, Carabaya, and finally the Apolobamba, which runs into the north of Bolivia.

Peru can in many ways be regarded as the centre of the Andes. Culturally, it was the base from which the Inca Empire engulfed the surrounding tribes, and throughout its Cordilleras there is constant evidence of the megalithic work undertaken by this great civilization of the New World. Climatologically, it forms a transition between the equatorial zones of Colombia and Ecuador and the arid zones of the Atacama desert in the south. But most important are its mountains, which on the evidence provided by the number of international expeditions must rank among the most attractive mountains of the world. In addition to the Cordilleras, other physical features help to make up the geography as a whole. Of these the most important is the Altiplano. Like the same region in Bolivia, this is bounded by the Oriental and Occidental Cordilleras to east and west and in the south by Lake Titicaca. Throughout the Peruvian Andes agriculture is primitive; the staple diet of potatoes is supplemented by maize and yucca in the lower and more favourable parts of the Cordilleras. Many peons live permanently at a height of 16,000 feet, where they scratch a living by growing potatoes and rearing llamas. In the highest regions they are a sullen people often under the influence of coca, a drug which enables them to carry heavy loads painlessly and for long periods without food or rest. They are not generally, however, much less temperamental than the llamas which form the alternative means for expedition transport.

Cordillera Blanca

This Cordillera has attracted more expeditions than any other region of Peru. The reasons for this are threefold. Access to the Blanca is relatively simple and roads lead up from Lima to high mining camps to the south-west of the main range. The climbing season is long and good weather can normally be expected from May to mid August. The most important reason, however, is that these peaks provide some of the world's most exacting snow and ice climbing and the peaks themselves are among the most attractive to be found anywhere. Huascarán is the highest mountain in the Blanca as well as the highest in Peru. It has two summits, of which the southern is the higher (22,205 feet) while the northern peak is 21,834 feet. In 1908 Annie Peck claimed to have climbed the northern peak with the guides Gabriel zum Taugwald and Rudolf Taugwalder. Setting off from Yungay she established camps on the south-west flank up to a final camp on the col between the north and south peaks (the Garganta) and ascended the south-east ridge to the summit. The first ascent of South Peak, the true summit, was made by the 1932 German expedition led by P. Borchers. Their route lay up the west face to the Garganta, passing a difficult icefall on the way. They also

A Peruvian woman feeding her child in the main street of Sicuani.

found the characteristically unconsolidated snow of the north-west ridge very taxing. This expedition also climbed Nevado Chopicalqui (20,998 feet), Nevado Huandoy (North Peak) (20,981 feet), Nevado de Copa (20,351 feet), and Nevado Artesonraju (19,766 feet) in the same season. In 1939 an Austrian expedition repeated the Peck route to make the first undisputed ascent of Huascarán north peak. Like the history of climbing on Aconcagua, the story of Huascarán closes with routes on the great south face. In 1958 an American expedition climbed the south face, and in 1959 a New Zealand party made a new route directly up to the Garganta.

Throughout the history of climbing in the Blanca, German and Austrian expeditions have played a significant role, and they were particularly active in the years before the Second World War. During the war there was a break of activity, but in the 1950s mountaineering was revived with increased activity. Americans now took the field in this area, and Leigh Ortenburger in 1951 and 1952 climbed the East Peak of

Cordillera Carabaya, Peru: on the first ascent of Huaynaccapac (18,955 feet). The summit is to the left of the photograph. Behind are Huaynaccapac II and, in the far distance on the left, Allinccapac II and on the right Allinccapac I (19,930 feet).

On the first ascent of Huaynaccapac II. The mountain was climbed by two routes simultaneously: the north-west ridge and the west face.

A camp at 17,000 feet at the foot of the serious difficulties on Tococcapac (18,504 feet).

Taulliraju (18,940 feet).

Huascarán (22,205 feet), the highest mountain of Peru and one of the earliest ascended. In 1908 Annie Peck is said to have climbed the lower northern summit. The first ascent of the south peak was in 1932.

Huandoy (19,685 feet) and made the third ascent of Nevado Pisco Oeste (19,000 feet). At this time the Peruvians themselves were starting to take a keener interest in mountaineering, and in addition to making second ascents of many peaks, also made some first ascents. By 1956 the reputation of the Blanca had grown to the extent of attracting expeditions from other countries and one of the great unresolved problems was the ascent of the last 6,000-metre peak, Chacraraju (20,056 feet). This fell to a strong French team consisting of Lionel Terray, M. Davaille, C. Gaudin, R. Jenny, M. Martin, R. Sennelier, and P. Souriac. This west peak of Chacraraju had been attempted previously by both German and American teams. Terray himself regarded this climb as the most difficult ice climbing of his career. The final assault involved twenty-six hours of continuous climbing. In 1963 Terray again returned to Chacraraju and climbed the east peak by the north-east face and the north spur, together with Guido Magnone, L. Dubost, P. Gendre, and J. Soubis. This route was then thought to have been the most difficult yet undertaken in the Andes and was equipped throughout with fixed ropes. In 1965 an American expedition, again led by Ortenburger, made the second ascent of Chacraraju Oeste by a new route up the north ridge. It is perhaps significant that what was generally regarded as the most formid-

Huandoy (20,981 feet).

Cordillera Blanca, Peru: Chacraraju (20,056 feet). First climbed by a strong French expedition in 1956, it has subsequently been climbed by successively more difficult routes: in 1963 by the French again, and in 1965 by an American party.

able of the high peaks of the Blanca should be one of the few mountains which has been climbed by three quite independent routes. This reflects the modern trend of Peruvian mountaineering. Gunther Hauser led a strong German team from Stuttgart in 1957, his most notable ascents in the Blanca being Alpamayo (19,600 feet) and the Pyramide de Garcilaso (19,297 feet). Alpamayo, although not high by Blanca standards, stands out as a supreme example of a typical Andean mountain. It has

The south-west face of Alpamayo (19,600 feet) in the Cordillera Blanca.

been called the world's most perfect mountain – a perfect trapezoid of fluted ice. Not surprisingly, Alpamayo had drawn the attention of German climbers as early as 1948, but they failed on the north ridge when a cornice collapsed. In 1951 a Franco-Belgian expedition climbed the north peak by the north-west ridge, but the true summit was reached by Hauser by way of the even steeper south ridge. Garcilaso had also been attempted by Germans in 1955, and again by George Band's British expedition in 1956. The final seal was set on climbing in the Blanca by the ascent of Nevado Cayesh (18,770 feet) by the New Zealand expedition of 1960, described as an almost impossible pinnacle of ice. In spite of such intensive climbing, there still remain five peaks over 19,000 feet and five over 18,000 feet which are unclimbed. These, together with innumerable new routes, seem to guarantee the popularity of climbing in the Blanca for many years.

Cordillera Huayhuash
The first recorded climbing in the Huayhuash was by the Germans in 1936, when E. Schneider and A. Awerzger climbed Nevado Siula (20,841 feet). It was not until the American expedition in 1950, led by Harrah, climbed Yerupaja (21,759 feet), the third highest mountain in Peru, that the full potential of this region was appreciated. In 1954 an Austrian expedition climbed nine of the main peaks, and in 1957 another Austrian expedition, including Toni Egger, visited Jirishhanca (20,099 feet). Known as the Matterhorn of Peru, the Quechua translation of 'Humming-bird beak of ice' is a

much more accurate description. Rondoy, another great problem which had been attempted by Walter Bonatti, finally fell to a relatively inexperienced British team. In 1966 there still remain in the Huayhuash five peaks of 19,000 feet and about thirty lesser peaks which have not been climbed. Like the Blanca, the climbing potential of this region is by no means exhausted.

Cordillera de Raura and Cordillera de Viuda
On the whole these are lesser ranges than the giants of Peru. Most of the important peaks of the Raura group were climbed by the 1957 Austrian expedition, and those of the Viuda group have been mainly climbed by members of the Club Andinista Cordillera Blanca.

Nevas de Cochas
The highest peak, Nevado Tullujuto (18,886 feet), was also the first to be climbed in 1938. Nevado Tunshu (18,725 feet) was eventually climbed by M. Emslie and W. Wallace in 1958, having witnessed the death of three German climbers in an avalanche in 1939.

15a. A camp on the west ridge of Pumasillo in the Cordillera Vilcabamba, Peru.

15b. Cordillera Darwin, Tierra del Fuego. A view from the head of Brooks Bay, which cuts deeply into the northern flank of the range.

Huagaruncho group

The Huagaruncho group is a compact region of granite peaks dominated by Nevado Huagaruncho (18,799 feet). In 1938 P. W. Long and W. F. Jenks made a reconnaissance of the south-west ridge. Again, in 1940, Jenks looked at the south-east ridge, but it was left to the 1956 expedition of J. Kempe with J. Tucker, J. Streetly, G. Band, and M. Westmacott to reach the summit by the west ridge.

Cordillera Occidental

The Cordillera Occidental consists of volcanic peaks which, from the climbing point of view, are unexacting. It was the custom of the Incas to bury their dead on these elevated peaks, but as early as 1901 Wagner, a mine manager, had climbed Nevado Chacani (19,972 feet) in search of Inca treasure, only to find that the grave had already been rifled. The highest peak, Nevado Coropuna (21,702 feet), was climbed by Hiram Bingham in 1911. Misti (19,166 feet), the volcano dominating the town of Arequipa, has a meterological station on its summit, a dependence of the Harvard College Astronomical Observatory.

Cordillera Vilcabamba

It was again the highest peak in the Cordillera Vilcabamba which first attracted mountaineers. In 1911 Hiram Bingham visited the region on archaeological work, and in 1946 A. Heim made an attempt on Pic Soray (18,961 feet). The first ascent, however, was on Salcantay (19,951 feet), the highest of the Vilcabamba peaks. On 5 August 1952 three ropes reached the summit of Salcantay: G. I. Bell and F. D. Ayres; D. Michael and W. V. Graham Matthews; and Mde Claude Kogan and Bernard Pierre. The Americans returned to the Vilcabamba in 1956, when they climbed Lasunayoc (19,029 feet), Nevado Colpachinac (18,045 feet), and three lesser peaks. In the same year George Band had made a brief reconnaissance and had climbed two small peaks, made an attempt on the north ridge of Nevado Choquetacarpo (18,111 feet) and brought back reports of Pumasillo (19,915 feet). In the following year, the Cambridge Andean Expedition, led jointly by S. G. McH. Clark and J. H. Longland, climbed Pumasillo by the west ridge. Surveying by the Cambridge group inspired a large Swiss expedition under the leadership of Ruedi Schatz to visit the Vilcabamba in 1959. They climbed most of the remaining large peaks, including Nevado Cabeza Blanca (19,488 feet), Nevado Choquetacarpo, Nevado Camballa (18,767 feet), and Nevado Panta (18,603 feet), as well as ten smaller peaks. In

Cordillera Vilcabamba, Peru. A section of artificial climbing on ice during the first ascent of Pumasillo (19,915 feet).

1963 Sacsarayoc (19,800 feet) and 'Mitre', the peak to the north of Pumasillo, were both climbed by a New Zealand expedition. Thus, in the space of only seven years, all the peaks in this relatively remote and unexplored region had been climbed. Publicity given to successful expeditions in mountaineering journals and their wide circulation makes this snowballing pattern of mountaineering exploration the general pattern in many Peruvian areas.

Cordillera Vilcanota

Like the Vilcabamba, the Cordillera Vilcanota is an isolated massif to the south-east of Cuzco. First visited by Piero Ghiglione in 1952, the region did not come into prominence until the expedition of H. Harrer, H. Steinmetz, F. März, and J. Wellenkamp in 1953. The two highest peaks, Ausangate (20,945 feet) and Nevado Colquecruz (20,049 feet), were both climbed, together with five lesser summits. In the same year, Piero Ghiglione climbed Nevado Colquepunco (19,751 feet). In 1957, the strong team of Gunter Hauser's from Stuttgart and an American expedition from Harvard were both so active that they climbed twelve of the main peaks. In common with other regions, the Vilcanota benefited from a post-war boom in mountaineering so that there are now no peaks unclimbed, although, as in all the other regions, there remain innumerable new routes to be done.

16a. Peaks of the Staunings Alps, East Greenland.

16b. The Sentinel Range, Antarctica, from the west, showing Mount Shinn and the Vinson Massif.

(*Above*) Cordillera Veronica de Urubamba, Peru. Nevado Cancán (16,650 feet) and Chainapuerto (*c.* 17,000 feet).

(*Below*) Veronica, or Padre Eterno (18,865 feet), as seen from the east.

Cordillera Carabaya

Surrounded by arid Altiplano country, the Carabaya is a perfect example of a *nudo* or isolated massif. It was visited first by geological expeditions, and in connection with this work G. Francis of the British Museum Expedition climbed Japuma (18,141 feet) in 1954. In 1955, H. Katz undertook glaciological work in the Quenamari district and climbed Nevado Quenamari (19,193 feet). The Quenamari ice sheet is a unique relic of the former extensive Pleistocene glaciations. In the same year Ghiglione climbed Yanaloma (20,048 feet). In 1959 a second British Museum Expedition visited the same area, but was unable to make any ascents. It was left to the Oxford Andean Expedition in 1960, led by K. I. Meldrum, to make the ascents of Allinccapac (18,964 feet), the dominating peak of the group. The expedition also climbed Nevado Huaynaccapac (18,955 feet), Tococapac (18,504 feet), and Juracapac (18,350 feet). In 1965 another British group, from Keele University, made some technically difficult ascents in the north-west of the range. There remain at present about four peaks of 18,000 feet which are unclimbed: 'Trident', 'Cornice Peak', 'Wedge Peak', and 'Incacapac'.

Cordillera Urubamba

Situated to the north of Cuzco, Nevado Veronica (18,865 feet) looks down on the gorge of the River Urubamba and dominates the whole range of the Cordillera Urabamba. Veronica was climbed by Egeler and de Booy in 1956. This opened up the way for an Italian expedition in 1958, which climbed eleven of the other peaks.

Lake Titicaca on the Peru—Bolivia border. The lake, high on the Altiplano, forms an important link between Puno on the Peruvian side and La Paz in Bolivia. The lake is famous for its large trout and for the primitive fishermen whose culture and economy is based around the lake.

The Andes of Bolivia

The most northerly of the Bolivian ranges is the Cordillera Apolobamba which is divided by the border between Bolivia and Peru. The peaks continue east along the ridge of the Cordillera Munecas, a lesser range, and turn south when joining the Cordillera Real on the eastern shores of Lake Titicaca. In the south the Cordillera Real terminates in Illimani (21,201 feet). The Andes continue southwards with the Cordilleras of Quinza Cruz and Santa Vera Cruz and the Cordillera de los Frailes. The latter merges with the volcanic cones that form the Puna or Cordillera Occidental of southern Bolivia. On the eastern side of Bolivia the only mountains with Andean characteristics are the Cocapata or Tunari group. In spite of the mountains, the most distinctive geographical feature of Bolivia is the Altiplano, a high plateau between 12,000 and 15,000 feet, 500 miles long and in places more than 150 miles wide. Formed of arid alluvial deposits, the area supports little vegetation. To the north it is bounded by the fresh water lake of Titicaca and to the south by the salt water lake and marshes of Poupo. The dominant race in the Altiplano are the Ayamaras, who together with the Quechuas eke out a meagre existence rearing llamas and alpacas in much the same sort of way as they must have done 500 years ago under the rule of the Incas. As a race, the natives fear the highest mountains, which were venerated as gods, and many of them are still disinclined to go beyond the snow-line, perhaps for fear of meeting the Hualapichi, a sort of elusive Abominable Snowman, no trace of which has ever been found by mountaineers. The most favourable months for climbing are June and July, a period which is usually one of drought; the heaviest rains occur during the southern hemisphere's summer.

Cordillera Real

The Cordillera Real is the most significant of the Bolivian ranges with five mountains over 20,000 feet. Rising abruptly

from the towns of Coroico and Inquisive at only 4,700 feet, it presents a mountain aspect which has often been compared to the celebrated view from Darjeeling. To the east a system of parallel valleys (*jungas*) drain into the River El Beni of the Oriente. In the Cordillera Real the snow-line is rather higher than in Peru and reflects a lower rate of precipitation in this region. Although the snow-line is at about 18,000 feet, the glaciers above this point are typical of the tropical Andes; huge cornices precariously cap ice-fluted faces, particularly on the southern flanks, which are equivalent to the north faces in Europe.

In the north of the range is the Sorata group, with Ancohuma (21,082 feet) and Illampu (20,873 feet), together with peaks of up to 19,000 feet which are still unclimbed. Illampu was climbed by E. Hein, H. Horeschowsky, H. Hortnagl, and H. Pfann in 1928, and Ancohuma by R. Dienst and A. Schulze in 1919. The central part of the range is dominated by the fine ice peaks of Condiriri (18,556 feet) and Huayna Potosi (Cacca Aca) (19,996 feet). The former was climbed by W. Kühm in 1941, and the latter by Dienst and Schulze in 1919. The undisputed giant of the range, however, is Illimani at the southern extremity of the Cordillera Real. It has three summits, of which the southern is the highest. There is still some doubt about its exact height, and figures range from the 21,191 feet of the Chilean Boundary Commission (1904) to the 21,277 feet of the American Geographical Society (1922). It is appropriate that this giant should have been the first object of mountaineering attention in the Cordillera.

Although the Ayamara shepherds must have climbed some of the smaller peaks whose ascents would have provided no technical problems, the mountaineering scene opened in 1877 when C. Wiener made an attempt on Illimani. The honour for the first ascent, however, went to Sir Martin Conway in 1898. The popularity of this mountain has remained, and by 1961 there had been fourteen ascents. After this achievement by Conway climbing gradually increased in popularity, particularly amongst the Germans, who were very active in the years before the First World War. In 1928 an Austrian expedition, led by H. Pfann, climbed Illampu and Pico Norte, together with a dozen other peaks. Another notable achievement by this expedition was the ascent of Ancohuma by a new route, a trend which is only now becoming established in some areas of the Andes thirty years later. They also created a precedent by using llamas as pack animals. Isolated groups continued to climb in this area, but greater interest was being shown in the Cordilleras of Peru and in the Himalaya. In 1951 the Club Andino Boliviano was formed, and this again focused attention on the Cordillera Real and in particular has introduced skiing to the region. Since 1951 most of the virgin peaks have been climbed, but diligent search may still reveal new summits. A Japanese party led by I. Muko as late as 1962 climbed six peaks over 19,000 feet, including Huayna Illampu (19,870 feet). Although most of the peaks have been climbed,

it is usually by one route only and there are innumerable new routes and new faces still to be explored.

Cordillera Apolobamba

Although the highest peak in the range, Nevado Chaupi Orco (19,830 feet), is situated in Peru and the range spans the southern Peruvian border, it is convenient to consider it as a single unit, particularly since many expeditions to the region have climbed equally in both Peru and in Bolivia. Little interest was shown in the area until the Italian and German expeditions of 1958. Between them these two groups climbed twenty-nine of the major peaks. In 1959, G. C. Bratt led an Imperial College Expedition, who were able to make a further thirteen ascents. The nomenclature in the Apolobamba is confused, since many peaks, although climbed, have not had their names officially accepted, and it does seem that first ascents may still be possible; in particular, Katantica (18,345 feet), to the south-west of Azucarni (18,307 feet), seems not to have been climbed.

Cordillera Munecas

The highest point of the Cordillera Munecas is Callinsayani (17,061 feet), but since the range is free from snow and ice there has been no record of any mountaineering activity.

Cordillera de Quinza Cruz

The highest peak in the group is Nevado Jachacuncollo (19,521 feet). Although the peaks are generally lower than the Cordillera Real, there is still only one pass which is free from ice. The peaks are mainly composed of slates and other sedimentary rocks, and the summits, in consequence, are more rounded, but they still carry quite considerable glaciers. T. Herzog made the first ascents here when in 1911 he climbed Inmaculado (18,618 feet), Cerro Carnaval, and Jachacunocollo. J. Prem visited the area in 1939 to climb Atoroma (18,701 feet). Apparently Nevado de Choquetanga (18,701 feet) and Cerro Pacuni (18,590 feet) are still unclimbed.

Cordillera de Santa Vera Cruz

This group is the most southerly of the glaciated eastern Cordilleras of Bolivia. Although only twelve miles long, two peaks, Cerro de Santa Cruz and Cerro Fortunata, are worthy of climbing. J. Prem climbed Santa Cruz in 1939.

Cordillera de Cocapata

This group does not offer much to the serious mountaineer. Incachaca (17,159 feet), the highest point, was climbed by T. Herzog in 1910.

Cordillera Occidental (Puna)

Rising from the arid Altiplano, the volcanic cones of the Puna contain the highest mountains of Bolivia, but from a climbing point of view they are disappointing. Nevado Sajama (21,424 feet) is the highest of them all and was climbed by Piero Ghiglione and J. Prcm in 1939. As early as 1904, H. Hoek climbed Nevado Nuevo Mundo (19,751 feet), the second highest peak, as well as six other peaks over 16,000 feet. Cerro Bonete (18,566 feet) was climbed by Indians for religious reasons, as were several other smaller peaks. The sulphureous deposits of the volcanoes is often of economic importance, and a high mine on Chorolque (18,373 feet), worked since the seventeenth century, has resulted in many ascents.

The Andes of Chile

The Andes of Chile can be simply divided into the Northern Andes, or Puna, Central Andes, Southern Andes, and the Andes of Patagonia and Tierra del Fuego.

The Northern Andes

The Northern Andes rise from the naked salt and gravel deposits of the desert of Puna de Atacama, and like the Puna region of Peru these mountains do not for the most part offer a very serious challenge to mountaineers. The snow-line in Chile is higher than anywhere else in the Andes, and in places reaches as high as 18,000 feet. The melt waters at the foot of these volcanoes provide the only springs and oases in the dessicated Atacama desert. They are the fountain of life for the hamlets at their edges, and it is little wonder that the sun-worshipping Atacamenan Indians should have been inspired to set up shrines and sacrificial altars on the summits of these barely glaciated and easily climbed summits. It now seems certain that the Atacamen Indians, who have lived in this region since before the Inca Empire, must have made ascents

of some of the highest volcanoes. Licancabur (19,456 feet) was used by the Indians as either a shrine or a watch-tower. On the summit of Llullaillaco (22,058 feet) there are buildings dating from the fifteenth and sixteenth centuries which may have been occupied for quite long periods during the year. Ascents were also made by local miners in the late 1800s. Aucanquilcha (20,276 feet) has mines which are worked at a height of almost 19,000 feet, while Ollague (19,259 feet) has sulphur mines which are worked very near the summit.

The Central Andes

The Central Andes is probably the Andean region which is most intensively climbed. Situated near to the large populations of Valparaiso and Santiago, it is not surprising that some of the peaks, like Cerro Plomo (17,815 feet), should have had as many as 300 ascents, nor that these mountains should offer first-rate skiing facilities. The highest of the peaks is Tupungato (21,490 feet), on the Chilean and Argentinian border, first climbed by S. Vines and M. Zurbriggen in 1897, the same year that the latter made the first ascent of Aconcagua some sixty miles to the north. The region as a whole is less barren than the northern area, but above 1,200 feet even pasture for mules is sparse. Most of the main peaks have been climbed, usually by German and Chilean teams. Juncal Chico (18,767 feet) was the highest of the unclimbed peaks for a time, but fell to M. Bazan in 1957.

Central Cordillera, Chile: Alto de los Leones (17,717 feet) seen from the top of Nevado Juncal (20,046 feet). The peak is famous for its steep and unstable walls.

Central Cordillera, Argentina: Aconcagua (22,835 feet), the highest point of the Andes, as seen from the Valle Horcones. The peak was first climbed by the Swiss guide, M. Zurbriggen, who was a member of E. A. Fitzgerald's 1897 expedition.

(*Left*) Climbing in Chile in January on a 16,000-foot peak with the unclimbed west face of Alto de los Leones in the background.

Central Cordillera, Chile: Polleras (19,521 feet) (*left*) and Tupungato (21,490 feet). The picture shows the barren north slopes typical of this part of the Andes.

The Southern Andes

The southern section of the range, although rising to only some 15,000 feet, offers some very serious rock climbing, and again snow and ice techniques are required. In the region of Rancagua some very difficult climbs have recently been made. In 1962 the south-east face of Torre de Pangal was climbed, and the ascent of Alto de la Mama (15,595 feet) required the use of thirty pitons. In 1964, all of the remaining peaks were ascended, including Puntilla III (13,977 feet), a wedge-shaped peak which had been attempted previously.

The formation of national and university climbing clubs has helped the advancement of mountaineering in this region and in particular the Academica Nacional de Alta Montana has helped to co-ordinate the interests of mountaineers generally.

The Andes of Argentina

The Argentinian Andes fall into three groups similar to those of Chile: the Northern Andes, or Puna, and the Central Andes which run into the Bariloche or Los Alerces district in the south. The Argentinian mountains in Patagonia are considered as a separate unit.

The Northern Andes

Although there are eleven peaks over 20,000 feet, the area has not attracted modern mountaineers, largely because the high snow-line makes these peaks less interesting and partly because these peaks do not present such great technical problems as the peaks to the south. The highest of the peaks, Nevado de Pissis (22,241 feet), was climbed by the Polish team of Osiecki and Szczepanski in 1937. Nevado del Acay (20,801 feet) was climbed by two Argentinians and a Chilean climber and marks the advent of high mountaineering in this region by local mountaineers. Many of the peaks were ascended by Atacamenan Indians; such peaks as Antofaya (20,013 feet), Aracar (19,948 feet), and Cerro Galan (18,537 feet) have all provided evidence of these early ascents.

The Central Andes

The Central Andes are dominated by Aconcagua (22,835 feet), the highest mountain in South America and in the Western hemisphere. Not only does it dominate physically, but also psychologically. Güssfeldt was the first to attempt the mountain, though through the illness of his companions he had to content himself with the solo ascent of Maipo. Encouraged by this success, he again decided to look at Aconcagua. His approach was from the north, up the valley of Putaendo and into the Val Penitente (Canon del Volcan), where he established a camp at 11,752 feet. Although at first sight the valley seemed to present a dead end, he found that a couloir did in fact lead to the foot of the mountain. Unable to establish a camp above the couloir, Güssfeldt set off with two Chelenos and climbed through the night by moonlight. At ten the next

morning one of the Chelenos collapsed with exhaustion and frostbite. Güssfeldt continued to a height of 21,535 feet, only 1,300 feet below the summit, before he too had to retreat because of bad weather. Snow continued to fall in the Val Penitente. Ten days later he returned to the attack, but was again turned back by a snowstorm at a lower point than he had reached previously.

The German Turnverein, from Santiago, attempted the same route as Dr Güssfeldt in 1897, but was defeated by poor weather, lack of equipment, and lack of time. Again in 1897, E. A. FitzGerald mounted an English expedition and employed Mattias Zurbriggen as their guide, together with four Swiss porters. Their expedition approach was from the south up the Valle Horcones, and from a base camp at Puente del Inca he established a camp at 12,000 feet in the Valle Horcones and a third camp at the head of the valley at 14,000 feet. The next 2,000 feet were gruelling and the party arrived so tired that they slept out at 16,000 feet. Two days later, on Christmas Day, they were established in a small sheltered hollow at 18,700 feet. Zurbriggen climbed 2,000 feet solo from this camp and found a tin box containing Güssfeldt's visiting-card. Two more attempts were made. On 30 December Zurbriggen got frostbite. On 14 January Zurbriggen reached the summit on his own and in a raging snowstorm, FitzGerald having had to turn back at a height of 22,000 feet. Since the first ascent it has been climbed on numerous occasions. In 1946 two refuges were erected by a group of Argentinian army climbers, one at a height of 22,000 feet. In 1952 a statue of Our Lady of Carmel was carried to the summit by two priests.

Because of its popularity, it is not surprising that several alternative routes should have been worked out. Aconcagua itself has two summits, the main one to the north while the southern one is slightly lower 22,730 feet. The lower peak was not attempted until 1927, when M. F. Ryan failed to reach the top. It was left to a German party in 1947, exactly fifty years after Zurbriggen's achievement on the main peak. In 1934 a Polish expedition climbed the east face with three camps at 18,040 feet, 19,355 feet, and 20,665 feet. In 1952 several parties started to take an interest in the south ridge and the south face. F. Marmillod, who had first been interested in this project in 1948, failed to get up the south ridge in 1952. It was in 1952 that the strong French team of Guido Magnone, Lionel Terray, and René Ferlet, after their success on Fitzroy, made a reconnaissance of the south ridge, but through lack of time were unable to make the complete ascent. In 1953 Marmillod returned and made a new route up the west face and on to the south ridge.

Probably the greatest mountaineering feat in the Andes has been the ascent of the great 9,800-foot south face by the Second French Andean Expedition in 1954. The expedition was led by Lucien Bérardini, the other members being A. Dagory, P. Lesueur, R. Paragot, G. Poulet, and E. Denis. The climb involved nine continuous days of climbing and bivouacking on the face, during which all the members suffered from some degree of frostbite. They reached the summit in a state of near collapse. This was the first time that a large Andean mountain had been attempted on Alpine instead of Himalayan lines, with planned bivouacs instead of well-established camps.

Bariloche–Los Alerces District

Within the Bariloche District there exist some relatively small but interesting rock peaks. Cerro Tres Picos (8,530 feet) is the highest of these, but Cerro Catedral (8,045 feet), Cerro Tronador, and Cerro Lopez all have some difficult rock climbs of about 1,000 feet. For example, the north-west face of Punta Luhrs on Cerro Lopez provides a 1,000-foot climb of Grade V. A guide to the climbs of the district is published by the Club Andino Bariloche.

Kim Meldrum

The Andes of Patagonia

The term Patagonia refers to the whole of that part of the mainland of South America from the Río Negro, latitude 40°S., southwards to the Straits of Magellan, a distance of nearly 1,000 miles. As in the rest of the continent, a spine of mountains extends the whole way along the western side of Patagonia, while the rest of the country is relatively flat. Unlike the Northern and Central Andes, which form a continuous chain of high elevation, these mountains are mostly broken into comparatively small groups by rivers which, rising in the eastern pampas, flow westwards through the range to the Pacific. This fact led to the boundary dispute between Chile and Argentina which, at the turn of the century, nearly led to war between the two countries. Chile claimed that the frontier should run along the continental watershed, and Argentina that it should be defined by the line of the highest peaks of the range, often far to the west of the watershed. The dispute was resolved by British arbitration in 1902. A compromise solution was arrived at, with the result that for much of its length the international frontier follows neither the main watershed nor the line of high peaks.

The Southern Andes forms a sharply defined weather frontier, so that the country to the east, which includes the bulk of Patagonia, is dry and treeless, while the western coastal area, including the mountains themselves, is very wet and much of it heavily forested. The tree-line varies from about 5,000 feet in the north to 2,500 feet in the south. For the most part the trees are *Notho fagus*, of which there are several varieties, both deciduous and evergreen, though in the extreme north there are some fine forests of *Araucaria* (monkey puzzle), while in the south the woods contain cypress and magnolia.

The northern part of the Patagonian Andes is largely composed of forested mountain ridges intersected by lakes and rivers and dominated by massive volcanoes, such as Osorno

(8,727 feet) and El Tronador (11,253 feet), some of which are active. Further south (latitude 42°–46°S.), the same characteristics prevail, and though volcanoes are less in evidence, there are many groups of fine glaciated peaks, mostly about 8,000 feet high, several of which have not been visited by mountaineers. The area is sparsely populated by farmers, and there are many uninhabited valleys; communication over the rugged terrain is for the most part difficult. There are a few small ports along the coast, and in the north there are some tourist centres, notably San Carlos de Bariloche, a well-developed winter sports resort.

From latitude 46°S. there is a dramatic change in the character of the range, which stretches southwards for more than 400 miles as a vast region of glaciers. In this distance its continuity has only one interruption; that is in latitude 48°S. where it is split by Baker Channel, an inlet 100 miles long, whose north-eastern and south-eastern arms receive respectively the waters of Río Baker, draining Lago Buenos Aires, and of Río Pascua, draining Lago O'Higgins (San Martín). The two sectors of the range thus formed are known in Chile as the 'Hielo Patagonico del Norte y Sur' (North and South Patagonian Ice). Each contains a large ice-cap from which radiate scores of glaciers, some as long as fifty miles; many of them, flowing through dense forest, thrust their massive fronts into the intricate system of lakes and fjords surrounding them. Here, for hundreds of miles, the deeply indented Pacific coast is completely uninhabited. On the other hand many of the outer valleys on the eastern side of the range are populated by pastoral farmers, and some contain rich grazing land capable of further exploitation as communications are improved.

The Hielo Patagonico del Norte contains the highest peak in Patagonia, Monte San Valentín (13,204 feet), and a great number of other mountains including scores of splendid granite peaks. Access to the range is difficult from both sides, with the result that little climbing has been done there. In 1952 Monte San Valentín was climbed, after many attempts, by an Argentine expedition led by Otto Meiling, and in 1958 Cerro Arenales (11,277 feet) was climbed by a large Japanese/Chilean expedition led by M. Takagi. In 1963/4 the ice-cap was crossed from Laguna San Rafael (north-west) to Lago Colonia (south-east) by a party composed of C. Marangunic, E. Garcia, M. Gomez, and E. Shipton, who also climbed Cerro Arco (10,000 feet) and repeated the ascent of Arenales. Most of the glaciers are still untrodden and the area offers a splendid field of new mountaineering to anyone willing to face the severe weather conditions which prevail.

The Hielo Patagonico del Sur extends from Baker Channel (latitude 48°S.) to Union Sound (latitude 52°S.). Parts of the range are relatively easy of access from the east, notably from Lagos Viedma and Argentino. For this reason the region has received more attention from mountaineers, though the great majority of peaks there still remain unclimbed, and most of the glaciers on the western side of the range have not been

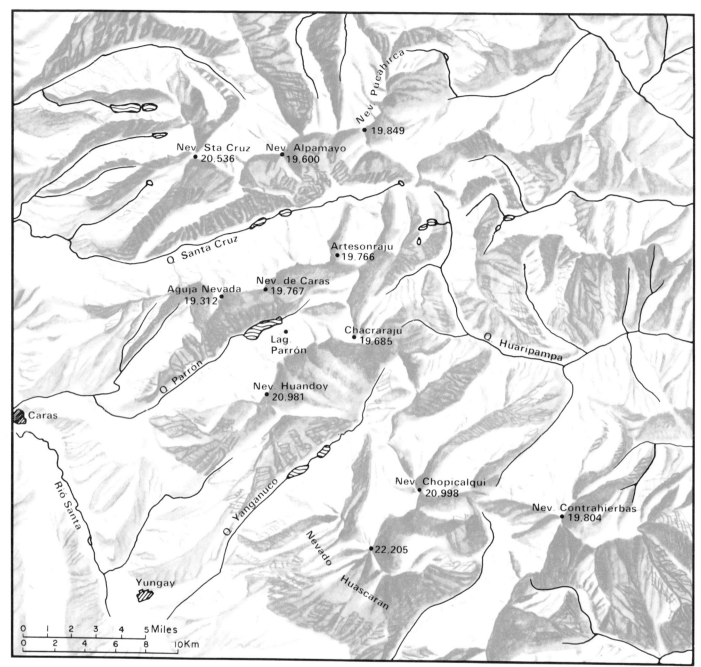

Nev. Pucahirca
● 19,849

Nev. Sta Cruz   Nev. Alpamayo
● 20,536   ● 19,600

Q. Santa Cruz

Artesonraju
● 19,766

Aguja Nevada   Nev. de Caras
● 19,312   ● 19,767

Q. Parrón

Lag.   Chacraraju
Parrón   ● 19,685

Q. Huaripampa

Nev. Huandoy
● 20,981

Caras

Río Santa

Q. Yanganuco

Nev. Chopicalqui
● 20,998

Nev. Contrahierbas
● 19,804

Nevado   ● 22,205

Yungay   Huascaran

0   1   2   3   4   5 Miles
0   2   4   6   8   10 Km

29. South America: Nevado Huascarán in the Andes and the
neighbouring peaks of Huandoy and Alpamayo.

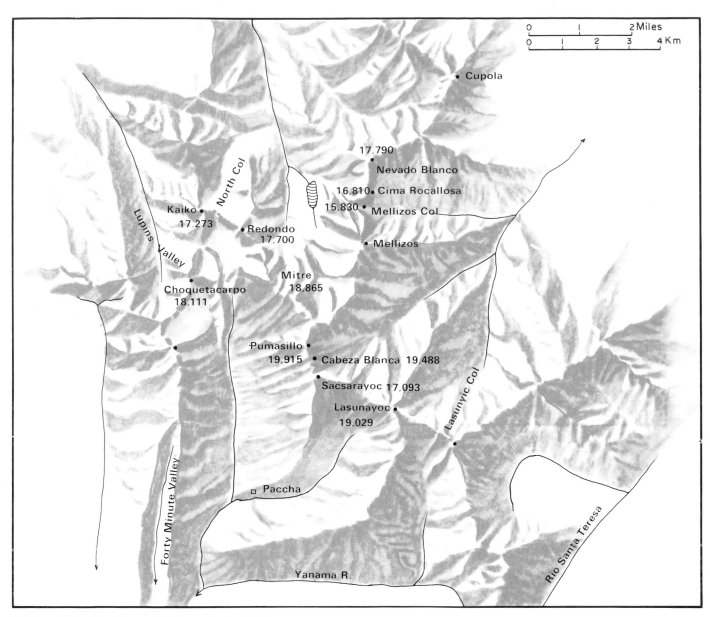

• Cupola

17,790
• Nevado Blanco
16,810 • Cima Rocallosa
15,830 • Mellizos Col
• Mellizos

North Col

Kaiko •
17,273

• Redondo
17,700

Lupins Valley

Mitre
18,865

• Choquetacarpo
18,111

Pumasillo •
19,915 • Cabeza Blanca 19,488

• Sacsarayoc 17,093

Lasunyic Col

Lasunayoc •
19,029

Forty Minute Valley

□ Paccha

Yanama R.

Rio Santa Teresa

0   1   2 Miles
0   1   2   3   4 Km

30. South America: Pumasillo Group in the Andes.

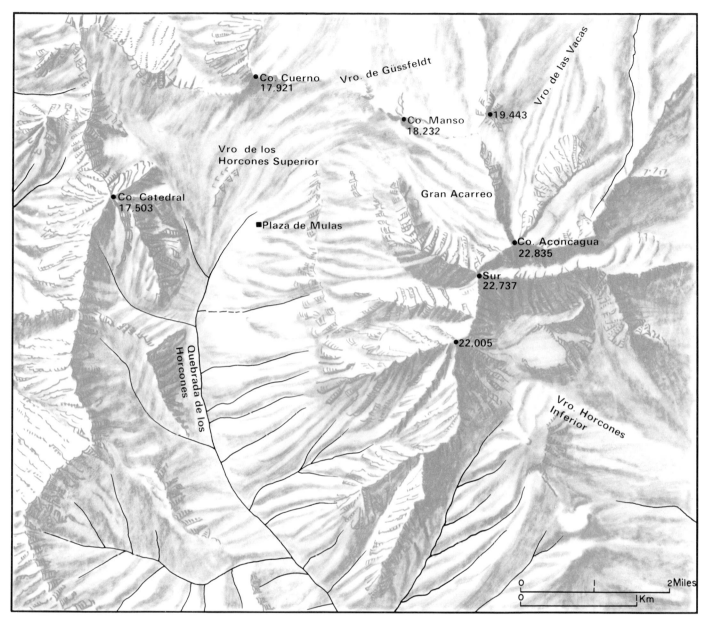

Co. Cuerno
17,921

Vro. de Güssfeldt

Vro. de las Vacas

•19,443

•Co. Manso
18,232

Vro. de los
Horcones Superior

Gran Acarreo

•Co. Catedral
17,503

■Plaza de Mulas

•Co. Aconcagua
22,835

•Sur
22,737

Quebrada de los
Horcones

•22,005

Vro. Horcones
Inferior

0   1   2 Miles
0   1 Km

31. South America: Aconcagua in the Andes.

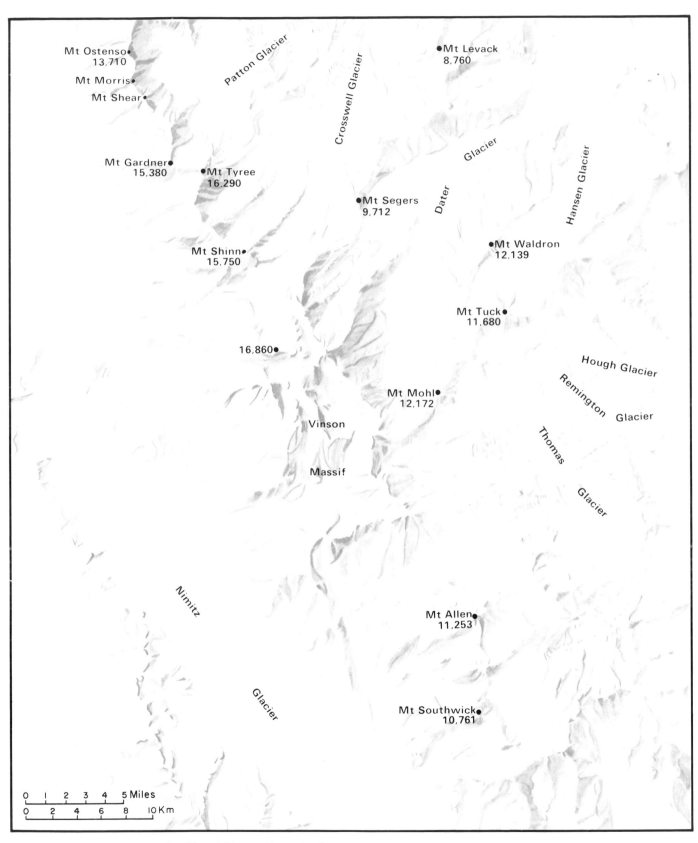

Mt Ostenso•
13,710

Mt Morris•

Mt Shear •

Mt Gardner•
15,380

•Mt Tyree
16,290

Mt Shinn•
15,750

16,860•

Vinson

Massif

Patton Glacier

Crosswell Glacier

•Mt Levack
8,760

Glacier

Dater

Hansen Glacier

•Mt Segers
9,712

•Mt Waldron
12,139

Mt Tuck•
11,680

Hough Glacier

Remington Glacier

Mt Mohl•
12,172

Thomas

Glacier

Nimitz

Glacier

Mt Allen•
11,253

Mt Southwick•
10,761

0 1 2 3 4 5 Miles
0 2 4 6 8 10 Km

32. Antarctica: the Vinson Massif and Mount Tyree in the
Sentinel Range.

The south, central, and north Towers of Paine, Patagonian Andes.

(*Right*) The north-east face of the Fortress, Patagonian Andes.

Patagonian Andes: the Paine Grande from the north. This, the highest peak in the area, was first climbed by an Italian party in 1957.

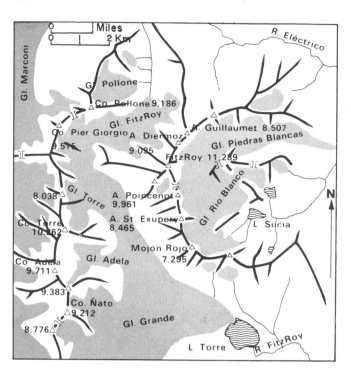

Hielo Patagonico del Norte: an unnamed peak rises some 4,500 feet above the ice-cap.

Hielo Patagonico del Norte: a sledge party approaching Cerro Arenales (11,277 feet) on the northern ice-cap. In the background is Cerro Arco (9,950 feet).

The Patagonian Andes: the FitzRoy and Cerro Torre.

(*Opposite*) Climbing fixed ropes on the south-east ridge of Cerro Torre, Patagonia, during the unsuccessful British expedition in 1967/8. Cerro Torre presents unique problems, severe rock and ice climbing in continually bad weather.

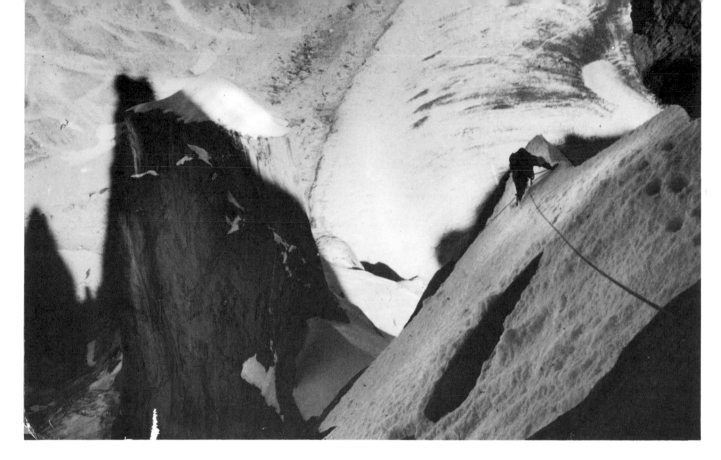

explored on the ground. The most notable climbing achievements there have been the ascent of FitzRoy (11,066 feet) by L. Terray and G. Magnone in 1952, and of Cerro Torre (9,908 feet) by C. Maestri and T. Egger in 1959, both of which involved climbing of an exceedingly high order in very bad weather conditions. The Cordon del Paine, a spectacular group of aiguilles in latitude 51°S., has also witnessed some fine rock-climbing feats, and the summits of the main peaks of the group have been reached.

The first expedition into this sector of the range was led by Dr Frederick Reichart in 1914. In 1916 and 1933 he made two unsuccessful attempts to cross the ice-cap. In 1956 a party led by H. W. Tilman crossed the range further south from Calvo Fjord to Lago Argentino and back, and in 1960/1, a party led by Eric Shipton made a journey over the whole length of the ice-cap from Baker Channel to Lago Argentino. In the middle of the ice-cap, in latitude 49°S., there is an active volcano, Cerro Lautaro (11,090 feet).

Between Lago Buenos Aires and Lago O'Higgins, detached from the main range, there is a glaciated massif known as Monte San Lorenzo. The highest peak (12,008 feet) was climbed by de Agostini in 1943, but there are a number of fine rock peaks there which are well worthy of attention.

South of Union Sound the main chain of the Andes continues southwards for another 100 miles through an almost unknown region of forested valleys, lakes, and fjords; some of the mountains rise to 8,000 feet and many of them are well glaciated. Two remarkable features in this area are the isolated volcano, Mount Burney, near the shores of Union Sound, and a miniature ice-cap in the mountains west of Skyring Sound.

Tierra del Fuego

Nearly all the high mountains of Tierra del Fuego are situated on an uninhabited peninsula, 150 miles long, running westwards from the main island between Admiralty Sound and the Beagle Channel. Towards its western end stands Monte Sarmiento (7,546 feet), a beautiful icy spire which was seen and named by the early navigators of the Magellan Straits. Most of the peninsula, however, is occupied by the Cordillera Darwin, which contains the highest peak of the island, Monte Darwin (8,700 feet). This range covers an area that would easily accommodate the Mont Blanc and Pennine Range of the Alps and most of the Bernese Oberland as well, while the extent of its glaciers is probably greater than that of the entire Alpine chain. Most of the large glaciers flow down to the sea.

Little mountaineering has been done in the region, partly because of the difficulty of access, but mainly because of its evil reputation for foul weather. It is lashed by the same westerly gales that rage around Cape Horn, savage storms that bring long spells of fog and rain and snow. After several unsuccessful attempts, Sarmiento was climbed in 1956 by C. Mauri and C. Maffei, members of an Italian expedition conducted by de Agostini. In 1962, Shipton, Marangunic, Garcia, and F. Vivanco explored the central area of the Cordillera Darwin, crossed the range from Brooks Bay to the Beagle Channel, and climbed several peaks including Monte Darwin and Cerro Yagan (formerly known as Luis de Savoya). The following year another party brought by Shipton climbed Monte Bove and Monte Francia at the eastern end of the range.

Eric Shipton

7 The Mountains of the Polar Regions
The Arctic

Greenland

The most important Arctic mountains are those of Greenland, the world's largest island. Occupying the greater part of the country is the ice-cap, which extends down the spine and forms a huge ice plateau rising, in places, to over 10,000 feet. This was first crossed by Nansen in 1888. The 1930–1 expeditions of Gino Watkins and A. Wegener were the first to experience its bitter winter conditions and low temperatures. Both parties had winter stations on the ice-cap; A. Courtauld, who had with J. M. Wordie's expedition in 1929 climbed Petermann Peak (9,760 feet), manned Watkins's station alone for five months. In 1934 M. Lindsay crossed the ice-cap by sledge from Jacobshavn to Angmagssalik – a very long journey with no support. Since then expeditions of many nationalities have done much to map the fringes of this great island.

The mountains, forming a rim to the dome of the ice-cap, were slow in attracting attention for their own merits. Scientists had little time for climbing, and active mountaineers could not afford the long journey. Many of the peaks are hard to approach, and once approached prove flat-topped and composed of friable rocks unsuitable for climbing.

Although Whymper visited the west coast as early as 1867, it was only after the turn of the century that detailed exploration got under way, and not surprisingly, it was to the scientist that the first peaks succumbed. In 1929 E. Sorge, of Wegener's expedition, climbed the astonishing Umanaktind, and five years later T. G. Longstaff and P. D. Baird climbed the 'Devil's Thumb' on the shores of Melville Bay. In 1931 Watkins's party had located Greenland's highest range, later named the Watkins Mountains, and Lindsay located the highest peak during his ice-cap crossing. In 1935 L. R. Wager returned to make the first ascent. The peak, subsequently named Gunnbjorns Fjeld, was fixed at 12,139 feet. The second highest peak, Mont Forel (11,024 feet), first seen by de Quervain in 1912, was attempted by Watkins in 1931, and together with others lying close to the Arctic Circle, climbed by a strong Swiss party in 1938. North-east Greenland was virtually unknown until 1952, when a powerful scientific expedition led by C. J. W. Simpson explored Dronning Louise Land. The highest summit here is Gefionstinde (9,180 feet), which was climbed by F. R. Brooke's party, who sledged almost to the top.

The most attractive mountains on the west coast are those of the Umanak Fjord region, and further south, the Sukkertoppen, whose highest peak, Mount Atter (9,182 feet), was climbed by M. W. Holland's expedition in 1956. At the southern tip of Greenland, Cape Farewell has many fine peaks which, though easily accessible, experience traditionally

The highest peak in Greenland, Gunnbjorns Fjeld (12,139 feet) in the Watkins Mountains.

Mount Forel (11,024 feet) from the south-east. In the background can be seen the inland ice.

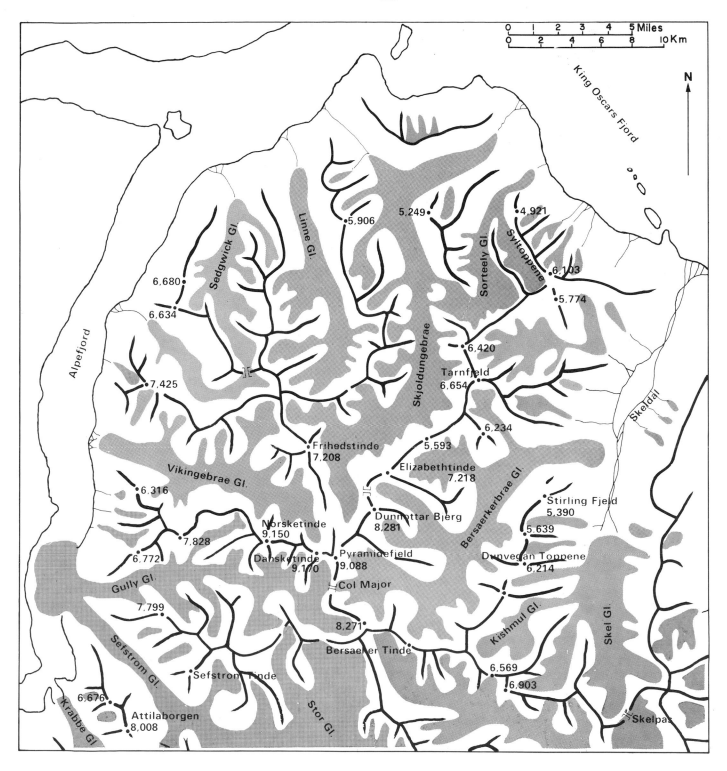

Part of the Staunings Alps, East Greenland.

bad weather. On the east coast there are the Staunings Alps in Scoresby Land, accessible from Alpefjord or King Oscars Fjord, and the Caledonia group and 'Switzerland' area lying between Mont Forel and the coast.

L. Koch's expeditions were the first to discover and explore the Staunings. In 1954 two members of his party, J. Haller and W. Diehl, made the first ascent of the highest peak, Dansketinde (9,170 feet). In the same year they and a Danish-

Norwegian expedition climbed Norsketinde (9,150 feet). It was obvious that these mountains, though much lower, had all the good qualities of the Alps. The routes were as long, since they started much nearer to sea level, and as varied. A 'Golden Age' of exploration was to set in.

In 1957 an Austrian party centred itself on a glacier at the head of Alpefjord and climbed sixteen peaks. Next year a vigorous Scottish party under C. G. M. Slesser explored several glaciers in the northern area, made two passes over the range, climbed seventeen peaks in all and carried out scientific programmes. Among the now increasingly numerous expeditions was that of Sir John Hunt in 1960, organized partly for the benefit of twenty-one boy members, which made the first ascent of the Pyramidefjeld (9,088 feet), a fine peak overlooking the Col Major at the head of the Bersaerkerbrae. In 1963, having made three expeditions to the west coast, G. Monzino visited the Staunings. He returned a year later to climb two peaks overlooking the Vikingebrae and make the second ascent of Dansketinde by a route on the north face.

'Switzerland', and the less accessible mountains surrounding the Femstjernen, were being visited more frequently. The newly-formed Danish Mountaineering Club organized a number of expeditions, and in 1966 a Japanese party made the second ascent of Mont Forel.

Mountaineering in Greenland has a bright future, and much remains to be done. High Arctic weather is usually stable in the summer months, while the continuous daylight makes it possible to do very long climbs without fear of benightment. The blue fjords, clearness of the atmosphere, and soft light add to the charm of these peaks. To set in the scale

Mount Asgard (6,598 feet) from a tributary of the Turner Glacier, Cumberland Peninsula, Baffin Island. This difficult peak was climbed in 1953 by four members of a Swiss–Canadian Scientific Expedition, J. Marmet, H. Rothlisberger, H. Weber, and F. Schwarzenbach.

Unclimbed peaks on the Qioqe Peninsula north of Umanak. West Greenland.

against these is the bad state of the glaciers; by the time early autumn snowfalls have improved the surfaces, cold has set in and made difficult climbing problematical.

At present the Danish government limits the number of parties allowed to visit Greenland each year. This is perhaps as well on two counts, since it is no place for the inexperienced and since the simple charms of the Eskimo race are worth preserving.

Ellesmere Island

The mountains of Ellesmere Island, first seen in 1861, are the most northerly in the world. The island features in the journeys of Nares, Greely, and Peary, but with so great a trophy as the North Pole in the offing only 450 miles away few spared a glance to the interior. Since 1950, when the weather station at Alert was established, the Canadian Defence Research Board and Geological Survey have mapped much of the island. The Oxford University Expedition was the first to visit the mountains in 1935, when A. W. Moore and the Eskimo Nookapingwa, travelling from Etah in north-west Greenland, climbed Mount Oxford, whose height they estimated at

9,000 feet. In 1957, on a second ascent, this was reduced to 7,250 feet.

Though extensive, and of great glaciological interest, the snow mountains of the United States Range, whose highest summits are Point 8,540 feet and Mount Whisler (*c*. 8,500 feet), and the British Empire Range to the west, with similar heights, do not promise ascents of great difficulty.

Baffin Island

Although John Davis visited the Cumberland Peninsula in 1585, the interior of Baffin Island remained unexplored for a further 300 years. Even then, surveyors and anthropologists seeking material about the Eskimos had come and gone before the first mountains were climbed. The peaks around Clyde Inlet and Eglinton Fjord had been noted for their possibilities long before the peaks of the Cumberland Peninsula were seriously tackled. Of these, the mountains round the Pangnirtung Pass are the most impressive, but there is another high range near Cape Dyer.

In 1953, Swiss climbers from the Arctic Institute's expedition, led by P. D. Baird, climbed near the Pangnirtung Pass,

notably the sheer, flat-topped Mount Asgard (6,598 feet), Mount Queen Elizabeth (7,014 feet), and the island's highest peak, the Tête Blanche (7,074 feet). In 1961 R. E. Langford's party, approaching up the North Pangnirtung Fjord, continued these explorations and climbed Mount Friga (6,650 feet) and other peaks.

Owing to increasing air facility, access to Baffin Island is becoming easier. There are many magnificent peaks of firm, smooth granite awaiting the climber. In spring, dog sledges can be used in the valleys, and aircraft equipped with skis can land on the frozen lakes. After the thaw, either float-planes are needed to reach the lakes or Eskimo whaleboats can be used up the fjords. But the crossing of lakes and rivers presents a problem. From mid June to mid August seems the time at which big glaciers, fine peaks, and long valleys offer the most rewarding prospect.

Baffin Island: a camp beside Summit Lake on the Pangnirtung Pass, Cumberland Peninsula. In the distance is Mount Queen Elizabeth (7,014 feet).

Peaks of West Spitsbergen from Kongsfjord.

The Kings Glacier and the Three Crowns, West Spitsbergen.

Jan Mayen

Jan Mayen is an arctic island thirty-five miles long and some three to twelve miles wide. The first serious scientific expedition, an Austrian one, visited the island in 1882/3, but the ascent of its most notable feature, the Beerenberg (7,680 feet), was not made until 1921 by J. M. Wordie's party. This huge extinct volcano, often fog-girt, is most easily approached up the South Glacier. The mountain is climbed fairly regularly by scientific parties, or by parties bound for Greenland.

Spitsbergen

Spitsbergen is the most mountainous of the islands which make up the Norwegian archipelago of Svalbard. Although they seldom exceed 5,000 feet and are more often in the region of 2,500–4,000 feet, the mountains give the impression of being much higher.

The sedimentary rocks which form the greater part of the island have, on the western side, been highly folded. The result is a country to delight the climber – of steep pyramid peaks and long serrated ridges separated by broad glaciers which descend to meet the many fjords that bite deep into the coastline. In contrast, Edge Island and North-East Land are relatively flat, the latter being covered by a considerable ice-cap.

Discovered by the Dutchman, Willem Barents, in 1596 (although there is an early mention (1194) of Svalbard in the Icelandic Sagas), Spitsbergen became, in the seventeenth and eighteenth centuries, the centre of a whaling industry which resulted in the virtual extinction of the Greenland whale.

Although whalers such as W. Scoresby added much to the knowledge of the coastline, it was left to the scientists who came later to explore the interior. Much early travel was done by A. E. Nordenskiold, who also climbed a number of peaks, but the real innovator of summer arctic travel and mountaineering was Sir W. M. Conway. In 1896 he made the first crossing of Spitsbergen, and the following year climbed Hornsundstind (4,694 feet) in the extreme south and a number of peaks in the Kings Fjord area in James I Land in the north-west.

Newtontoppen and Perriertoppen (both 5,633 feet) are the highest peaks on the island. Newtontoppen was first climbed by a party led by A. Vassiliev during the Russian Arc of Meridian Survey in 1900. Apart from these few ascents, however, little was done until the series of Oxford expeditions, which, commenced in 1921, resulted in a number of peaks, such as Mount Irvine (5,200 feet), being climbed by Odell and Irvine in 1923. Since then Spitsbergen has become increasingly popular and more frequently visited. It is particularly suitable for small expeditions with limited means such as the 1962 Swiss party which climbed extensively in Haakon VII Land in the north-west.

Despite Spitsbergen's position only 700 miles from the North Pole, the warm Gulf Stream water ensures that the west coast remains ice free during the summer months, thus solving the major problem of access.

Wilfrid Noyce

The Antarctic

Introduction

On the opposite side of the world from the principal habitations of mankind lies the vast ice-covered continent of Antarctica. In area, it is greater by half as much again as Australia. In shape, it is roughly circular: the surrounding seas, choked with pack-ice for most of the year, extend the perimeter of polar ice as far as the 60th Parallel. The Antarctic is a clean, dry, cold desert – a continent compressed beneath a great dome of ice which in one place is 14,000 feet thick. It is also a cold radiator – the core of all weather in the Southern Hemisphere. Cold polar air pushes the climatic and oceanic boundary as far north as the 50th Parallel; while the circumpolar sweep of the Southern Ocean, driven eastwards in the storm paths of prevailing winds, builds up a barrier of mountainous seas between the South Polar Regions and the more hospitable climates of her neighbouring continents: South America, Africa, and Australasia.

Historical

The possibility of the existence of a southern continent had been postulated by Greek philosophers some 2,000 years before the continent was discovered. Sixteenth-century geographers gave the name *Tierra Australis* to this hypothetical land mass.

In 1768, Captain James Cook sailed with instructions to search for the southern continent, but though he circumnavigated the world, charted New Zealand, changed the face of geography, and affected the politics and strategies of empires, he failed to discover the 'Great Object'. During his second voyage of 1772–5, Cook not only crossed the Antarctic Circle for the first time in history but at one time penetrated the pack-ice to latitude 71°10′S., but without once sighting the elusive land.

Discovery

Cook's reports of an abundance of seals and whales in southern waters attracted the competitive, tough sealers and whalemen; and so began the 'Maritime Era' in Antarctic history. The Southern Ocean became the scene of gory industry, particularly in the region of South Georgia and the South Shetland Islands; and the commercial incentive, driving the sealers further south in search of fresh hunting-grounds, resulted in the definite discovery of the continent in 1820 by the Englishman, Edward Bransfield – although it is very likely that the Russian naval captain, Baron von Bellingshausen, sighted the ice-covered mainland in longitude 2°14′W., but without recognizing it as such, just two days before Bransfield sighted the northern tip of Graham Land. In the succeeding years, explorer/sealers like Weddell, Biscoe, Kemp, and Balleny, and even a few well-appointed naval expeditions like those of d'Urville, Wilkes, and Ross, penetrated the pack-ice, and by 1900 Antarctica had taken shape on the charts. The stage was set for the 'Heroic Era' to commence.

Today the names of Scott, Shackleton, Amundsen, and Mawson are synonymous with the continent their expeditions probed during this era, and their epic journeys set an example which has been the inspiration of polar explorers for two generations.

Exploration

It was the American, R. E. Byrd, who developed the technique of aircraft reconnaissance and logistic support that have brought such fruitful results to Antarctic exploration in recent years. But there were three other expeditions in the south during the period between the wars that made a distinctive mark on Polar history: Mawson's 1929–31 expedition; J. Rymill's British Graham Land Expedition of 1934–6; and Ellsworth's 1935 trans-Antarctic flight from Graham Land to the Ross Sea, during which he discovered the Sentinel Mountains.

The post-war period of renewed interest in Antarctica began slowly, but the pace quickened as British, Americans, and other nations returned to the assault; Chile and Argentina set up bases in 1947, and two years later the French and the Norwegian–British–Swedish Expedition set up their bases on the Princess Marthe Coast. Helicopters had been used by Byrd in 1948, and a new phase of expansive exploration was getting under way.

This phase reached a peak during the International Geophysical Year of 1957–8, and within five years there were few major glaciers or mountain ranges that had escaped notice. At last it was possible to look at the map of Antarctica and see the nature of the topography.

The map of Antarctica

We now know that structurally the Antarctic Continent is divided into two parts. For geographical convenience these two different structural zones are called East and West Antarctica, though strictly speaking they are separated not by the Greenwich Meridian but by the Trans-Antarctic Mountains – a chain of spectacular block-faulted ranges of sedimentary rock overlaying a granitic basement complex. East Antarctica is the larger of the two parts, and structurally

A view of the Sentinel Range, looking north. This, the highest mountain range in Antarctica, was first seen and named by Lincoln Ellsworth during his trans-Antarctic flight of November 1935.

it is a continental shield of pre-Cambrian metamorphosed sediments on which lies relatively undisturbed sediments. West Antarctica is structurally different in that it comprises an archipelago formed of disturbed metamorphic, igneous, and sedimentary rocks of younger age which extends northwards to form the Antarctic Peninsula. Graham Land is an extension of the Andean mountain chain, uplifted in the Tertiary period, and is connected to the tip of South America by the partially submerged Scotia Ridge–a tectonic chain 2,000 miles in length which surfaces in the form of the South Orkneys, South Sandwich, and South Georgia islands. Distinct in structure as these two zones of Antarctica would seem to be, they are joined by an overlying ice-cap which is aground in all the sub-glacial troughs and basins; and so thick is this ice-cap that the surface elevation of Antarctica is on an

The ranges of Antarctica.

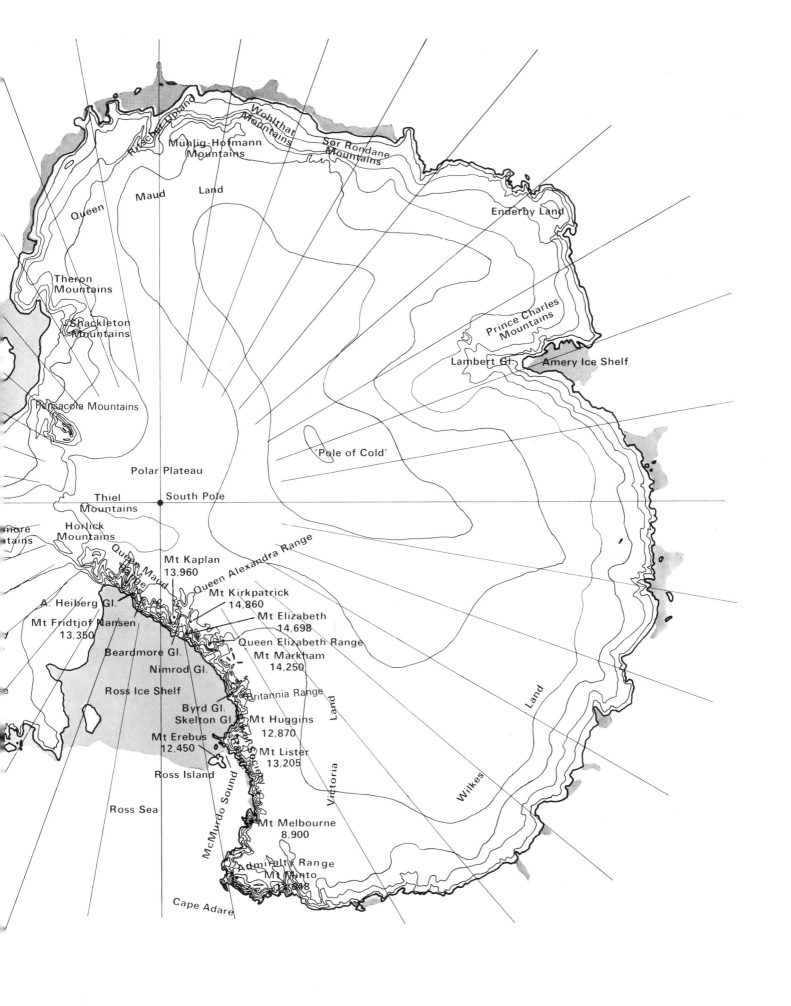

average higher above sea-level than any other continent.

Rock pierces this ice-cap in only a few isolated locations, for the vast bulk of East Antarctica is without a single nunatak – it is a white desert dome, at the approximate centre of which is the 'pole of cold': the coldest place on earth, where the average air temperature is about − 76°F. and where it can fall in winter as low as − 126°F. The greatest part of East Antarctica's 8,000 miles of coastline is either ice cliff, glacier tongue, or ice shelf. West Antarctica on the other hand, although taking up a smaller area, has a longer coastline, higher mountains, and more exposed rock. It will therefore almost certainly be to West Antarctica that in due course the mountaineers will gravitate.

The Antarctic Horst

The most impressive mountain chain in Antarctica is the Horst Range, which stretches like a bent spine 2,500 miles across the continent from the northern reach of Victoria Land towards the western coast of Queen Maud Land. In the past decade the entire range has been photographed and mapped, the territory being agreeably divided between the New Zealand field parties, in the mountainous country between Cape Adare and the Axel Heiberg Glacier, and the more distant Horlick and Thiel Mountains becoming the preserve of the Ohio State University geologists operating from McMurdo Station. The Pensacola Mountains, discovered on a long-range trans-Antarctic flight from McMurdo in 1956, were visited by American scientists from Finn Ronne's base on the Filchner Ice Shelf the following year, and the Shackleton Range and Theron Mountains at the other end of the Antarctic Horst were discovered and mapped by the Commonwealth Trans-Antarctic Expedition in 1956–7.

This great spinal chain is divided into many historic, geographic, and scenic blocks. Between Cape Adare and McMurdo Sound (a coastline discovered by James Clark Ross in 1841) is the Scott's Northern Party territory: spectacular scenery of bold wind-swept mountains, huge glaciers, and pockets of dry, cold, dusty valleys, where glaciers drain into puddle-sized lakes which remain mysteriously salty.

Between McMurdo Sound and the Nimrod Glacier the chain is broken by broader glaciers and the scenery becomes more expansive. This is the country of Scott, Wilson, and Shackleton, who reached their furthest south latitude in 1902 near the mouth of the Nimrod Glacier. It is the least spectacular link in the chain, although some of the mountains exceed 10,000 feet. South of the Nimrod Glacier, in the Queen Elizabeth and Queen Alexandra Ranges, massive mountains dominate a jumble of rolling snow-covered hills, icefalls, and flat neves. The imposing bulks of Mount Markham (14,250 feet) and Mount Kirkpatrick (14,860 feet) are the loftiest mountains in the area.

The Beardmore Glacier, discovered and pioneered by Shackleton's Pole party in 1909, is the historical focal-point

The Admiralty Range showing the Ironside Glacier and Mount Minto (13,648 feet) in the distance.

Looking across the Lower Beardmore Glacier towards the west face of Mount Elizabeth (14,698 feet), and to Mount Anne (12,704 feet) to the right at the head of the Evans Glacier. Behind and to the left is Mount Mackellar (14,082 feet), Queen Alexandra Range.

and the pilot's principal landmark on the many flights made each summer between McMurdo and the American South Pole Station. The scenery here is grand rather than beautiful. Sheer-sided rock walls, torn ice-flanks, and shining table-top blocks stand on either side of this broad highway to the polar plateau down which the last men to travel were the ill-fated members of Scott's Pole party in 1912.

The Queen Maud Range, although less lofty than the Queen Alexandra Range, is nevertheless more distinctive. Each valley glacier is quite unlike its neighbour: there are dry areas windswept and bare of snow; there are pockets of heavy precipitation and mountains that show no rock except on their northern faces; there are pinnacles and turrets of bare rock and massifs of solid grandeur overshadowing spectacular ice-falls, of which the Axel Heiberg–the route of Roald Amundsen's Pole party through the range in 1911–is an outstanding example. Mount Fridtjof Nansen (13,350 feet), which dominates the Axel Heiberg Glacier, was climbed by a New Zealand party in 1961. This range shrinks as it turns inland from the Ross Ice Shelf, and the mountains become engulfed by plateau ice, except for the steep escarpments and plateau summits that outcrop in the Horlick and Thiel mountains (which have in recent years produced a rich harvest in fossil flora and coal seams several feet thick).

The Pensacola Mountains, still part of the great Antarctic Horst, are more Alpine in appearance–in some areas almost grotesque–but undoubtedly of mountaineering interest. The Shackleton Range and Theron Mountains, on the other hand, are at the tail of the Horst and are relatively uninteresting from the mountaineering point of view.

Many hundreds of mountains have been scaled in the Antarctic Horst by New Zealand, American, and British surveyors and geologists during the course of their work, but understandably, they all took the easiest way up since it was their job and not merely their pleasure to climb, and their endurance had to be preserved for the two to eight hours of survey observations carried out on each windy summit.

The Antarctic Peninsula

The mountains of the Antarctic Peninsula are totally different. This, the second longest mountain chain in Antarctica, with its rugged off-shore islands, treacherous sea ice, deep fjords, icefalls, and steep glaciers, is the most difficult region on the continent in which to travel by dog team; and air operations are even more hazardous in this area of violent local winds. Since the Second World War small British expeditions have been mapping this region. The highest mountain in Graham Land, Mount Français (9,456 feet), and the highest mountain in Palmer Land at the base of the peninsula, Mount Andrew Jackson (11,316 feet), have both been climbed, as has Mount Gaudry (8,049 feet) on Adelaide Island. The scene here is more compact than in the remainder of the continent, the coastline is magnificent, and there are still many splendid peaks to be climbed, such as those of the Douglas Range, on Alexander Island, which exceed 9,000 feet.

The Sentinel Range

South of the peninsula, isolated and surrounded by sub-glacial trenches, basins, and troughs, is the loftiest and most

A survey camp in Neny Fjord. Dog teams are still much used by British parties for travel among the mountains of the Antarctic Peninsula.

(*Top*) The west face of Mount Tyree (16,290 feet) in the Sentinel Range, the second highest summit in Antarctica. The first ascent of this difficult peak was made in January 1967 by two members of an American Alpine Club expedition, B. Corbet and J. P. Evans.

(*Bottom*) N. B. Clinch climbing towards the summit of Mount Gardner (15,380 feet). Below are the eastern basins of the Sentinel Range which drain towards the Filchner Ice Shelf and the Weddell Sea.

chaotic range on the continent – the Sentinel Range in the Ellsworth Mountains. It is a range characterized by razor-sharp ridges and sheer-sided rock faces of 6,000 feet or more. At least two peaks of this range are in excess of 16,000 feet: the Vinson Massif (16,860 feet) and Mount Tyree (16,290 feet). An American party led by N. B. Clinch in 1966 was the first purely mountaineering expedition to visit the range. As well as climbing Vinson and Mount Tyree, the party also made first ascents of Mount Shinn (15,750 feet), Mount Gardner (15,380 feet), and Mounts Ostenso (13,710 feet) and Long Gables (13,620 feet). But there are still many unclimbed

summits in the range and it is surely here that the biggest prizes await the Antarctic mountaineer.

Marie Byrd Land

The mountains of Marie Byrd Land are, by comparison, tame, even though many peaks in that region are greater than 11,000 feet. Like the Sentinel Range, the mountain ranges of Marie Byrd Land are the peaks of an island cut off from the main continent by a sub-glacial basin, but in Marie Byrd Land the exposed rocks are all volcanic and most of the highest moun-

Mount Erebus from Hut Point (a water-colour by E. A. Wilson).

tains, such as Mount Sidley (13,850 feet), are extinct volcanoes with the classical profile and collapsed craters, in some cases several miles in diameter. The vulcanism that built these mountain ranges accompanied the more profound disturbances of the Tertiary Period that built the Andean chain, its extension in the Antarctic Peninsula, the Sentinel Range and the Antarctic Hortst; and although the Antarctic mountain building waned during the late Tertiary Period, the vulcanism persisted. To this day there are active volcanoes in the sub-Antarctic islands. Mount Erebus (12,450 feet) on Ross Island is active, and there is a report of another active volcano, Mount Melbourne, on the coast of Victoria Land.

Mount Erebus

The first ascent of an Antarctic mountain of any size was the praiseworthy first ascent of Mount Erebus (12,450 feet) by a western approach in March 1908. The party, led by Professor Edgeworth David, was from Shackleton's 1907–9 expedition. A no less remarkable second ascent was made up the northern slopes in December 1912 by members of Scott's last expedition, led by R. E. Priestley, for they were literally driven off the crater of the volcano by a minor eruption. Forty-seven years passed before the third ascent of the volcano was made – this by a New Zealand party of geologists and surveyors operating from a base camp at 3,000 feet. On the following day two Americans reached the summit from the west. Since then ascents of Mount Erebus have become commonplace.

Mountaineering in Antarctica

It is generally recognized that mountaineering in Antarctica has, as yet, no place as a sport. There are numerous good reasons why this should be so: the shortness of the Antarctic summer season, and the cost of putting one scientist on the continent with his support and equipment makes it a duty for

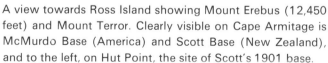

A view towards Ross Island showing Mount Erebus (12,450 feet) and Mount Terror. Clearly visible on Cape Armitage is McMurdo Base (America) and Scott Base (New Zealand), and to the left, on Hut Point, the site of Scott's 1901 base.

Looking eastwards to the Nordenskjöld Glacier and the cloud-capped Mount Paget (9,563 feet) from the summit of Mount Duse, South Georgia.

each man to use every minute of his day profitably. Surveyors and geologists who might conceivably have some business on the summits of Antarctic mountains are not only expected to take the easiest way up to save time, but also to minimize risk of injury; for search and rescue operations in Antarctica these days would be prohibitively expensive. The choice is therefore open for the mountaineer with an interest in the south either to join a regular expedition and be satisfied with easy first ascents, or to find a plausible 'excuse' for tackling the harder routes.

The sub-Antarctic islands

In many respects the sub-Antarctic islands are a far more promising field for the mountaineer, for here he is not dependent upon logistic support. The weather conditions on the sub-Antarctic islands, however, are appalling at all seasons of the year. Every kind of precipitation falls or lashes the glaciated slopes: and a shroud of fog or dank overcast persists for much of the year. Gales and storms tear at the surface and, to add to the most inclement weather that can be imagined, the mountains are themselves as challenging as any to be found on the Antarctic mainland.

But at least the private expedition here has a chance. This has been well proved by the splendid South Georgia Survey led by V. D. Carse; H. W. Tilman's Crozet Island Expedition in his 45-foot pilot cutter *Mischief*; and W. Deacock's Heard Island Expedition in the 65-foot schooner *Patanela* captained by Tilman. All three expeditions are quite recent and each was an outstanding success.

There are ten small groups of islands from which to select; the most attractive ones from the mountaineer's point of view being undoubtedly South Georgia and Heard Island, and, from the adventurer's point of view, the South Sandwich Islands. All one needs, so it would seem, is sailing skill, a stout vessel, and an even stouter heart.

Wally Herbert

Index

Newtontoppen

Beerenberg

Kebnekaise

Vatnajokull

Scandinavian Mts

Jotunheimen

Galdhopiggen

Ben Nevis

Snowdon

Ural Mountains

Verkhoyansk Range

Chersky Range

Kam

Alps

Dolomites

Carpathians

High Tatra

Transylvanian Alps

Sayan Range

Altay Range

Dzungarian Alatau

Mt Blanc

Pindus Mts

Caucasus

Elbruz

Takht-i-Suleiman

Peak Communism

c. de Gavarnie

Pyrenees

Tyan Shan

Astyn Tagh

Hakutozan

Japanese Alps

S Nevada

Pontine Mts

Kopet Dagh

Nan Shan

Fujisan

Atlas Mts

Ararat

Zagres Mts

Demavend

Hindu Kush

Pamirs

K2

Kun-Lun

Minya Konka

Toubkal

Taurus Mts

Nanga Parbat

Himalaya

Tahat

Nanda Devi

Everest

Niitaka

Hoggar

Tibesti

Emi Koussi

Ras Dashan

Ethiopian Mts

Ruwenzori

Mt Stanley

Mt Kenya

Kinabalu

Carstensz

Kilimanjaro

Nassau Range

Owen Stanley Ra

Chimanimani Mts

Musgrave Range

Gt. Dividing Range

Drakensberg

Kosciusko

Mt. Ossa

Big Ben